THE
PH.D. IN ENGLISH
AND
AMERICAN
LITERATURE

THE
PH.D. IN ENGLISH
AND
AMERICAN
LITERATURE

DON CAMERON ALLEN   *Johns Hopkins University*

Holt, Rinehart and Winston, Inc.

New York · Chicago · San Franciso · Atlanta · Dallas ·
Montreal · Toronto · London

To all the graduate students who have endured me
and who will wish I had seen the point sooner

Preface

At the 1965 meeting of the Modern Language Association in Chicago, the Secretary, Professor John Fisher, abetted by the first Vice President, Professor Nathan Edelman, urged me to undertake the study of the Ph.D. in English and American Literature under the aegis of the Advisory Committee. "Morally" weakened by fifteen years of service on the Editorial Committee and physically disturbed by the approach of my sixty-third year, I agreed to abandon my normal habits of life and become (for a season) a statistical debauchee. At the moment of decision, I assumed that there would be small risk to life and limb (brain damage already had been sustained) because it was then supposed that the Modern Language Association would bear the costs; hence, the labor would be fantastically modest. However, these expectations were dashed when the Danforth Foundation generously offered to support a report on a larger scale. For this support, I, the Advisory Committee, the officers of the Modern Language Association, and, perhaps, the profession are very grateful.

As the director of this study, I was, and still am, an amateur. I have spent forty years in the Renaissance—which is full of questions but no questionnaires. During my professional career I have received numerous questionnaires, but I can hardly be said to have given them a hard look. Faced with learning something about the art, I entered the Education stacks (marked "L" in my university's library for "loquacious") in order to see what was done by the real professionals. No student of literature is likely to pause for very long over the prose in most of these volumes, but the best of them print, as I have, the questionnaires eliciting the facts that produced the graphs, columns, and so forth (of which we have none) in their cabooses. With numerous examples of the sort before me, as the compiler of this study, I became the sedulous ape.

The months of March to September 1966, were devoted to reading article after article in the various educational journals and in trying to compose four questionnaires for distribution to important groups in the profession. The first version of the questionnaires was criticized by the Advisory Committee and mauled by the attendants at the Johns Hopkins meeting in May of that year. The second version of the questionnaires was field tested on the doctoral alumni of New York University and The Johns Hopkins University. This edition was further revised by experts in the United States Office of Education and the Advisory Committee. As the original deviser, I now realize that the questions are "leaky" and "loaded" (as the respondents have told me); and I now know that only after all questionnaires are in, read, and the flaws made manifest that a proper questionnaire can be composed. I am grateful to those who took time to fill out these forms because I realize what a bore and a burden it must have been to busy people. I am also thankful to those who wrote me letters or supplied their responses with fuller explanations. I have taken the liberty, as I warned them, of quotation, but I hope I have kept comments unidentifiable.

During the eighteen months that have been devoted to this survey, the author and compiler has been admirably advised by the members of the Advisory Committee: Professors Gustav Arlt, Theodore Andersson, Fredson Bowers, John Gerber, Albert Kitzhaber, Maynard Mack, Robert Ornstein, and Gordon Ray. The Secretary of the Modern Language Association, Professor John Fisher, and his efficient coajutors, Professors George Anderson, Kenneth Mildenberger, and Michael Shugrue have been patient towers of strength. The aid and comfort of Patricia Martel, Professor Fisher's secretary, is also cheerfully acknowledged. David Fruin, a member of the Johns Hopkins' statistical division, analysed the questionnaires and provided the material from which the tabulations were made; they have been checked and corrected by Hans Rütimann. Thanks again to the grant of the Danforth Foundation, we were able to hold five conferences on the Ph.D., which were attended by chairmen or representatives of departments now offering work toward the doctorate. The first of these meetings was held at Baltimore on May 6 and 7, 1966, under the auspices of The Johns Hopkins University. The second was at Chicago on October 21 and 22, 1966, and sponsored by the University of Chicago. The third meeting, at the invitation of Leland Stanford University, took place in San Francisco on December 2 and 3, 1966. The fourth meeting occurred on February 10 and 11, 1967, at New Orleans with Tulane University as the host. The final meeting, at the invitation of New York University, was in New York City on March 10 and 11, 1967. We wish to thank these institutions for their hospitality and the attendants at the meeting whose advice and comments helped to make this report to the profession possible. (See the list of conference participants that follows this Preface.)

We cannot expect that this survey will charm the complacent. The results of the survey astonished me. I have clearly been renting rooms in an ivory tower too long. I have had to put aside many of my ancient convictions—many of them lightly or thoughtlessly held— and seek a new philosophy. The tabulations cannot be shirked, and while they are not the raw material of universal laws, as many statistics pretend to be, they are votes. In the prose that precedes them, I have attempted to count them and sort out their significances, but I cannot be scientific in my conclusions, because I am not made that way. I anticipate objections from both sides of the house. The right will complain that I have done the profession a vast disservice by my results and opinions. The left will see me as a conservative afraid of my shadow. The middle will probably put me down as a wry observer. With this prospect before me, I will conclude with a remark from a well-known eccentric, which the more than nine hundred members of the profession who learned German after they were graduate students can easily translate, "Gewissen Geistem muss man ihre Idiotismen lassen."

Baltimore, Maryland   **D.C.A.**
February 1968

Participants in Conferences on the Ph.D.
in English and American Literature

DONALD K. ADAMS, Department of English, *Occidental College*
HAZARD ADAMS, Department of English, *University of California* (*Irvine*)
RICHARD P. ADAMS, Department of English, *Tulane University*
JACOB H. ADLER, Department of English, *University of Kentucky*
A. LYNN ALTENBERND, Department of English, *University of Illinois*
GEORGE L. ANDERSON, Associate Executive Secretary & Treasurer, *MLA*
JEROME W. ARCHER, Department of English, *Arizona State University*
DUDLEY BAILEY, Department of English, *University of Nebraska*
SYLVAN BARNET, Department of English, *Tufts University*
SAM S. BASKETT, Department of English, *Michigan State University*
MORTON BERMAN, Department of English, *Boston University*
DAVID BEVINGTON, Department of English, *University of Virginia*
J. W. BICKNELL, Department of English, *Drew University*
EDWARD A. BLOOM, Department of English, *Brown University*
MORTON BLOOMFIELD, Department of English, *Harvard University*
BRADFORD BOOTH, Department of English, *University of California*
  (*Los Angeles*)
LAURA BORNHOLDT, Vice President, *Danforth Foundation*
WILLIAM BRASWELL, Department of English, *Purdue University*
HOWARD O. BROGAN, Department of English, *University of Massachusetts*
GERALD CHAPMAN, Department of English, *University of Denver*
JOHN WILLIAM CLARK, Department of English, *University of Minnesota*
C. L. CLINE, Department of English, *University of Texas*
JIM CORDER, Department of English, *Texas Christian University*
EARLE DAVIS, Department of English, *Kansas State University*
RICHARD J. DIRCKS, Department of English, *St. John's University*
ALAN DOWNER, Department of English, *Princeton University*
G. H. DURRANT, Department of English, *University of British Columbia*
KENNETH E. EBLE, Department of English, *University of Utah*
VICTOR ELCONIN, Department of English, *University of Oklahoma*
JAMES H. ELSON, Department of English, *Syracuse University*
ROBERT D. FANER, Department of English, *Southern Illinois University*
C. W. FAULKNER, Department of English, *University of Arkansas*

JOHN H. FISHER, Executive Secretary, *MLA*
EPHIM FOGEL, Department of English, *Cornell University*
GEORGE H. FORD, Department of English, *University of Rochester*
EDWIN FUSSELL, Department of English, *Claremont Graduate School*
ALBERT F. GEGENHEIMER, Department of English, *University of Arizona*
JOHN GERRIETTS, Department of English, *Loyola University*
EVERETT A. GILLIS, Department of English, *Texas Technological College*
OTIS GREEN, Department of Romance Languages, *University of Pennsylvania*
DAVID GREENE, Department of English, *New York University*
JOSEPH E. GRENNEN, Department of English, *Fordham University*
JOHN C. GUILDS, JR., Department of English, *University of South Carolina*
E. F. GUY, Department of English, *University of Alberta*
GEORGE M. HARPER, Department of English, *University of Florida*
ROBERT HEILMAN, Department of English, *University of Washington*
C. CARROLL HOLLIS, Department of English, *University of North Carolina*
DANIEL F. HOWARD, Department of English, *Rutgers University*
THEODORE HORNBERGER, Department of English, *University of Pennsylvania*
CHARLES M. HUDSON, Department of English, *University of Missouri*
BERNARD F. HUPPÉ, Department of English, *State University of New York at Binghamton*
B. R. JERMAN, Department of English, *Kent State University*
THOMAS A. KIRBY, Department of English, *Louisiana State University*
KENNETH L. KNICKERBOCKER, Department of English, *University of Tennessee*
W. E. KNOTTS, Department of English, *State University of New York at Albany*
ALBERT J. KUHN, Department of English, *Ohio State University*
WILLIAM G. LANE, Department of English, *University of Colorado*
LEWIS LEARY, Department of English, *Columbia University*
CLIFFORD LEECH, Department of English, *University of Toronto*
E. HUDSON LONG, Department of English, *Baylor University*
ROBERT LUMIANSKY, Department of English, *University of Pennsylvania*
MAYNARD MACK, Department of English, *Yale University*
DAVID MALONE, Department of English, *University of Southern California*
PATRICIA C. MARTEL, *MLA Staff*
STANLEY MAVEETY, Department of English, *University of Oregon*
ROBERT D. MAYO, Department of English, *Northwestern University*
MAURICE B. McNAMEE, S.J., Department of English, *St. Louis University*
GEORGE MEYER, Department of English, *Tulane University*
KENNETH MILDENBERGER, Director, Office of Programs, *MLA*
JOHN W. MORRISON, Department of English, *University of Nevada*
THOMAS C. MOSER, Department of English, *Stanford University*
WILLIAM T. MOYNIHAN, Department of English, *University of Connecticut*

CHARLES D. MURPHY, Department of English, *University of Maryland*
CHARLES MUSCATINE, Department of English, *University of California (Berkeley)*
J. KERBY NEILL, Department of English, *Catholic University of America*
CLAIR C. OLSON, Department of English, *University of the Pacific*
WILLIAM R. PARKER, Department of English, *Indiana University*
W. R. PATRICK, Department of English, *Auburn University*
ROY H. PEARCE, Department of English, *University of California (San Diego)*
ROBERT PREYOR, Department of English, *Brandeis University*
JOHN REESING, Department of English, *George Washington University*
WARNER G. RICE, Department of English, *University of Michigan*
WALTER RIDEOUT, Department of English, *University of Wisconsin*
EDWARD H. ROSENBERRY, Department of English, *University of Delaware*
WILLIAM ROSSKY, Department of English, *Temple University*
ERNEST SANDEEN, Department of English, *University of Notre Dame*
HERBERT M. SCHUELLER, Department of English, *Wayne State University*
J. BURKE SEVERS, Department of English, *Lehigh University*
MICHAEL SHUGRUE, Assistant Secretary for English, *MLA*
HUGH B. STAPLES, Department of English, *University of Cincinnati*
MILTON STERN, Department of English, *University of Connecticut*
ALBERT E. STONE, JR., Department of English, *Emory University*
STUART M. TAVE, Department of English, *University of Chicago*
ANDRESS TAYLOR, Department of English, *Howard University*
D. F. THEALL, Department of English, *McGill University*
JARVIS A. THURSTON, Department of English, *Washington University*
WARREN I. TITUS, Department of English, *George Peabody College*
FRANCIS G. TOWNSEND, Department of English, *Florida State University*
EDMOND L. VOLPE, Department of English, *City College (New York)*
J. A. WARD, Department of English, *Rice University*
SIDNEY WARHAFT, Department of English, *University of Manitoba*
JAMES W. WEBB, Department of English, *University of Mississippi*
ROBERT H. WEST, Department of English, *University of Georgia*
E. H. WHAN, Department of English, *Ohio University*
ROBERT WHITMAN, Department of English, *University of Pittsburgh*
ROBERT WIGGINS, Department of English, *University of California (Davis)*
EUGENE WILLIAMSON, Department of English, *University of Alabama*
GEORGE J. WORTH, Department of English, *University of Kansas*
JOSEPH B. ZAVADIL, Department of English, *University of New Mexico*

Contents

THE
PH.D. IN ENGLISH
AND
AMERICAN
LITERATURE

CHAPTER 1

The Graduate
Departments
of English
Before 1900

Higher education in America began when the General Court of the Massachusetts Bay Colony set aside the sum of £400 in October 1636 "towards a schoale or colledge."[1] This offhand gesture—the funds were not immediately forthcoming—begot an emulative movement that established more than 2000 institutions within three centuries. Some of these institutions grew and flourished; some withered and bloomed again; some either merged with others or adopted new shapes or colors. A few died; but in America, once a college is founded, it is the closest thing to an immortal creature known to man. The general histories of education and the histories of particular colleges and universities provide us with a grand picture of this amazing phenomenon.[2] The autobiographies, biographies, letters, and daybooks of those men who were involved in the great development inform us of the contentions, the broken and fulfilled hopes, the praise, the blame, the success, and the failure that attended the growth of higher education in the United States.[3] The later emergence of *higher* higher education or graduate study is equally as interesting as the evolution of colleges; and moreover, it was attended by more controversy. The historians are now beginning to tell us about it, but there is still much to learn.[4] A solid account of the disciplines providing the basis of advanced study is a prime requirement; and histories of some of these disciplines have been recorded by competent experts. There is, however, no sketch of the evolution and growth of the graduate department of English and American literature; yet an understanding of its past, no matter how imperfect, may be of some help to those who consider its present problems and plan for its future.

The study of all modern languages and literatures is probably the offspring of the study of Greek and Latin. One can point to Boccaccio, the first professor of modern languages, and also to a long line of critics and scholars who supported the literature of the vernacular against the attacks of the classicist. Moreover, there was a professor of modern poetry at Kiel in Milton's generation, and the continental academies heard and printed essays on modern languages before the eighteenth century began. In England, however, the formal study of English literature came late to the universities;[5] and in the nineteenth century, America, although it was learning to look elsewhere, still looked to England. All early teachers of rhetoric were trained classicists; and though some of them were certainly skilled enough to teach Latin and Greek, it is possible that many of them saw better professional prospects as teachers of rhetoric. They were not teachers of English literature, for departments of English as such do not begin to materialize until the elective system, inaugurated by Harvard, triumphed, and colleges and universities altered their philosophy of education. A system of education that had once provided "mental discipline" for the elite became both professional and individualized training for the many.

With slight differences, the curricula of colleges of a century ago were uniform. From Boston to Atlanta, from New Brunswick to Ann Arbor, freshmen and sophomores were translating and analyzing grammatically almost the same Greek and Latin texts. They wrote prose and verse compositions in both languages and memorized the standard aphorisms that would serve them as badges of cultural and social superiority for the remainder of their lives. Rhetoric and forensics were important subjects in the undergraduate curriculum. At Yale in the 1830s, sophomores read Jamieson's *Rhetoric* and seniors studied Blair.[6] The advice of these rhetorical masters was followed in writing and speaking. The classical studies that occupied most of the first two years of the college schedule tapered off in the junior year; and upperclassmen were given a smattering of modern languages, logic, ethics, metaphysics, history, economics, and natural history. Most of the undergraduate courses were taught by younger men who tutored in a variety of subjects. Lecturing was unusual, although the president of the college often gave such a course on "the evidences of Christianity." The ordinary classroom, however, was the scene of questions by the tutors and memorized answers from the students. The undergraduate was sorely disciplined; he may also have been edified.

The tutors who taught rhetoric and forensics are the ancestors of the modern professor of English literature. Their lives were not very exciting, and they definitely went on to something better when the chance came their way. The Reverend Mr. Chauncey Goodrich, who was teaching rhetoric at Yale in 1830, eventually gave up his subject and was promoted to the Professorship of Pastoral Charge. All of these tutors were trained classicists, and one can hope that these studies enabled them and their students to speak and write brilliantly. But if a fine type of English prose resulted from this classical training, it is probably not to the credit of the professional classicists. Julian Sturdevant, a student at Yale in the 1830s, wrote that his classical tutors were good drillmasters, but were lacking in culture and the literary spirit. When Kingsley, Professor of Latin, complained of his students' shocking inability either to read Latin or to translate it into English, Sturdevant agreed with his master but quickly inquired, "Whose fault is it?" This same Professor Kingsley wrote the second part of the Yale report of 1828 that sustained the conservative British educational tradition against the new German methods commended in the Harvard statues of 1825. Kingsley supported the universal teaching of the Greek and Latin writers because they provided standards of merit closest to what the "thoroughly informed and disciplined" human mind approves.[7] English literature, "which depends on Greek and Latin rather than on French," is not mentioned as a proper subject in this report; it was probably considered in the same class as modern languages, subjects that could be picked up "without a derangement of the established system." Yale kept to these classical ideals for some time, because in 1853 Andrew White found that the tutors "made everything of gerund-grinding and nothing of literature."[8]

Rhetoric and oratory were taught everywhere, but literature, even classical literature, seems not to have been an important subject. After all, when the revered writers of Greece and Rome mainly furnished good examples of the use of the middle voice or the ablative absolute, one could hardly expect English literature to be much more than an avocation of the light-minded. As early as 1756 the inspired William Smith of Philadelphia emphasized English and English literature in his classical college. Later on, a division of English was established at the University of Vermont by James Marsh, whose theories of higher education were well in advance of his age. A department comparable to a department of English was proposed at Amherst by a clique of "young Turks" headed by Jacob Abbott, author of the famous "Rollo" books. A young nation, this group maintained, ought not to cling to "the prescriptive forms of former centuries."[9] But none of these ventures seems to have thrived or to have resulted in a general approval of English as a college subject.

English literature and other modern languages began to find a solid place in the curricula in the 1870s. The Harvard catalogue for 1875 states that a sophomore will read Campbell's *Philosophy of Rhetoric*, Whately's *Rhetoric*, Spencer's *Philosophy of Style*, and Abbott's *How to Write Clearly* with A. H. Hill. The same underclassmen were expected to absorb Hill's *General Rules for Punctuation and the Use of Capital Letters*. During his last three years, the Harvard student wrote a total of twelve themes and did eight forensics. These requirements were repeated at most other colleges; but in 1875, a Harvard undergraduate might also have elected one of Professor Francis Child's literature courses. In English I, he could read the *Canterbury Tales, Hamlet,* Bacon's *Essays,* selected poems of Milton, and the *Areopagitica.* The "rudiments" of Anglo-Saxon and Hadley's history of the English language were taught in English II, and *Beowulf* and Matzner's *Altenglische Sprachproben* in English III. Child reported that in 1875–1876 he had an average enrollment of forty in English I, only four in English II, and no one in English III. It is rather clear where undergraduate interest centered.

One can almost assume that these elective courses in English literature were taught very much after the manner of courses in the classics. Child's training had been philological, and undoubtedly in America, as in England, the teaching of modern literatures had to appear as solid as the teaching of Greek. Fortunately for us, the Harvard catalogue for this period informed the undergraduate about the nature of examinations and set-papers. The topics on which the undergraduate wrote themes were apparently culled from the thoughts of great men; consequently, he might be asked to expand on Mill's remark that "No society in which eccentricity is a matter of reproach can be in a wholesome state." He would also be expected to detect solecisms in sentences like "She was smaller in stature than either of her three sisters, to all of whom had been acceded the praise of being a fine woman." If, after this rhetorical study, the undergraduate elected to take English I, he would learn to modernize Chaucer, to annotate his language and allusions, and to summarize his plots. He would be expected to memorize one of Milton's sonnets and know his principal dates. He could, finally, expect to turn out an essay on "The Death of Othello" or "The Character of Cassio." The early curriculum at New Haven was more demanding and more conservative than the one at Cambridge. Rhetoric and forensics were required every year, but there was something called "Criticism" in the senior year. In 1877–1878, English literature appears formally in the Yale course of study; the junior was expected to read Craik's *History* and Morris and Skeat's *Specimens.* In 1878–1879 these texts are replaced by "Shakespeare," who is himself replaced by "Chaucer" in the year following. In these latter years "optionals" in English literature could be had with Beers and Northrop. By the academic year 1884–1885, Yale had accepted President Eliot's radical Harvard elective theories and English literature really came into its own—thanks mainly to the activities of the Sheffield tutors. However, by the time of Yale's conversion, Harvard had granted the first American Ph.D. in English literature to Robert Grant.

The doctorate of philosophy as a professional teaching degree has an interesting American history. The title is, of course, medieval and like the Master of Arts was once simply an indication of pedagogical rights. The degree could be earned in course or be awarded as a privilege by pope or emperor. Originally, the bachelor's degree signified that its possessor was an apprentice for a doctorate, but in time, it came to have an intrinsic value of its own. The other medieval degree, the M.A., was first given in America (as it was in England) to any graduate who stayed out of prison and paid the necessary fees; but as early as 1642, Harvard set up other conditions for its bestowal besides those of a strict moral life. The Overseers and Masters specified that the candidate for the degree give in writing "a synopsis or summary of Logic, Natural and Moral Philosophy, Arithmetic, Geometry, and Astronomy" and be ready to defend his "*Theses* or position."[10] Graduate study in a sense may begin with this requirement, which was undoubtedly honored in the breach.

Two hundred years later, in 1846, the Harvard Corporation began to consider the establishment of a school of science and literature where its graduates could be given advanced instruction. A year later, the Lawrence Scientific School was founded, but the study of literature, mentioned in the original prospectus, got submerged because it was thought the interest would be so slight there would be no point in offering it. While Harvard was setting up this embryo graduate school, Yale was feeling inner stirrings; and in 1846 a committee was appointed (Professor Kingsley was again a member) to recommend courses that could be given "to others than members of the undergraduate classes." Within twelve months, this committee suggested the organization of a Department of Philosophy and the Arts which would incorporate courses outside the ordinary Yale curriculum and satisfy the "demands of our graduates and others for instruction in particular lines beyond what is wanted or can be given in the college course." Within a decade the prescient James D. Dana proposed that this department be enlarged to prevent young Americans "from seeking in the atmosphere of Germany the knowledge for which they yearn." Yale did not accept this suggestion immediately, but it would.[11]

Dana's attitude was not unique; but even after the report on the Department of Philosophy and the Arts had been accepted, opportunities were still slight for the student who wished to go beyond the Yale A.B. Daniel Coit Gilman, a great admirer of Dana and a Yale graduate of 1852, found it difficult to get advanced study of any sort. President Woolsey suggested that he read Rau's *Political Economy* and "come and tell him the contents." Gilman did not consider this advanced study, but he had similar experiences with Professors Hadley and Porter. When he went to Cambridge and talked to President Sparks, he was told he could hear Agassiz's lectures, "and I believe Mr. Longfellow is reading Dante with a class."[12] Because of this domestic situation, Americans had long been going to Europe; and before the twentieth century began, more than 10,000 of them had matriculated at German universities. Cogswell, who was among the vanguard of American students in Germany, thought that "very few of what the Germans call scholars" were needed in America;[13] but as the nineteenth century wore on, his judgment became more and more incorrect. The degree of doctor of philosophy sought by Americans in Germany was first given in 1852 in the United States, *honoris causa*, by Bucknell University;[14] but eight years later, Yale had the higher honor of establishing it as an earned degree.

At a meeting of the Corporation of Yale University on July 24, 1860, the Scientific School asked that the doctorate be given "in accordance with the usage of German Universities" for "high attainments in

Mathematics or Philosophy and the Arts" in order to satisfy those students "who now resort to German universities for the advantage of study no greater than we are able to afford." The memorandum proposed that the requirement be a year of further study, an examination in the subjects studied, and the approval of an original dissertation.[15] Results were immediate; and in the year 1861, the doctorate was conferred on Eugene Schuyler in Philosophy and Psychology, A. W. Wright in Physics, and J. M. Whiton in Classics. Schuyler, a brilliant linguist, may have written a dissertation on Wedgwood's lexicon of English etymology. He then took a law degree at Columbia, entered the diplomatic service, and became not only a Russian specialist but also one of the earliest American translators of Russian classics. Whiton wrote a six-page essay in Latin on *Brevis vita, ars longa.* He became an ordained clergyman and composed a famous theological work, *Is Eternal Punishment Endless?* Wright, who submitted a dissertation on the orbits of meteors, remained at Yale as a professor and a distinguished scientist.[16] The Ph.D. was now rooted in America as an earned degree, but it is plain that it was regarded by at least two of these men as a cultural adornment, something between the A.B. and a really professional degree.

Harvard, which had been in advance of Yale in liberalizing its undergraduate departments, did not announce a graduate program until 1876. In this year it agreed to grant a doctorate to an A.B. "who was qualified," following a two-year course of liberal study terminating in an examination and a satisfactory dissertation. Francis Child, who was about to train the first American Ph.D. in English, contented himself by saying he would meet graduate students once a week for conference and instruction "in such parts of English literature as they may be studying." His three courses in English were undoubtedly open to these students, and one of them registered in English II in 1876. A. S. Hill's course in "Modern English Literature" seems not to have carried graduate credit. In 1876 Robert Grant (1852–1940) presented a thesis that summarized the various theories about Shakespeare's sonnets for which he was awarded a doctorate in English literature. Grant now took a law degree at Columbia, set up practice in Boston, but used his spare moments to write novels, plays, verse, autobiographies, essays, and travel books. The Ph.D. in English had not spoiled his talents as a man of letters, but like Schuyler and Whiton, he did not regard it as the beginning of an academic career.

There is no information about Grant's training or examinations for the doctorate, but by 1878 Harvard's doctoral requirements are made somewhat more explicit. On the first of June, each candidate for a doctorate was asked to submit an account of how he had spent the year; but the rendering of this account, the catalogue stated, does not exempt the student "from liability to examination on the whole ground of his studies at the time of his offering himself for the degree." His thesis, "plainly written," was to be retained in the president's office for a month so that it could be perused by members of the Academic Council. Approved by all powers, the candidate was given the degree of doctor and was "recognized as qualified to give special private instruction to candidates for the degree in the departments in which he himself has taken the degree." With this affirmation of rights and purposes, the Harvard faculty of 1878 made the Ph.D. the essential requirement for university teaching.

These Harvard announcements of 1878 arose, undoubtedly, from the importance placed on teaching by American colleges in the nineteenth century. The career of Francis Child, the first American scholar in English literature, suggests the pedagogical pressure on a college teacher of that time. After graduating in 1846, Child remained at Harvard as one of the typical tutors of his age and taught mathematics, history, and economics. His real interest in English literature was manifested in 1848 by the publication of *Four Old Plays,* one of the first works of American literary scholarship. He went to Germany in 1849 for philological study; he was given an honorary Ph.D. by the University of Göttingen; and he returned to Harvard in 1851 as Channings' successor in the Boylston Professorship. He then taught courses in rhetoric for the next twenty-seven years. When Johns Hopkins University was established, Gilman attempted to supply departmental vacancies by month-long series of lectures. There was no professor of English, and Child was invited to lecture in February 1876 and 1877 to make up for this want. It is reported that his lectures on Chaucer were more popularly attended than those on Dante by Lowell. At any rate, Gilman was impressed and offered the professorship of English to Child. Harvard apparently met the offer by releasing Child from the teaching of rhetoric. By this action Gilman established an English department at Harvard although thus far he had failed to do so at Johns Hopkins.

Freed from the teaching of rhetoric, Child divided his former three elective courses into several components. He continued to teach eleven hours a week, but he had a separate course for Chaucer and another for Shakespeare. The department began to grow around him. Mr. Wendell, Hill's assistant, offered a course in "English Drama before 1865." Undergraduates were still forced to take the prescribed courses, but even these were brightened with readings in Addison, Goldsmith, Burke, Scott, and Irving. Mr. Briggs began to teach a course of his own, "Shakespeare to Dryden exclusive of Milton." Milton, of course, had long been the private property of Child. Mr. Clymer announced a course in "Nineteenth Century Prose." The Harvard department was now a department and was setting the pattern for other colleges. Child also introduced a course in Grein's *Bibliothek*, which was for graduates only, but it probably was not overcrowded. As a matter of fact, after Grant had taken his degree, it was thirteen years before Harvard made any more doctors in English; then in 1889, Herbert Greene handed in a dissertation on allegory in Spenser, Bunyan, and Swift, and C. F. R. Hochdörfer wrote a thesis on the language of "The Court of Love." By this time, too, George Lyman Kittredge, who had been registered as a graduate student in 1884, was employed by Child as an assistant, and Josiah Royce, the first Johns Hopkins' doctor of literature, was teaching forensics and English VI, entitled "Oral Discussion of Social and Literary Topics."

Royce was really Johns Hopkins' first Ph.D., and the understaffed university had to get his learned accomplishments certified by outsiders. Porter of Yale approved his dissertation and Morris of Michigan examined him—probably in modern languages, but possibly in philosophy.[18] Dr. Royce, having acquired his degree in 1878, went to California as an instructor in the English department. In the fall of the same year, A. S. Cook, a Rutgers' A.B. and a former student in Germany, was appointed instructor in English at Johns Hopkins and organized the department. Cook had twenty-nine graduate students in his seminars on Anglo-Saxon, Chaucer, and Shakespeare. Sylvester, an eminent Cambridge mathematician and very minor poet, gave lectures to these students on the science of prosody. Among these students was James Bright whose doctoral thesis on Alfred's version of Gregory's Pastoral Care was accepted by Cook in 1881. Bright thus became the second man to take an American doctorate in English; but he immediately went off to Germany with Cook, who had not been reappointed by Gilman, for further philological study. After dropping Cook, Gilman failed in his attempts to get Sweet, W. D. Howells, Edmund Gosse, and Robert Browning to accept the Johns Hopkins Chair of English literature; so he made do with W. H. Brown, M.D., former editor of the *Southern Review* and an antiphilologist, and Henry Wood, teacher of German and very much a pro-philologist. Wood gave a course in Cynewulf, conducted fortnightly seminars, heard regular papers and reports. Then, after an absence of four years, Bright returned from Germany and was made instructor in English, and Wood devoted himself to graduate work in German.

Long before the German graduate system was imported to Baltimore,[19] advanced work in English literature, as in many other subjects, had found a home in America. The founding of Johns Hopkins was so spectacular, however, that the interest of Americans in advanced professional study greatly increased. By 1890 Bryn Mawr, Cornell, Michigan, Princeton, Pennsylvania, and other universities, had graduate departments of English and American literature. It has often been assumed that these early departments were heavy with German-trained philologists and that literature as literature was shunned. There is in this assumption only a kind of half-truth. Philology was there, indeed; in order to prove that the study of English was as difficult as the study of Greek, but that it was not the exclusive and dominant method of study. Bright might boast that his seminar's library contained fifteen editions of Beowulf, and Murray of Princeton might point to his collection of 140 volumes on Anglo-Saxon; but Child, no enemy of linguistics, could state as his inducement to graduate students that Harvard had 278 volumes of Miltonia; and Demmon, out in Ann Arbor, could hold out the bait of a 3500-volume Shakespeare library. In New York, George Woodberry, made professor at Columbia in 1890, gave very literary courses and even taught "Practical Criticism." Brander Matthews lectured on American literature as literature, and T. R. Price, sometime professor of Greek at Virginia, discussed modern poets like Tennyson, Browning, and Arnold. At Yale, where Lounsbury and Beers were now assisted by Cook and Cross, most of the dissertations accepted were non-philological. F. H. Stoddard, professor of English at New York University, directed theses on "The Philosophy of Judgment as Portrayed in Shakespeare" and "The Evolution of the Essay"; and Felix Schelling of Pennsylvania gave doctorates for studies of Donne, Breton, Lodge, Sidney, the pastoral, formal satire, and the religious lyric. James Hart, Professor of Rhetoric at Cornell, seems to have been the only truly determined philologist, and granted doctorates in 1891 to Emerson for a study of the Ithaca dialect and in 1898 to Northrup for a thesis on the Old English prefixes, a, oe, on, and ond.

Michigan is probably the first middlewestern university to give doctorates in English literature. The smooth surface of its courses in rhetoric were rippled at an early date by a literary survey based on Arnold's Manual and by three elective courses in English and American literature. Graduate work in linguistics under Isaac Demmon and George Hempl were offered in the early 1880s, but J. Rose Colby, who took the first doctorate in 1886, wrote on "Some Ethical Aspects of Later Elizabethan Tragedy." The establishment of the new University of Chicago with a large English department was, of course, a great stimulus to the advanced study of literature in America. When J. M. Manly came to the department from Brown University at the end of the final decade, the enrollment figures had been for some time equal to those of Harvard and Yale combined. The example set by Michigan and Chicago was quickly followed in the middle states by Wisconsin, Minnesota, and Vanderbilt. Each of these universities established a graduate department and began to give doctorates before the century ended.[20]

In the far west, both the University of California and Stanford had graduate schools of English before 1900 although neither institution had given a doctorate by that date. One would expect graduate work to begin at Berkeley with the appointment of A. S. Cook, but it was only after Cook went to Yale, that California developed a graduate department under Gayley, Bradley, Armes, and Lange. Gayley offered a course in esthetic theory and there were seminars in "tendencies and movements," but the program was probably linguistic in emphasis. At Stanford, the important graduate courses in English literature ranged from "Beowulf" to "Shakespeare," but Professors Anderson, Hudson, Flügel, and Lathrop presided over seminars in which the topics to be studied were of a rather modern nature.

Many of the professors in all these new graduate departments were giving a degree that they did not have and about which some of them may have had doubts or regrets. Not a single member of the early Harvard graduate staff had a Ph.D. At Yale, Cook, with a Jena degree, was the only doctor. There were two Ph.D.'s in English at Bryn Mawr, nine at Chicago, two at Johns Hopkins, one at Stanford, one at Michigan, two at Minnesota, two at Pennsylvania, one at Princeton, one at Vanderbilt, three at Western Reserve, and one at Wisconsin. In spite of this paucity of teachers with Ph.D.'s—and some of the doctorates may have been honorary[21]—it is amazing how well the instruction was managed and how carefully and uniformly the standards for the degree were settled.

Residence requirements varied from one to two years, but it was regularly assumed that the candidate should add an additional year for the writing of the dissertation. Language requirements were fairly regular. Although a few universities asked for Latin, this language was so commonly studied that most departments seem to have taken it for granted. German and French are the languages normally required, but the University of Pennsylvania requested simply "a knowledge of two European languages." In all departments the candidate was expected to present himself for "private examinations" in his major and minor subjects. The final examination was usually said to be public. Most universities, Harvard and Yale excepted, required that the thesis be printed; but Johns Hopkins and Michigan allowed "publication in part." The degree was, of course, the basic requirement for an academic career. Most of the people earning it—a few women excepted—could subsequently be found in academic posts.

The pedagogical value of the doctorate was, of course, first emphasized by the Harvard statement of 1878, but the same idea was given a kind of consecration when the Modern Language Association conducted its third census of the teaching personnel of colleges and universities in 1887. The degrees of each teacher were carefully recorded, and it was discovered that only about twenty-five teachers of English had Ph.D.'s. Some of these doctorates may have been of German origin; some may have been honorary; some may have been in a totally different subject. The reason for this interest in degrees cannot now be ascertained, but the association was as much absorbed then by pedagogical matters as it was by scholarship. The original pedagogical interests of the association can be clearly detected in the papers read at the first MLA convention. Ten of the fourteen papers were on teaching problems; the other four were of a learned nature. Of the seventeen papers in the first volume of *PMLA*, ten are concerned with the curricula and the methods of language teaching. Subsequent volumes also contain essays on educational matters; and though the number of these essays decreases, they do not vanish entirely until the seventh year of publication. The members of the association continued, however, to hear papers in its "Pedagogical Section" until 1900, but even here it never answered the question put to it by President Magill of Swarthmore in 1892. The scholarly concerns of the profession, he said, were worthy enough but of interest to not more than 5 percent of the students who were being taught. "Now," he asked, "what are you going to do with the other 95 percent?"

It has been proposed by historians of education that the medieval doctors were masters in a trade guild and that the bachelors of arts were their apprentices. This hypothesis seems to gain modern support when we discover that the apprentices of the 1890s began to form local associations which eventually became the Federation of the

Graduate Clubs. Delegates from the graduate student locals at Cornell, Harvard, and Johns Hopkins met in April 1893 and drew up a set of resolutions that were sent to the journeymen in all universities granting the doctorate. These masters were urged "only to grant the degree to persons competent to advance knowledge," to be more liberal in permitting student migration, and, consequently, to reduce the residence requirement to one year. All of this is reported in a little volume that the Harvard Club compiled about graduate work in America; moreover, this little volume, *Graduate Courses*, appeared for most of the 1890s as the official organ of all graduate students. It regularly attacked the custom of giving the doctorate as an honorary degree, insisted that all graduate departments require an A.B. for admission, and recommended that the universities pay the cost of publishing doctoral dissertations. In its later years, the annual volume summarized the proceedings of the organization's national convention. Some of the papers read at these meetings are on topics too recent to be seventy years old.

At one meeting, J. F. Tufts of Chicago observed that they were all on the way to becoming specialists who would be regarded as lacking "breadth and cultivation" and "wanting the ability to interest or the patience to instruct their students." This, he felt, was the public image of the Ph.D. To correct this sorry impression he implored his colleagues to look harder at the "philosophy" in their title than at the "doctor" and to color all they had to say with philosophic enamels. On another occasion, after President Eliot had welcomed the delegates and spoken well of their migratory plans, Professor J. W. White of Harvard urged them to demand reasonable teaching schedules. No one, he pointed out, expected a clergyman to preach nine sermons a week. J. P. Warren, a graduate student, presented a paper at the same meeting on "Specialized Scholarship *versus* Preparation for Teaching as a Basis for Graduate Study." He regretted that those who knew more but taught less got the most attractive teaching posts and suggested that research professorships be established to separate the two functions. The delegates later listened to a paper on "The Master's degree: Is it obsolete?" The author, a woman scholar, felt that the M.A. protected the value of the Ph.D., and whereas she thought it a prime requirement for elementary teaching, she predicted that as the worth of the M.A. declined that of the Ph.D. would decrease. This pessimistic paper was seconded by Emily Fogg, a Bryn Mawr graduate student, who regarded the M.A. as a mere "culture degree," but her sober objection was to the growing tendency to admit undergraduates to graduate courses. Standards went down, she said, when this was done.

The Federation of Graduate Clubs held its last convention before the twentieth century began. When it was organized, the Ph.D. in English was offered at fourteen of the nineteen universities in the federation. By the time of its last convention in December 1898, twenty-four English departments had a graduate program. The year before, a census taken by the locals had shown that English was the third most popular subject in the graduate schools and that of the more than 3000 registered graduate students, 547 were in English literature. By 1910 there were forty graduate departments of English and American literature, and today there are more than one hundred. But the problems of the first quarter of a century are still with us; they have simply become larger and more manifold.

CHAPTER 2

The Problems
Before Us

———————————◆•◆—————————————

Probably few English graduate students of 1900 were not looking
toward an academic career; and by that date, it was clear that the
doctorate was the necessary first qualification. In 1884, six years after
Harvard had proclaimed the pedagogical nature of the Ph.D. and set
the course of study that secured the degree, only 19 of its faculty of
189 teachers had the three magic letters after their names. But Harvard was an ancient establishment, and the faculties of newer and
less influential universities could not be so cavalier about giving something they did not themselves have. The steady increase of the doctorate of philosophy as an academic ornamentation can be observed
by turning through the catalogues and announcements of other universities for the years 1895–1905. For example, by 1900 the doctors
of philosophy are in the majority at Brown University. In 1904 the
College of the City of New York demanded this degree of its professors, and a year later, the University of Illinois announced it would
make no one a professor who was not a Ph.D.[1] After World War I,
the doctorate quickly became the sine qua non of many four-year
colleges as well as of all universities.

Undergraduate registration was not, however, too enormous at the
beginning of the twentieth century. Only about 4 percent of the college age group was on the campuses because a university was the

15

place to send one's bright children only. In the fall of 1965, according to the Office of Education, 6 million students, about 40 percent of the eighteen to twenty-one year olds were on the registration books of institutions of higher learning.[2] The government experts at forecasting enrollments, who have been regular underestimators by about 10 percent, predict that there will be 7 million undergraduates in 1969 and 9 million in 1975. Unless some forms of mechanical education are highly perfected by these dates, it will take a considerable number of instructors to teach the 80,000 sections of freshman writing that must be organized within a few years. But if prophetic figures of this nature are disturbing, there is consolation in the fact that the annual emergence of Ph.D.'s in English has been reasonably steady for the last six years. Since 1960 between 400 and 500 have been annually graduated. Whereas the procession of new doctors continues to be of an average length, that of the M.A.'s in English lengthens by about 10 percent a year. This increase in the master's degree is not attributable to the graduate departments alone; they have been substantially aided by the colleges. In 1964, one hundred and seventy-four colleges helped the major graduate English departments make over 4400 masters of arts. One can assume that as the undergraduate body increases at the rate of about 250,000 students a year, the people with M.A.'s in English can be depended on for help.

In the 1890s the supply of Ph.D.'s in English was undoubtedly smaller than the demand; in fact, it was only in the unhappy period between 1931 and 1940 that there was any reasonable relationship between what was wanted and what was to be had. The acute shortage has been very visible since 1950, but a picture of the academic year 1962–1963, a typical one, will reveal what has become the annual predicament. Of the 4.5 million students registering this year (the usual 250,000 increment was observed), 28,000 were seniors in English and American Literature and 33,000 were juniors. These 61,000 English majors were undoubtedly increased by junior and senior "tourists" from other departments, but their number is unknown. The 61,000 majors plus the visitors from other areas were augmented by more than 2 million sophomores and freshmen, who might be taking survey courses and having their literacy inspected and corrected in freshman English. In the spring of 1963, 72 graduate departments of English gave 516 Ph.D.'s and, helped out by 230 nongraduate departments, made 4019 M.A.'s. The next fall saw the customary increase of 250,000 in the freshman class and a 15 percent increase in English majors. Once again the supply of trained English teachers was inadequate for the number of students to be taught. It is not amazing that 137 institutions of higher learning notified the NEA in the fall of 1963 that they had acute shortages in the English department.[3]

The regular deficit in fully trained teachers of English is not the result of a "greener pastures" syndrome. The English Ph.D. does not often venture out into the cold, nonacademic world. Faithful to his careful traditions, he enters the teaching profession at the rate of ninety-one to the hundred. The nine who stray in strange lands probably end up grading their husbands' themes. This fidelity of English Ph.D.'s to the teaching profession is almost miraculous when it is viewed against the general infidelity of the other learned professions. The NEA report on 1958–1960 displays the singularity of this condition.

Table 2.1.   *Where the new doctors of philosophy go**

FIELD	DEGREES GRANTED	ENTERING OR CONTINUING TEACHING
English	726	91.2%
Philosophy	196	86.8%
Languages	361	84.0%
History	580	77.2%
Economics	455	67.7%
Political Science	317	62.4%
Mathematics	479	60.2%
Physics	885	26.5%
Chemistry	1864	19.3%
All fields	16,252	45.6%

* Table derived from NEA biennial research report; reprinted by permission of the NEA Research Division. But see how the sciences have changed since 1938 in Logan Wilson, *The Academic Man* (New York, 1942), p. 48.

Mathematics, Physics, and Chemistry lose from forty to eighty percent of their new doctors to nonacademic employment and lead in all lists of teacher shortages in one, two, three order. English is, however, just behind them. In the last decade it has been regularly in fourth place.

The shortage of fully trained teachers of English has unfortunately been increasing in an order that is not consonant with the increase in undergraduate enrollment. In 1953–1954 only 29 percent of all new teachers of English had a doctorate; ten years later, this surprising percentage had fallen to little more than 12 percent. Once again the figures are disappointing. The decline in trained personnel revealed

Table 2.2.   Degrees held by new teachers of English
               (in percentages)*

DATE	PH.D. DEGREE	M.A. DEGREE	A.B. DEGREE
1953–1954	29.0	63.0	8.0
1954–1955	23.4	68.4	8.2
1955–1956	18.9	72.7	8.4
1956–1957	17.7	80.7	11.6
1957–1958	16.8	70.0	13.2
1958–1959	13.7	74.1	12.2
1959–1960	13.6	76.8	9.6
1960–1961	13.6	74.8	11.6
1961–1962	13.5	75.4	11.1
1962–1963	12.6	76.6	10.8

* Table based on NEA biennial research report findings. Reprinted by permission of the NEA Research Division.

by these percentages for English is true of all other disciplines but not to the same degree. While the number of beginning English teachers with Ph.D.'s was being halved, the average for all fields was falling from 31 percent to 25 percent. It seems almost a natural law that the more trained English teachers are required, the fewer are available. Can this shortage be solved or should we regard it as chronic?

Industrial production is increased by building more plants and by operating those already built more wisely. In agriculture more acres are put into cultivation and farming methods are improved. The essential product of the undergraduate institutions is the A.B. and other associated degrees; one cannot help but feel that the enormous increase in this division of the education industry is closely related to the increase in acreage and plant. Campuses piled with brick, stone, steel, and concrete to make shelters for body and mind have appeared from out of nowhere. Management and nonacademic personnel has grown formidably. Everything has seemed to grow in measure with everything else except trained faculty and the means of training them. In 1776 about seven colleges had created an alumni body of 3000. Between 1954 and 1964, about 4.5 million bachelors of arts and science were produced. The alumni group of 1976 is likely to be at least 3000 times larger than that of 1776 and most of them will be made in the next decade. There are, however, many paths to the A.B., but there is now only one path to the Ph.D. in English. The question that consequently arises is this: Will an increase in graduate departments of English similar to the increase in undergraduate departments produce enough trained teachers to staff the undergraduate departments? The statistics in Table 2.3 suggest what the graduate departments of English have been doing about this problem.

Table 2.3.   *Number and sources of Ph.D.'s in English graduated*
               between 1955–1965

(There are two sets of figures on hand for this information. The USOE issues an annual report and all departments except those asterisked send the compiler of this table its own census. The department's own census was preferred to that of the USOE, but the government count had to be used when the department had none of its own U = university; S = state university.)

1	Alabama (U)	5	24	Duke	75
2	Arizona (U)	4	25	Duquesne	1
3	Arizona (S)	2	26	Emory	15
4	Arkansas (U)	29	27	Florida (U)	47*
5	Auburn	1	28	Florida (S)	30
6	Baylor	1	29	Fordham	76
7	Boston	52	30	Georgia	11
8	Bowling Green	4	31	Harvard	265
9	Brown	45	32	Illinois	177
10	Bryn Mawr		33	Indiana	86
	(Pennsylvania)	12	34	Iowa	93
11	Berkeley (California)	96	35	Johns Hopkins	46
12	Davis (California)	1	36	Kansas	29
13	Los Angeles (California)	70	37	Kent (S)	1
14	Catholic (U)	29	38	Kentucky	18
15	Chicago	100	39	Lehigh	7
16	Cincinnati	13	40	Louisiana	21
17	Claremont	19	41	Loyola	17
18	Colorado	46	42	Maryland	25
19	Columbia	397	43	Michigan (U)	195
20	Connecticut	22	44	Michigan (S)	22*
21	Cornell	62	45	Minnesota	87
22	Delaware	2	46	Mississippi	3
23	Denver	45*	47	Missouri	19*

48	Nebraska	19	69	South Carolina	7
49	New Mexico	21*	70	Southern California	51
50	New York (U)	123	71	Stanford	103
51	North Carolina	96	72	Syracuse	29
52	Northwestern	65*	73	Temple	4
53	Notre Dame	50	74	Tennessee	21
54	Ohio (U)	1	75	Texas Christian	3
55	Ohio (S)	87	76	Texas (U)	100*
56	Pacific	1	77	Texas Technological	14
57	Oklahoma	35	78	Tulane	41
58	Oregon	19	79	Utah	13
59	Peabody	19	80	Vanderbilt	62
60	Pennsylvania (U)	167	81	Virginia	27
61	Pennsylvania (S)	34	82	George Washington	3
62	Pittsburgh	43*	83	Washington (St. Louis)	22
63	Princeton	91	84	Washington (Seattle)	125
64	Rice	21	85	Wayne (S)	23
65	Rochester	36	86	Western Reserve	34*
66	Rutgers	11	87	Wisconsin	277
67	St. Johns	34	88	Yale	213
68	St. Louis	20			

The realities that Table 2.3 intimate, but do not shout, appear quite clearly when the tabulation is carefully scanned. If we select an earlier year like 1949 as a subject for analysis, we discover that thirty-three graduate departments of English awarded 157 doctorates. Twenty-five years later, in 1964, seventy-three departments gave 556 degrees. The surface of this increase is indeed bright. The number of degrees has almost quadrupled; the number of degree-granting departments has almost doubled. But a rhetorical announcement of this nature simply covers the reality. The same thirty-three departments conferring all the degrees in 1949 gave 400 of the 1964 degrees. The forty new graduate departments accounted for 156 degrees. If a long view of almost twenty years, 1947–1964, is scrutinized for data, it is obvious that a rather small number of graduate departments of English have trained most of the teachers now teaching. A tabulation of all departments granting more than 100 degrees in this period shows slight but interesting variations in rankings.

The rankings in Table 2.4 indicate that since the late 1940s the relationship between the nine most active graduate schools of English—Columbia, Harvard, Wisconsin, Yale, Michigan, New York University, Pennsylvania, the Californias, and Illinois—has not changed

Table 2.4.   *Relative rankings of graduate departments according to number of Ph.D.'s granted in English and American Literature*

WHOLE PERIOD	LAST TEN YEARS (1954–1964)	LAST FIVE YEARS (1959–1964)
1. Columbia	1. Columbia	1. Columbia
2. Harvard	2. Harvard	2. Harvard
3. Yale	3. Wisconsin	3. Wisconsin
4. Wisconsin	4. Yale	4. Yale
5. Michigan	5. Michigan	5. Michigan
6. New York University	6. Pennsylvania	6. New York University
7. Pennsylvania	7. Californias*	7. Californias*
8. Californias*	8. New York University	8. Illinois
9. Illinois	9. Illinois	9. Pennsylvania
10. Chicago	10. Texas	10. Indiana
11. Texas	11. Indiana	11. Texas
12. Indiana	12. Washington	12. Washington
13. Stanford	13. Chicago	13. Stanford
14. Iowa	14. Stanford	14. Minnesota
15. Washington	15. Iowa	15. Iowa
16. North Carolina	16. Minnesota	16. North Carolina
17. Minnesota	17. Princeton	17. Chicago
18. Princeton	18. North Carolina	18. Princeton
19. Northwestern	19. Northwestern	19. Northwestern

* U.C. at Berkeley and Los Angeles were combined in the USOE report until recently.

greatly. Yale has created about ten fewer Ph.D.'s in the last five years than Wisconsin and dropped back one place. Pennsylvania with seventy-seven doctors in the five-year period has fallen behind New York University with eighty-seven, the Californias with eighty-four, and Illinois with eighty-one. In the lower half of the table, Chicago has slipped considerably; whereas the University of Washington and Minnesota have risen spectacularly, but it will probably be a long time before any of these departments are competing seriously with the leaders. Columbia, Chicago, the Californias, Harvard, Illinois, Michigan, New York University, Pennsylvania, Stanford, Texas, the University of Washington, Wisconsin, and Yale, fourteen graduate departments of English, have granted 54 percent of all doctorates earned in the last decade. To this series of very active departments, we may add those at Boston, Cornell, Duke, Fordham, Indiana, Iowa, Minnesota, Notre Dame, Northwestern, North Carolina, Southern California, Princeton, and Vanderbilt, because they granted about 21 percent of the Ph.D.'s won in this period. The remaining eighty-eight departments were responsible for slightly more than 23 percent of the doctors in English. To put it flatly, during the last ten years one fifth of the English departments have trained two thirds of the Ph.D.'s.

It is as clear as a manufacturer's annual report that not all the plants are in full production. If all the graduate departments in the third file—the 80 percent—would train, as some of them do, four or five Ph.D.'s a year, the shortage of teachers of English and American literature would be eased but not eradicated. Some of these departments may have stricter admission requirements or standards than the leaders—this is a matter that cannot be investigated—but in general it can be assumed that they are as eager to train teachers as Columbia and Harvard. It was they who breathed more freely when the Wilson Fellowships, invented partly to comfort them for lack of endowment, were announced. But their problem was not solved by this establishment,[4] nor is it actually helped much by NDEA grants. Aspirants for the doctorate are likely to apply to them only after they have failed to be admitted by a well-known department. Studies have indicated that the main reasons for this student attitude are academic snobbery and professional legend. All candidates for the doctorate, regardless of subject, seek to wrest their degrees from departments that are higher in repute, certainly no lower, than the one that gave them their A.B.'s; because it is assumed that a new doctor's chance for appointment is based on the source of his doctorate. It is also assumed that appointing officers are nervous men and search first for appointees at the great universities so that they can account subsequently for mistakes by pointing to the colors on the appointee's hood. When they fail to induce the graduates of the great universities to join them, it is believed that the heads of these lesser organizations turn to the lesser graduate schools for aid.

It is quite possible that all of these notions can be supported by the past, but there are no statistics to show that any of these beliefs has contemporary validity. When the available material for the class of 1965 was studied, it was clear (though the sample was not perfect) that a doctorate from a "Cartter University" was three times better than a "non-Cartter" degree in securing a post at a "Cartter" university and twice as good as a "non-Cartter" degree in avoiding appointment at a college with fewer than 1000 students. In all other respects there is almost no difference. The data presented in Table 2.5 may suggest that myths about the value of degrees are fading and the data in Table 2.6 may also indicate that the equally old notions about the importance of an "Eastern" degree are just as invalid.

Table 2.5.   *First appointments of the 1965 class of Ph.D.'s in English*

	ORIGIN OF THE DEGREE	
	"CARTTER	OTHER
APPOINTMENT	UNIVERSITY"*	UNIVERSITIES†
"Cartter University"	34	10
Other university	68	67
State college	12	18
Liberal arts college: Enrollment 1000+	14	13
Liberal arts college: Enrollment −999	10	19
Two-year colleges	3	3

* The data are based on fourteen departments and 141 cases traceable out of 265 degrees given.   † The data are based on forty-three departments and 130 cases traceable out of 181 degrees given.

Table 2.6.   *First appointments of the 1965 class of Ph.D.'s in English*

	GEOGRAPHICAL LOCATION OF			
	GRADUATE DEPARTMENTS*			
APPOINTMENT	EAST	MIDWEST	SOUTH	WEST
	(19)	(15)	(14)	(9)
"Cartter University"	16	16	4	3
Other university	43	43	27	22
State college	7	6	11	6
Liberal arts college: 1000+	9	12	4	2
Liberal arts college: −999	11	11	6	1
Two-year college	1	0	0	5

* Number of departments involved is indicated in parentheses. The number of students is the same as for Table 2.5.

The fact that students crowd toward the great graduate departments makes it plain that these departments, which already lead in the training of Ph.D.'s and probably have the largest number of ABD's on their records, should double their degree and awards and lead further. But leading and doubling is exactly what they have been doing during the last quarter of a century. In 1948 Columbia gave nineteen Ph.D.'s and Harvard gave fourteen; in 1965 Columbia gave fifty-three degrees and Harvard gave thirty-seven. Similar miracles occurred at other graduate universities. Nothing more can be asked of the great departments, and it is quite possible it is a lack of talented and properly motivated candidates for the doctorate in English rather than a want of graduate departments that may be the basic difficulty.[5] It would probably require the total effort of the unaccredited department of magic to effect a great awakening among English majors and send more of them to graduate schools; but until such an event occurs, there are probably already many students long at work on a doctorate—enough to satisfy the immediate need for qualified teachers were half of them to finish their degrees this year. In the fall of 1963, for example, there were 5749 full- and part-time students who had progressed beyond the M.A. and were registered in our graduate departments. In the spring of 1964, some 556 of them became Ph.D.'s. What has been the fate of the remaining 5193? Have they all now completed their training? Statistics do not indicate it. Possibly it is this group that should be carefully considered and the methods used in training them revalued.

The candidate for the doctorate in English must live longer than his friends in science or social science, because they will have their degrees and be on the road to a professorship about six years before he finishes his dissertation. Rosenhaupt's 1958 account of Columbia's graduate students showed that it took about ten years of elapsed time to get a doctorate in English.[6] Berelson's 1960 study of American graduate education revealed that any doctorate in the Humanities required at least a median of six years.[7] The USOE censuses for graduate enrollments of 1961, 1962, and 1964 (the only ones made) indicate that the average time lapse between the A.B. and the Ph.D. in English is nine to eleven years. But once a graduate student has finished the course and been handed his diploma, what are his professional prospects?

During the 1930s, a new Ph.D. in English was fortunate to find a teaching post at all, but lack of employment was a predicament he shared with mankind in general. During the recent two decades, the whole profession has become prosperous and, thanks to NEA reports, what now happens is more or less comprehensible. The data for 1961–1963 suggest that of every hundred new Ph.D.'s in English, thirty-five will be employed by state universities, seventeen by state colleges, twelve by private universities, two each by municipal colleges and teachers colleges, nineteen by private colleges, and twelve by junior colleges.[8] These figures are not exact because no account was taken of the new doctors in English who remained in those institutions that had been employing them and did not move to new positions. Those new Ph.D.'s who were employed by or remained at large universities or strong colleges were, perhaps, a little more fortunate than their fellows. They may have been given more reasonable teaching loads and salaries, but their professional advantages beyond these were slight. What is absolutely clear, when it is coldly considered, is that three fourths of these new Ph.D.'s will mainly teach underclassmen for a long time. How long a time is *long*?

The exponent of increment for majors in English and graduate students in English is about the same as the annual growth exponent in higher education. Between 1954–1955 and 1963–1964, the graduating majors in English and American Literature increased in number from 13,000 to 33,000. This increase equaled that of History but ran ahead of that in Philosophy and Classics. While the English department increased its graduated majors by one and one-half times, the departments of German and Romance languages doubled or tripled their numbers.[9] All of these increases are rather remarkable and were plainly made at the expense of other disciplines, because the actual number of Humanities A.B.'s conferred in this period increased by only 38 percent. But the comparatively slow increase in graduating seniors in English was not duplicated in the lower terraces of the universities and colleges. The freshmen and sophomore classes, where the teacher of English is so heavily committed, doubled in size. Percentages are, however, as bewildering as the figures that beget them. When enrollments are calmly contemplated, it is certain that in many institutions the underclass courses in English will continue to outnumber the advanced courses in population by a ratio of eight to one. In other words, we shall always require eight times the number of full-time teachers for freshmen and sophomores as we do for juniors and seniors; in fact, as the 772 junior colleges now in existence are added to at the rate of 50 new colleges a year for the next decade, the ratio between underclass and upperclass teachers of English will get well beyond these current proportions.

It is clear that we cannot expect the well-established graduate departments to increase their enrollments enough to meet this need, and for the moment the newly established departments do not attract enough students to supply the necessary trained teachers. It has been assumed that there are many students who might become highly competent underclass teachers but who are reluctant to enter graduate training because of the nature of the requirements in training and the time involved. The critical attitude toward the doctorate in English expressed by a certain group of articulate teachers may also have something to do with the shortages. The Ph.D. was opposed in the beginning by prominent educational philosophers like A. Lawrence Lowell and William James, and the initial opposition of these men to the degree has been echoed in each succeeding generation. In 1959, Earl McGrath, U.S. Commissioner of Education, voiced his opinions in the significantly titled, *The Graduate School and the Decline of Liberal Education*,[10] a book that produced affirmative and negative responses. The rigidity of the whole doctoral process has recently been described by Everett Walters in "The Immutable Ph.D."[11] and the dehumanizing nature of graduate departments in the humanities, a theme that is almost a hundred years old, has once again been diagnosed by William Arrowsmith in "The Shame of the Graduate Schools."[12] But these criticisms are now part of the national tradition and they have not been limited to single voices nor have they gone unheard in academic assemblies.

For more than thirty years the Ph.D. and the precedures of graduate education have been the subject of debate and discussion at the annual meetings of the American Association of Universities. These discussions became sharper, if the solutions of the difficulties did not, when the AGS and then the CGS came into being. The Ph.D. in English and in other subjects might have been made as rare as the title once accorded the Chinese literati if one or both of these higher organizations had insisted on the accreditation of graduate departments. If this event had occurred, the M.A. would have been the teacher's degree and the Ph.D., like the ultimate French doctorate, would have been reserved for a few pale, middle-aged, and distinguished scholars. But this is not the Anglo-Saxon way of doing things. The AGS, which had often talked about accreditation, heard a report of four of its deans in 1957[13] and a "Report of the Ad Hoc Committee on the Ph.D. Pattern" in 1963. In the latter year, it united with the CGS in the publication of two brochures, "The Doctor of Philosophy Degree" and "Minimum Standards for the New Doctoral Programs." Both of these publications are suggestive, how-to-do-it pamphlets, and any academic group needing to read them should avoid inaugurating graduate study. In 1964, the CGS once again heard a resolution on accreditation, but quickly announced it would have nothing to do with decisions of this nature. It recommended that delicate judgments of this kind ought to be made by regional or professional groups. The best advice of these organizations was on the expensiveness of graduate instruction, but any institution or department that chose to ignore the question of finance could begin graduate work.

Both organizations of graduate deans have not shut their eyes to the essential difficulties of the traditional Ph.D. program in a modern world. In 1956, the AGS heard a panel discussion, "The Great Split—Scholarship and Teaching." This was, of course, the topic engaging the attention of the MLA in 1884 and the Federation of Graduate Students in 1898. Stimulated by Russian success in outer space, the AGS also looked hard at the doctorate in 1957 and concluded that the degree had never been defined and the course toward it was "tortuously slow and riddled with needless uncertainties." These questions, "What is it?"[14] and "Why does it take so long?"[15] are still unanswered. In his book on graduate education, Charles M. Grigg supplies a sad summary of the whole problem.

> The emphasis on the acquiring of the degree, without reference to the original purpose for which it was granted, has led to continual pressure either to downgrade the Ph.D. or to offer other doctoral degrees. The situation became more acute as tremendous increases began to occur in the demand for research personnel. As a result of these forces, modification of graduate programs took a particular turn, in that the requirements for graduate degrees, such as foreign languages, thesis, and examininations were continued in spirit if not in practice. An illustration of this was the continual holding to the requirement of two foreign languages, whereas the student's actual proficiency in the language and in the use of the language is often questionable, and its utility in his later professional career may be minimal.[16]

Grigg's commentary is probably more applicable to graduate study in general than to the graduate curriculum in English and American literature, but it prompts us to ask questions—perhaps irreverent ones—about our own disciplines. Does the Ph.D. in English guarantee a combination of two excellences, one in teaching and one in research and criticism, or does it assure one and not the other, or does it provide neither? Considering the current state of affairs in higher education do we need to emphasize the knowledgeable teaching of English and American Literature or specialists and researchers in these literatures? Granting that an interest in scholarly investigation does not usually limit a teacher's pedagogical skills, should a lack of interest or ability in original study of this nature close the academic doors to good and competent teachers lacking what Dean West of Princeton long ago called "the union card"? None of these questions are in the least novel; they have been asked and promptly answered again and again. Various plans have regularly been brought forward to save the supposedly large body of gifted but undegreed teachers who either spend their lives in academic darkness or, angered and discouraged, turn their backs on a profession with such rigid, outmoded, and unrealistic educational requirements.

Since the conclusion of World War II, various plans have been offered to supply our burgeoning universities, state colleges, colleges, and junior colleges with properly trained teachers. Most of these plans have a particular application to the shortages in English departments in that they propose to certificate teachers who do not want to spend an expensive length of time in learning to be critics and research specialists. One of the earliest and more modest proposals is the restoration of the Master's degrees as the essential qualification of the undergraduate teacher. As late as 1959, Dean Elder of Harvard hoped that the M.A. could be rehabilitated by being made more rigorous and pedagogical and hence more acceptable to college deans and presidents.[17] In line with this idea, President Oliver Carmichael proposed in 1961 that qualified undergraduates be allowed to follow a special curriculum to the M.A. or M.S. beginning with the junior year.[18] None of these ideas has been broadly accepted because the master's degree—there are now 300 kinds of them—cannot, to use the words of Dean Arlt, "be sold."[19] Its value in higher education was questioned in 1898, and since then it has been smothered by the Ph.D. It is still the professional degree for secondary teachers and passes current in junior and community colleges, but it can be wondered for how long this will be the case.

In 1966 Yale University abandoned, with a few departmental and group exceptions, the granting of the traditional master's degree and adopted a Master of Philosophy degree, "to dethrone," as Dean J. P. Miller puts it, "the Ph.D. degree as the only respectable degree for positions of college and university teaching." The new degree is to be awarded to candidates who have completed "all requirements for the Ph.D. degree, except the submission of an acceptable prospectus and dissertation." The Yale M.Phil. differs from the same degree granted for several years at the University of Toronto in that it follows the track of the doctorate instead of a track of its own.[20] The University of Michigan, convinced that "master's" is a blighted word and that other intermediate degrees—the "Doctor of Liberal Arts," the "Doctor of English" and similar "doctorates"—were dubious, has agreed to grant a Ph.C. or "Candidate in Philosophy," well known in Scandinavia and Eastern Europe.[21] This degree, like the "Doctor of Arts Degree" being considered at the University of California at Berkeley, is again an intermediate degree between the old style master's degree and the Ph.D. The propounders of these degrees hope that these titles will legitimize the position of the present holders of ABD in the teaching world.

The interim degrees are of the greatest interest to all departments of English faced with teacher shortages. They are of equal importance to the more than one hundred graduate departments now offering a doctorate, because these departments have succeeded in producing the second largest group—Education has first place—of ABD's in the United States.[22] In 1960, fifty-three of these departments admitted to the USOE that they had 448 ABD's on their rolls. This was probably a reasonably modest confession and does not suggest the true plight of the more than 4000 graduate students of English in or beyond their second year of work. A recent study of graduate attrition by Tucker, Gottleib, and Pease shows that about half of all students attempting a doctorate in the Humanities are either dropouts or in the ABD condition.[23] This same percent could hold for the men working toward a Ph.D. in English. These are the people who would benefit by the interim degrees, but there are many questions about these degrees that must be considered.

It is now assumed that holders of the interim degree will be granted doctorates as soon as their dissertations are approved, but the matter of a time limit, now imposed by many graduate departments on their ABD's remains to be discussed. Will a Ph.C. or a M.Phil. be convertible into a Ph.D. at any time or is there a five-, ten-, or twenty-year limit? Can a "Candidate in Philosophy" or a M.Phil. be transferred? Will it, for instance, be possible to take this degree at X University, but submit one's dissertation at Y University? Or if one's interim degree is voided by a time limit at X University, could one still use it toward a Ph.D. at Y University where there was a longer time limit or no limit at all? Will the granting of these degrees be limited only to universities now giving the doctorate or can any university give the interim degree? Some universities that now are ill equipped to do a Ph.D. feel that they can do a very satisfactory Ph.C. or M.Phil. These are a few of the problems connected with the granting of interim degrees that must be studied and solved. The ultimate vogue of an interim degree must also be estimated. How many graduate students of English will accept it as a terminal degree and live happily with necessity. The felicity of M.Phil.'s D.L.A.'s, and Ph.C.'s with either phase of the degree will depend on the corresponding felicity of employing institutions. Will the large universities, both public and private, employ teachers with these degrees? Will they give them "promotion and pay" if they decide not to or are unable to convert their interim degrees into Ph.D.'s? Will the attitude of state colleges, liberal arts colleges on their various levels, and junior and community colleges be congenial toward these degrees or not? In the long run, will the fate of this type of degree be better than that of the real but somewhat invisible ABD?[24] All of these questions must be answered.

An alternate possibility followed by a few graduate departments and talked about in the June 1965 ADE meeting is the "streamlined" Ph.D., which enables a student with proper financial support to finish the course in four years. The proponents of this type of degree think, as Professor Barber observed, that standards and requirements are different matters.[25] They realize that the modern requirements for the doctorate in English have been accumulating and enlarging since the simpler times of the last century. In the 1890s a candidate for the Ph.D. in English was seldom expected to know much about his subject after the death of Shakespeare; and, as a matter of fact, there was not too much to know. In the 1920s, knowledge of English literature more or less ended with the death of Sir Walter Scott and American literature was terra incognita. The philological requirements of past times (inherited from the Germans and thought of as highly scientific) have been generally reduced, sometimes eliminated, in modern departments. It is presumed, since the reduction of the philological demands did not debase the doctorate, that the same thing could now be done with unrealistic course, language, and dissertation requirements. By limiting these obstacles to suit the needs of the profession, it is supposed that the time element will be lessened and more qualified teachers produced. Again there are questions. No matter how one describes it, does not a lessening of requirements cheapen the degree? Even if there are fewer requirements, will they not be rigid enough to make the new Ph.D. just as difficult for the gifted student, whose possible individualized curriculum was discussed at the Tufts Conference,[26] in 1965, as the old Ph.D.? Once again, it must also be asked whether or not the syncopated degree will be as acceptable to the various employing institutions as the old style Ph.D. with its longer course of study.

These are all questions that the profession must ask itself and attempt to answer; but all of them can be subsumed under one question: Can the curriculum for the doctorate in English and American Literature be shorn of its unrealistic accretions and converted into a serviceable and uniformly administered procedure sensibly adjusted in all its requirements to the public obligations of the profession of this century? The succeeding chapters attempt to display what we think of ourselves. Those of us who have reasonably free minds may draw conclusions from them.

CHAPTER 3

The Personnel
of the Departments
# of English

I No college or university in the United States is without a Department of English. Its personnel of full- and part-time teachers usually outnumbers that of most other departments, but the actual number of English teachers is really unknown. It has been estimated that there are more than 20,000 of them; and though they are organized into various professional and scholarly associations, they are too numerous, too mobile, and too amorphous a body to count. Those who have managed to become Doctors of Philosophy in English and American Literature are known to the files of their graduate departments, but many of these teachers are known only in this way. All of them should be heard more frequently than they are, and this compilation of their training and experiences is intended to bring this about.

II In this chapter we shall draw the professional profiles of the chairmen of graduate and undergraduate college departments of English and of the graduate professors in the universities. But we shall begin with a sketch of what we have called, to the amazement of some, "recent recipients of the

Ph.D.;" namely, 1880 men and women who obtained their doctorates in the decade between 1955 and 1965. This is an important group of teachers because their memories of the graduate school are fresher and not yet obliterated by the colors that time mixes. This is also a generation brought up to examine before it reverences, to inquire the reason for what has always been assumed to be what it seems. All of these people are academic successes and speak with the voice of accomplishment. They "have leaped all the hurdles and been voted into the Ph.D. Club." We know nothing about the large number of starters who tripped over the bars and, to preserve the metaphor, were "blackballed." We are, consequently, listening to the right side of the house, the one that speaks with the tongues of unfallen angels.

The composite biography of these academic winners is based on a 55.2 percent response (Table 3.1) and represents a group in which 83.2 percent are men and 16.8 percent are women (Table 3.2). Most members of this group, 82.7 percent, were undergraduate majors in English or American Literature (Table 3.3), and received their preliminary training at state and private universities and large colleges. State colleges, now increasing at a very rapid rate, and the numerous small liberal arts colleges produced only 15 percent of the 1880 recent recipients of the doctorate (Table 3.4). It has been discovered that the decision to undertake an academic career, even in the sciences, comes at a fairly mature age. The professional teacher of English follows the common pattern. Fewer than seventy members of the class of 1955 to 1965 thought they would get a doctorate before they entered the freshman year. Most of these teachers elected the academic career during the first year of postgraduate study (Table 3.5), but no matter how late their decision, it is clear that it was almost half made when three fourths of them started to work for M.A.'s and almost all of them in English or in American Literature (Table 3.6).

When they learned that graduate study was enjoyable or at least endurable, these newly made Masters of Art looked about for a doctoral program that would admit them to studentship, train them in their profession, and benevolently, perhaps, grant them the ultimate degree that makes a college or university teacher eminently employable. More than half of them testify that they selected their graduate department for "academic reasons" and they are firm in the belief that these reasons were the "reputation" of the university and/or of the department (Tables 3.7, 3.8). Only one fourth of them considered the reputation of the professor under whose personal guidance they would write a dissertation and who would be their mentor and sponsor during the opening stages of their careers. The geographical location of the chosen university—its nearness to friends and family, its situation in a comfortable climate or familiar terrain, and its material and intellectual opportunities—mattered no more to most of them than their choice of a scholarly master. In spite of their admitted indifference to geography, a study of the sources of all their degrees shows that the homing instinct in English graduate students is as well developed as it is in other animals. The recent recipients of the doctorate sometimes venture out of their accustomed habitat, but they are usually inclined to take two of their degrees at one university (Table 3.9).

A small percent of these recent Ph.D.'s tried some other "trade" before they embraced that of teaching. Some were real estate or automobile salesmen; some entered small and large businesses; some tried the pulpit or the printing press; but most of them began to study and teach shortly after they had acquired their bachelor's degrees. One fourth of them had their doctorates by the age of thirty, but the average man or woman was three years older than this; in fact, the majority of them did not finish their dissertations until they were somewhere between the ages of thirty and forty (Tables 3.10). The women were somewhat later in taking their final orals than the men, and they supply their reasons. Many of them had no husbands to support them; others waited until they had supported their husbands through graduate school or until their children were old enough to go to school. The Ph.D.'s created between 1961 and 1965 were a trifle faster in completing their degrees; there is a small, but not very significant, decrease in the median age for this second group. The lowering of the time elapsed does not, however, suggest that in the very near future the Doctor of Philosophy in English will be graduated at the same age as the Doctor of Medicine.

If we can assume that the ordinary age for taking the A.B. is twenty-two, then the more than thirty-three-year age average for the Ph.D. indicates that eleven years have evaporated in the process. If we look at the reasonable extremes, omitting the more than 300 people who required sixteen to more than forty-five years to achieve the Ph.D., we discover that 83 percent of all the recent doctors earned the degree in the elapsed time of three to fifteen years and that one half of the men and one third of the women had a diploma by the tenth year (Table 3.11). Even with this optimistic report before us, we cannot as yet think of the Ph.D. in English as a four-year degree.

Statistics in the main support what most people have always assumed, and it is no secret that the course to the Ph.D. in English has always been thought to provide time with provender. The reason for this temporal attenuation has usually been given as a lack of financial support for full-time study. The responses of this group of 1880 people do not support this traditional assumption. Of this number, 1580 or 84 percent, state that they had at least one year of uninterrupted time. About 15 percent never had a completely free year, but, on the other hand, 61 percent had two to four years of free study and over fifty had more time than this (Table 3.12). Out of a sense of anticipatory gratitude, parents of embryo physicians and lawyers usually pay for the advanced education of their hopeful children, but the universities' coffers are the sources of the grants and fellowships that provided 64.1 percent of these recent Ph.D.'s with the boon of uncluttered hours. About one quarter of these men and women had wives, husbands, parents, or relatives writing the checks, but one third of them dug into savings probably accumulated during the years when they were full-time college teachers (Table 3.13). We have no notion of the amount of money that was poured into these individual academic campaigns. It may have been very meager, indeed; but it appears that most of these students were better supported than we have thought or would like—thanks to our myths—to confess.

The length of the temporal course to the doctorate may be the result of the system rather than the product of material privation. We know from the advices of this group that they spent four years in course work and examination preparations and more than two years in researching and writing their dissertations (Tables 3.14, 3.15). In many cases these years were sandwiched in with part- or full-time teaching. Some 36 percent of this group were never teaching assistants, but the other 64 percent spent almost three years as "field hands," (Table 3.16) and 1379, or 73 percent, of the working group were full-time teachers for an average of about five years (Table 3.17). The reaction of the majority of this group, some 60 percent, is that they spent too many months in getting the degree; five years, they think, is a more reasonable sum of time to pay for a doctorate (Tables 3.18, 3.19). One third of them indicate that the lack of money was their prime problem, but the "life work," otherwise known as the dissertation, and military service are the hindrances indicated by one fifth of the respondents (Table 3.20). No one complained about it, but the laws of nature must also play a large, retarding part. Three fourths of the males and more than one third of the females were married when they took their doctorates (Table 3.21). The marriages tended to be fruitful and more than half of the males fathered between one and seven children whereas almost a quarter of the females had one to four offshoots. When the dean of the graduate school read off the names of new Ph.D.'s, 1971 children witnessed 904 mothers or fathers get their hoods (Table 3.22).

Once they were enrolled in the "Ph.D. union" and equipped, we trust, with the necessary skill and kit of tools, the recent Ph.D.'s in English and American Literature settled down, for the most part, in academic berths. Some 7.5 percent of them remained in the department from which they took their degrees (Table 3.23), but the large remainder went into the terra incognito of a different department. Over 20 percent entered the service of a private university; 41.4 percent joined a state university; 13 percent were employed by large colleges and 9 percent by small ones. State colleges, junior and community colleges, and other tasks, almost always educational, absorbed the rest (Table 3.24). Once engaged in their professional duties, most of them have remained faithful to their first employers, and 61.3 percent of them are still members of the department whither they went after they owned a doctorate. Only a few have been interested in change: 28.3 percent have a second post and 7.7 percent a third. A very few are truly footloose. One woman is in her sixth college, and three men are in their fifth (Tables 3.25a, 3.25b).

Forty years ago a Ph.D. in English was very successful if he managed to reach a full professorship at something more than a freshwater college by the age of forty or forty-five. The recent recipients of the Ph.D. have, in their ascent of the educational ladder, gained rungs over their seniors. More than three hundred of them, or 17.4 percent, are already at the top; and more than six hundred of them, or 35.9 percent, have arrived at an associate professorship, the rank that suggests its holder is "going to make it." Those who graduated in the classes from 1960 through 1965 have done a little better in the climb than those who finished in the earlier five-year period. It should also please those who are worried about equality that the women with doctorates are no longer subject to discrimination, for 17.5 percent of them as opposed to 17.4 percent of the men are now full professors (Table 3.26). Given this prosperity, it is not astonishing that this whole group voted to the extent of 91 percent that the time and money that their degrees cost them were well worth it (Table 3.27).

III   The rapid rise of the new Doctors of Philosophy in
             English to academic heights unimagined by their
             earlier counterparts probably explains the fact that
they conduct graduate courses and direct dissertations much sooner than did their own graduate teachers. Of the 1170 graduate teachers

whose answers supply the basis of this section—231 also responded to the questionnaire for recent recipients—493 took their Ph.D.'s after 1954 (Tables 3.28, 3.29) and 62.5 percent of them were teaching courses yielding graduate credit by the second anniversary of their own degree (Table 3.30). By contrast, only 36 percent of those who had their doctorates before 1955 had arrived at the same status after one year of teaching.

The ease with which a young Ph.D. now reaches graduate status also accounts for their very early nomination as dissertation directors. Slightly more than two thirds of the ante-1955 Ph.D.'s have judged or are now in charge of judging the original efforts of graduate students, but almost half of the recent recipients have at least one dissertation with a preface respectfully acknowledging their talents and industry. The median time in service before the English professor gains this eminence is highly important. The older group were in their sixth year before they were trusted with this chore; the younger group is directing a thesis by the end of the fourth year (Table 3.31).

In the past, the pleasures of directing graduate study were seldom granted to anyone who had not distinguished himself as a competent scholar. This competence was often established by the required publication of the dissertation and a certain reckless eagerness to get oneself in print forever afterward. The recent recipients of the doctorate, who are seldom required nowadays to put their theses in type, managed to the number of 768 to reveal, either in whole or part, their library findings and personal cerebrations to the learned world (Table 3.32). In addition to their dissertations, 59.2 percent of the recent Ph.D.'s have done further research and brought out books, monographs, or articles. When such a large number of young men and women are engaged in publishing, much to the horror of their non-publishing colleagues, it must be difficult to follow the traditional method of sorting out the graduate teachers from the undergraduate teachers. Nonetheless, when the publication records are scrutinized, it appears that the old values are still cherished, because 82.3 percent of the recent graduates now entrusted with graduate teaching have printed, on the average, one book and a half-dozen papers besides the grist from their dissertations. The fact that 44 percent of those not teaching on the graduate level have yet to publish at all tells us that history continues to write the same habitual pages (Table 3.33).

The personnel of the graduate divisions in English and American Literature is composed of both Ph.D.'s and non-Ph.D.'s. Of the 1170 individuals who supplied us with information, some eighty or 6.8 percent have no doctorates and are the exceptions that test the rule

(Table 3.28). In their cases individual talent was enough, and they demonstrate, as many of the respondents put it, that "it is the man or woman who counts in the long stretch." The members of this unorthodox group are somewhat older than their more numerous colleagues; their ages vary from twenty-four to seventy-one years, but their median age is fifty-eight (Table 3.34). Ten members of this exclusive society have only the A.B., but the others have both the A.B. and M.A. (Table 3.35). The majority of them are men (Table 3.28), and 37.5 percent have given up the idea of taking a doctorate; the others describe themselves as either ABD or "Ph.D. imminent" (Table 3.36). It can be assumed, we suppose, that most of them will eventually reverse their collars and subscribe to the ordinances of the academic church. Some of the older non-Ph.D.'s, about 21.8 percent are now full professors, and 62.8 percent are either assistant or associate professors (Table 3.37). We have said, and we repeat it with pleasure, that the older members of this group of non-Ph.D. graduate teachers demonstrates that if one has courage and skill, one does not need "the union card." The younger group, which time will probably transform into Ph.D.'s, suggests that in many institutions the demand for graduate study is so pressing that teachers are drafted into giving the degree they are attempting to earn.

The Doctors of Philosophy who teach graduate courses earned their A.B.'s mainly at state and private universities and large colleges. In this respect, they are similar to the general run of all Ph.D.'s in English. However, there is a slight difference. About 77 percent of all Ph.D.'s received their undergraduate training at one or another of these three types of institutions, whereas 83 percent of the graduate professors come from one of these major sources (Table 3.38). The state colleges and the small colleges which are edged out as suppliers of people successful in earning doctorates are pushed a little closer to the end of the bench when it comes to the training of people who will move into graduate professorships. The discrimination between the sexes also appears at this advanced level, because 95 percent of all graduate teachers are men (Table 3.28). Among the average respondents with Ph.D.'s, some 1090, the age at the awarding of the degree was thirty-two, slightly earlier than the average age for all Ph.D.'s in English (Table 3.39). This age average holds true for both the ante- and post-1955 groups, a division which we have made in order to establish comparisons between the older Ph.D.'s and the more recent ones. Both groups also spent about the same measure of time—nine years—working for their doctorates (Table 3.40).

When we analyse the elapsed time between the A.B. and the Ph.D. of the current graduate professors, we learn that the ante-1955 group spent a median time of three years in full-time study, part-time study, and part-time teaching. Their median time in full-time teaching and military service was about four years. The post-1955 group passed a median of three years in both categories of teaching and study and two years in the military. The earlier group (1950–1955) to the extent of 132 individuals, or 22.1 percent, used about two years of the elapsed time in some nonacademic pursuit; whereas 151 persons, or 30.8 percent, of the younger group spent the same amount of time at other occupations (Table 3.41). It is interesting to note that 20 percent of the whole group did no teaching until they had their ultimate degree, but that the other 80 percent held from one to five teaching positions before they were given their doctorates (Table 3.42). This 1090 men and women are more content with the time expenditure required for gaining the Ph.D. than the whole 1955 to 1965 group. They voted that they thought it reasonable by 79 percent (the ante-1955 contingent) and by 67.3 percent (the post-1955 recipients) (Table 3.43).

The graduate professors of English and American Literature appear to be a far more mobile group than the Ph.D.'s as a whole. Slightly more than 60 percent of them have been in two to four departments since graduation; only 37.6 percent of them, as compared with the recent recipient average of 61.3 percent, are still at the first institution that engaged them (Table 3.44). The talents—or perhaps it is the restlessness—that attracted the attention of their elders and got them graduate status has undoubtedly brought it about that they were seductive and hence seducible by other departments. When we look at the ranks that this group has obtained, we see the striking difference between the ante- and post-1955 graduates. The latter group was promoted to professorships about six years earlier than their predecessors (Table 3.45). Supply and demand, as we have stated before, is without question the superior string-puller.

We have been using the expression "graduate professor" to signify those who teach courses to which graduate students are admitted and for which they are given credit toward advanced degrees. Most professors of English and American Literature are, however, amphibians. Sometimes they are on the sunny banks of undergraduate teaching and sometimes they are in the cold currents of pro-seminars and seminars. Of the ante-1955 Ph.D.'s seventy-five, or 12.6 percent, are simonpure graduate teachers, totally unknown to the undergraduate population. A very limited number of the non-Ph.D.'s and the post-1955 graduates occupy these unusual positions (Table 3.46). Almost 60 percent of the whole group, as might be expected, devote one quarter to one half of their teaching time to postgraduate instruction. Their teaching loads are, however, certainly lighter than those of the purely undergraduate professors. The median instructor-student ratio for the whole group is one to thirty-nine in undergraduate courses, one to thirty-five in undergraduate-graduate courses, one to nineteen in graduate courses, and one to twelve in seminars (Table 3.47).

The graduate professor's real burden, if he takes his duties seriously, is the dissertation. In directing the compilation of this final work, he reproduces his own kind, and since it is his own kind, he normally exercises the utmost parental care. The time spent in the classroom, in the seminar, or in the lecture hall can be added up in any week and multiplied by the number of weeks in a term; but the hours spent with thesis students can only be estimated, if the professor is conscientious, by a celestial computer. The compiled statistics suggest that all we have just been saying is nonsense, because if our respondents are correct, 26 percent of all theses are directed by 4 percent of all graduate teachers. The record of the non-Ph.D.'s is plainly fantastic. Four men have directed 173 theses or 81 percent of all dissertations directed by the 80 non-Ph.D. graduate teachers. When we look at the other group, we discover that 67 percent of the 1090 graduate professors with doctorates have yet to supervise more than three dissertation candidates (Table 3.48). The overloading of a few professors with this trying but important task may account for some complaints about the dissertation and the dissertation director that will be intimated in Chapter 6. It may also have something to do with the complaint of over 20 percent of the recent recipients that the dissertation was one of the main factors in delaying their degrees.

IV   The third group of teachers of English and American Literature whose opinions we have solicited is a very small one composed either of departmental chairmen or the directors of studies in graduate departments. At the moment of our inquiry, there were 109 universities where a doctorate in English could be earned; some of these departments have been granting the degree for almost a century and have hundreds of alumni; other departments are only a year or two old and have yet to carry their first graduate students to a doctorate. Of the 109 departments consulted, 88 or about 80 percent responded to our request for information (Table 3.49).

The chairmen or graduate directors in these eighty-eight departments are predominately masculine. In only two cases are women in direct charge of graduate study (Table 3.50). Though the ages of these leaders vary from thirty-four to sixty-seven, the average age is fifty (Table 3.51), and almost everyone is a recognizable person of academic or scholarly distinction. All have an earned doctor's degree, but eleven of them did not bother to take the M.A. and one apparently did not take an A.B. (Table 3.52). The sources of their undergraduate training are more uniformly at larger institutions than those of the whole group. Only seven of these executive officers went to graduate school from a state college or a small college; eighty-one, or over 90 percent, took their A.B.'s at a private or state university or a large liberal arts college. As a matter of fact, they are also different from the general group in that 40 percent of them were undergraduates at one or other of the greater private universities (Table 3.53). This small group is particularly helpful in that its members do their bit toward justifying Chancellor Cartter's recently uttered academic pecking order for English Departments; 83 percent of them have their doctorates from one or other of his twenty leading graduate departments (Table 3.54).

This small assembly of chairmen and graduate study directors was, however, not particularly hurried in earning the doctorate although one had a Ph.D. before most Americans are college juniors. Their average age at securing the degree that they now administer was almost thirty-two years and their median age was thirty-one, about two years below the general average (Table 3.55). This two-year difference is probably explained by the fact that the median elapsed time between the A.B. and Ph.D. is a rather modest seven years (Table 3.56).

Like their colleagues in the graduate division, these eighty-eight executive officers are more inclined to migrate than is the profession as a whole. One has joined six different departments since taking his doctorate, and seven have been members of four departments. The median number of occupied posts for the whole group is two, but 58 percent have moved once or twice since leaving graduate school (Table 3.57). Mobility and academic success seem to have a relationship when we reach the upper echelons of the profession, but at a certain point stasis takes over. This first law of pedagogical progress is supported by the fact that the median number of years in their current posts is for this group a symbolic twelve, but one member has recently celebrated his fortieth year on his campus (Table 3.58).

Almost all of these executive officers responded to our questionnaire addressed to all graduate professors; and if we chose to sort these documents out, we might furnish a more sharply drawn etching of this group of eighty-eight. The number is, however, so visibly minor that we have blended it in with the larger category. We shall now conclude with a short account of the chairmen of departments without a doctoral program, our fourth group but the one depended upon to provide the products of the doctoral program with the major necessities of the intellectual life: food, clothing, shelter, and an audience.

V   There are now more than 2000 private, state, junior, and community colleges in the United States that hunger for Ph.D.'s in English and American Literature, but that have not yet gotten round to producing them at home. The chairmen of 550 of these departments were questioned about their personnel, their curricula, their opinions, and their departmental ambitions. The response was about 66 percent (Table 3.59) thanks to the fact that most colleges with an M.A. program, 123 of them, were unstinting in their replies. Ten of these colleges began to grant this intermediate degree more than fifty years ago, but 62 of them have installed study for the master's degree since 1955 (Table 3.60), and 53 other colleges inform us that they plan shortly to begin this type of graduate work (Table 3.61). The colleges now offering work toward the M.A. estimate that they have bestowed 3682 of these degrees in English and American Literature since 1960 and have now some 6208 students in the process of earning this degree (Table 3.62). Eleven departments with this experience in graduate study hope soon to open their doors to Ph.D. candidates, but 90 percent state flatly that they have no plans in this direction (Table 3.63).

The chairmen of the three hundred and sixty-three responding departments are generally men, but 15 percent (almost the same percentage taking doctorates in the 1955 to 1965 group) are women (Table 3.64). Most of these executives are middle-aged and tested (Table 3.65), and 87 percent of them have their doctorates in English (Table 3.66). On the average they were somewhat slower in earning their degrees than the classes of 1955 to 1965; the men had them at a median age of thirty-five and the women at a median of thirty-six years (Table 3.67). The men were somewhat quicker about earning their doctorates than the women, but the whole group spent about eleven years at the task, a timespan that is clearly standard (Table 3.68).

Not all the members of this group have earned a doctorate though a number of them have been granted honorary doctorates either by their own or by another college. Some 13 percent of these chairmen, thirty-nine men and nine women, have not yet finished their graduate training, and many of them are not likely to do so. The prejudice of college administrations and the pressure of accrediting agencies is, consequently, demonstrated by the academic ranks of these chairmen without doctorates. Some 36.2 percent of them have been promoted to full professorships, but the rest are in lower orders (Table 3.69). The prestige value of the Ph.D. is underscored by the fact that the chairmen with doctorates have generally moved into the academic king-row. Almost all of these men and women who had their Ph.D.'s before 1955 now are professors, and about 65 percent of those who took their degree after this date have reached the top (Table 3.70).

These 363 executive officers preside over college staffs that number 6742 persons, of whom slightly over 40 percent have finished their graduate training; in fact, only 131 of their full professors, or 10.4 percent, do not have this degree (Table 3.71). In most of these institutions, 92.1 percent, the doctorate is the sine qua non for a professorial chair. About 40 percent of the deans and presidents stop the non-Ph.D. at the rank of associate professor, and another 40 percent will hold him to an assistant professorship (Table 3.72). Not all these chairmen by any means approve of this situation, but they bend their necks to the wills of the Parcae.

Teachers in small colleges, and particularly in the new community colleges, must be men and women who are intellectually nimble and versatile. It is recognized that an instructor in a community college must stand ready to give almost any demanded course. The problem of multidexterity is not so great in small colleges, but 101, or 27.8 percent, of the college chairmen report that they share personnel with other departments (Table 3.73). The teacher in these colleges must be able to double in some other subject, and the chairmen list the departments with which they share personnel. We can assume, however, that not many members of the English Department cross over into other fields except at the most forlorn colleges. When 20 percent of the sharing departments state that they have common personnel with Classics or with Modern Languages, it is probably these departments, lacking enough students for Greek or German, that fill out instructional schedules by lending their teachers to the Department of English.

It must finally be observed that the colleges have more than a modicum of undergraduates with which to reckon. Some three hundred and fifty-two of the chairmen were able to report their recent enrollments in all English courses, and the total is well over half a million. The same group of chairmen estimated that their staffs taught 155,799 students in advanced and elective courses (Table 3.74). Not all chairmen stated the number of English majors in their care, but 351 made estimates that total 38,624 students (Table 3.75), and 58 percent indicated that their majors were on the increase. At 66.6 percent of the colleges the general enrollment in English had increased by 20,322 students since 1964 (Table 3.76); hence, these chairmen are not without the problems that confront the heads of the greater university departments. The general ratio of their 6742 full-time teachers to their English enrollments is one to eighty-seven. When we consider the number of majors and assume that they are taught by professors and associate professors, the ratio here ameliorates to one to eight; but majors, of course, are not the solitary dwellers in advanced courses. The teaching loads in the college departments are also heavy. In about one third of the responding colleges, the teaching load was under twelve hours, which is the average load in slightly over half of the departments. On the other hand, in 11 percent of these institutions the teaching requirement is a primitive fifteen hours. The college teacher, both Ph.D. and non-Ph.D., works at his trade (Table 3.77).

With these summaries we know something about the men and women who support the professional teaching of English and American Literature. The profiles are composite and this does each individual a disfavor, because the great similarity between any group of teachers is their differences. But differences among so many hundred voices cannot be heard; and now that we have seen them all as a kind of mass chorus, we shall want to hear what they have to say about the profession's past experiences and its hopes for the future.

CHAPTER *4*

The Recruiting and Admission of Candidates for the Doctorate

Most of the teachers of English and American Literature who took their doctorates during the last ten years were, as we now know, undergraduate concentrators in these fields. Since they decided to try their hands and their wits at the Ph.D. depths while they were testing the shallower waters of the M.A., we cannot feel that undergraduate study is either the preparation for or the essaying ground of the highest degree. The prelegal and premedical curricula presumably ready undergraduate men and women who finish as lawyers and physicians, but the major in English and American Literature appears to be only the porch, as the master's degree is the foyer, to the doctorate.

The chairmen of departments without doctoral programs inform us that they have sent 4131 of their better undergraduate majors to the doctoral departments since 1961 (Table 4.1); and we learn that in two hundred and twenty-nine, or 68 percent of their institutions, undergraduate interest in earning a doctorate is steadily increasing

45

(Table 4.2). Some of these departments encourage their senior students to try only for the M.A., but almost 90 percent of them urge the student to get both degrees. Only a negligible number discourage them from any graduate study whatsoever (Table 4.3).

Since an important number of college departmental chairmen—and they are better aware than almost anyone else of the paucity of trained teachers—advise their majoring students to think of advanced study, it is not surprising that over 70 percent of them (Table 4.4) think they have invented some sort of pedagogical program designed to fortify their students against the rigors of the graduate school. In this respect they seem to be prudently far ahead of the undergraduate divisions of some graduate departments, and the means that they employ to get their advanced undergraduates "to think Ph.D." should be news to many graduate professors. For a long time, the honors courses with a thesis in the senior year has been an accepted method of pointing undergraduates toward graduate work, and many colleges have adopted and developed it. A few chairmen see to it that their undergraduates also learn French and German, take oral examinations for practice, and master the rudiments of bibliography and research methods in a course called Introduction to English Studies. Some colleges state that they provide seminar training for senior students, but one college even has a pre-honors course whose director selects freshmen and sophomores to shape them, not only for honors, but for subsequent graduate study. To these propaedeutic efforts, some of the colleges add further practical and instructive methods.

It is the custom of several colleges to name an advisor (who is given released time for this purpose), personally to direct the work of students who appear to be promising future professors of English. One college even issues a monthly newsletter, which informs its undergraduates about opportunities and innovations in the various graduate schools. Other college chairmen say that they hold monthly or, at least, semiannual meetings of all majors so that the intending graduate students can listen to either a panel of their own professors or lectures by invited representatives from graduate departments. Experienced alumni who are or were graduate students are also asked to these affairs. All of these practices are very much to the good, and we can only wish that they were widely popular. Actually the majority of the departments without a doctoral program do not have the predoctoral program they would like to think they have and state that they prepare their students for advanced degree study by "teaching them to write annotated term-papers" or by "making them learn English Literature."

Once a new Ph.D. leaves his graduate professors behind him and strikes out on his own, he appears to sever most of his ties with his graduate department. He is obviously never so sentimental about his postgraduate years as he is likely to be about his undergraduate days; and it is as plain, and perhaps as loud, as a college cheer that he is in no sense "a loyal alumnus." Fewer than 20 percent of the college chairmen and their staffs (Table 4.5) send their aspiring senior students to their own graduate departments. A number of chairmen tagged the question that produced this statistic as "loaded," and indeed it was, but the explosion came from an end that they did not anticipate. Several chairmen wrote reproachfully that they suited their students to appropriate graduate departments, and that is definitely a noble notion. The findings on various aspects of graduate study suggest, however, that the chairmen who attempt this delicate adjustment are no better than the directors of graduate study (who are their coadjutors) as successful fitters. The college chairmen, in spite of their disavowals, are actually very catholic at putting round pegs in round holes and managed during 1965 to fit at least 1170 of their students into one hundred and one graduate departments of English and American Literature (Table 4.6). Some of these students went halfway across the continent to continue their reading; but when we compare the address of the forwarding colleges with those of the receiving graduate departments, we find that the majority of the students could almost have jumped from one campus to the other.

According to the count of chairmen of graduate departments, their undergraduate division produced over 8000 A.B.'s with majors in English in 1966 (Table 4.7) and sent about 20 percent of this number into graduate work (Table 4.8). These chairmen followed the custom of the college chairmen and advised their seniors to go, in most cases, to another department for further study (Table 4.9). Their advice was eagerly accepted, because only 18 percent of all resident graduate students are working for the doctorate at the institution from which they took their baccalaureate degree (Table 4.10). A few graduate departments permit a student to take only two degrees with them, and, as we mentioned in Chapter 3, only 14.5 percent of all recent recipients have their A.B. and Ph.D. from the same university, whereas more than half of them took both graduate degrees at one place. These figures lead us to ponder how graduate students are recruited by the departments with a doctoral program.

Though twenty-five graduate directors or chairmen state that they make no attempt to enlist candidates for the doctorate, fifty-seven recruit on a national basis. They take a firm stand against parochialism and consider their own majors, according to 50 percent of their responses, only after they have inspected the applicants from the country at large, or if their sweep is not that great, from their immediate region (Table 4.11). The methods of recruiting are rather feeble, because most of these departments do little more than send out flyers and brochures that list faculty, requirements, courses, and scholarships. These announcements pile up on some official desk or get nailed, one on top of the other, on the departmental bulletin boards where they are lost among the more gaudy proclamations of exciting undergraduate events and opportunities. Fewer than 15 percent of the graduate departments pay visits—by means of a single visitor or a team of delegates—to neighboring college campuses. Very few, five to be exact, depend on their graduate alumni (Table 4.12). The remainder seem to have sensed what this study has brought out about alumni affection for the "old school."

The intellectually or professionally motivated English or American Literature major advised by his college department's Graduate Committee, informed by his perusal of flyers and brochures, "learned" in the ways of graduate school catalogues, and, if lucky, instructed either by panel discussions or by visiting graduate dignitaries, fills out the necessary forms, purchases copies of his academic record, secures letters from his more benign teachers, and bundles them all off to the graduate departments to which he is suited. If also supplied with a Wilson or a Danforth Fellowship, he or she is much more certain than an empty-handed classmate of being attractive to a large number of departments. All of the places to which he commits his future are chosen, as we know, for "academic reasons." If he is not funded by one of the great national foundations, he hopes to get a scholarship, a grant, or a teaching assistantship. He almost always expects to be given full tuition; he almost never volunteers to pay his own way or, as a matter of fact, any part of it. He has paid for his A.B.; and though his undergraduate record may be shaky, he knows that there are graduate departments where a "C" average will be blinked at, and he can expect the remainder of his education to be costless. His dossier, one of the many he will get together in his professional lifetime, arrives a panting, paper ambassador in the waiting rooms of the graduate department. How is it received and what happens to it?

In 20 percent of the graduate departments, the "paper face" of the applicant will be scanned by the officials in the Admissions Office or by the graduate dean and may never be seen again. If it is a shining face, it may be shown to the chairman or to the graduate committee of the English Department; and even though the first viewers may have liked it, it can be effaced here. In only five of the eighty-eight responding graduate departments does the whole graduate staff have an opportunity to consider all the files of applicants and vote on their acceptance or rejection (Table 4.13). It is difficult to understand this burking of what should be a democratic process. Does it result from some sort of hierarchical sense of power distrustful of the judgments of subordinates or is the right of the ballot at this crucial election cast away by the graduate staff because of intellectual ennui or academic distractions?

The undergraduate grade record in English and American Literature is the principal item most cautiously observed when the judges in the graduate departments consider the admission of students. The second measure of indicated success for them is the total academic record. Although one respondent describes the testimonial letters from undergraduate teachers as "nothing but polite noise," these documents, sometimes thoughtful, sometimes hasty, sometimes stereotyped, and sometimes highly individualistic, impressed the general run of graduate professors somewhat more than they do the more jaded chairmen or directors of graduate study. The source of the applicant's bachelor's degree, which certainly comments on his grades, his lack of language training which may hamper his progress, his own letters or submitted papers (which can speak volumes about his literacy or emotional state) his success in extracurricular affairs (which delineates his personality and gauges his ambition and drive), all of these other pertinent calibrations of his character and ability are held to be subordinate to the first five or six letters of the alphabet. The GRE score, required by many graduate departments and almost universally included in most dossiers, is almost at the bottom of trusted indices to the candidate's prospects as an eventual Ph.D. (Table 4.14).

When the graduate department projectors look at the alphabetical or numerical diagram of the student's academic past, about 30 percent of them have some sort of quota in mind (Table 4.15); but this quota is by no means so exclusive as the applicants are likely to imagine. Only nine of the responding departments close their books when they have accepted 50 or fewer students; in fact, the twenty-four departments that confessed to observing a quota stand ready to receive and entertain 2600 advanced graduate students. For sixty-one of the remaining departments, the sky is apparently the limit; the corridors to the "Ph.D. Club" are as spacious as the halls of dreams (Table 4.16).

The immense length and breadth of the doctoral park can be

estimated by the current graduate enrollments reported by some seventy-five departments with doctoral programs. It could be assumed that the thirteen departments that did not report are unable to count the multitude, because they could hardly fail otherwise to have a census. There are now 12,000 graduate students in English or American Literature (almost enough for four brigades), on the rosters of these reporting departments which represent fewer than two thirds of all departments with doctoral programs (Table 4.17). Of this number 4548 are full-time students (Table 4.18), 5875 are part-time students (Table 4.19), and 1172 are regarded as doctoral candidates and are probably on the departmental books as ABD's (Table 4.20). This truly gigantic enrollment, increasing during the last decade, has enabled the graduate teachers to make some strong comparisons between the students now in residence and those whom they knew in their own graduate days.

More than half of the current graduate professors find their present students just about the same in professional puissance as their former classmates of past generations. One quarter of these teachers cast a more jaundiced eye on the men and women now under their tutelage and give them no decorations, whereas about 20 percent of them are more sanguine and think the present student body is superior to the one they formerly knew (Table 4.21). When they sort out the superiorities and inferiorities of their students, both the ante- and post-1955 Ph.D. groups agree that contemporary graduate students are worse at classical and modern languages than the men and women of their time. However, it must be admitted that they are not very fussy about the applicants' preparations in these subjects when they meditate on their academic histories and vote on their admission. The younger group of graduate professors is, likewise, not overwhelmed by their students' knowledge of the fields of English and American Literature or by their control of wider humanistic areas; but the older group, which taught many members of the post-1955 contingent, find the recent students superior in these branches of learning to the men and women they remember from their own student years (Table 4.22).

When it comes to evaluating the skills of contemporary graduate students, the older teachers—either broken in spirit by experience or softened in opinion by advancing age—are far more liberal in their assessments than their younger colleagues. They think that the new students are more careful and accurate readers, more intellectually curious, better at synthesis and analysis, and superior in making critical decisions than they were. They agree with the post-1955 congregation (which finds the present students inferior in all these other skills) that the modern doctoral candidates are unable to write precisely or lucidly (Table 4.23).

Graduate professors from both groups supplied often heated marginal comments to support or qualify their more automatic responses. The more optimistic ones think the students in their classes are "more alert," "aggressive," "sophisticated," "independent," "less passive and with more desire to know what they know firsthand," or "more concerned with the justification of what they are doing" than the men and women who took their degrees with them. One respondent puts it rather plainly, "more interesting people are now entering graduate school than in my day." But many of these professional graduate teachers are far from complimentary. They describe their students as worse in "logic," "general knowledge," "seriousness," "patience," "intelligence," and "literacy." They complain that the contemporary graduate students have "a civil service attitude," are "alarmingly uniformitarian," "softer and more reliant on institutional benevolence," and without any interest in "historical information." "They all think they are literary critics!" One graduate professor believes that "they are not hungry enough and hence play it safer"; but others protest that "they lack an interest in work, but expect enormous material advantages" or that "they dislike the intellectual life and merely are with us to avoid the draft."

The majority of graduate professors accept these dark views when they think about the prospective dropouts among their newly admitted students. They know from the tough annals of academic experience that not too many of the 12,000 aspiring students in their seminars will someday have gold tassels on their mortarboards. Our knowledge about dropouts is very vague. The educationists have made studies of the problem, but no one has any exact figures for English Departments for any period of time. Abou ben Dropout's name does not head the roll call of graduate departments; in fact, his name drops out of the files almost as soon as he does. We should like to know more about these departed ones; their voices—critical, frustrated, sour, desperate, and discouraged—would make an excellent antiphonal chorus to the chanting of those who have succeeded (though even some of them can sing off-key with full throats). Unfortunately, our dropouts are the blank faces in the procession; and even if we knew them by name and place, it is not very likely that many of them would answer a questionnaire.

Since we know nothing about the true reasons of those who discontinue study for the doctorate, we can make no analysis of causes behind the fact and are forced to depend on the shadowy impressions and troubled memories of the men and women who taught them. We do possess from the chairmen of graduate departments or the directors of graduate study some information, or rather estimation, of their departments' attrition rate. Few departments lose more than half of their inducted students, but more than 60 percent of the responding chairmen confess that they lose between 10 and 50 percent of their potential Ph.D.'s (Table 4.24). But why do graduate professors think these postulants for their chairs leave?

The heads of departments or chairmen of graduate study, whose opinions must be more universal than those of their workaday colleagues, are inclined to explain this defection by the financial difficulties confronting the advanced student who is eventually outfaced by the demands of Ceres and Bacchus. Venus, as we have suggested, is already well satisfied in her claims. In the second category of discouraging causes, they appoint "loss of interest" in academic life or study and a genuine "lack of ability" to carry on the work required of a graduate student (Table 4.25). The graduate professors differ in some degree from the chairmen and directors of graduate study in that they place financial problems in third place and bring "no ability" and "lack of physical and emotional force" to the front as the domineering causes of attrition. They nominate "loss of interest" for the third position (Table 4.26); and since this reason is given the red ribbon by both groups, we cannot help but wonder what imbues it with such destructive force.

When both groups set down marginal comments on this dropout problem, they were sometimes sarcastic but also very realistic. "Dropouts lack," says one professor, "a holy drive." "They are confused," say others, "have conflicting goals," "are too often failed poets," or rather, "find more creative work far more charming." They "set too high standards for themselves," and the consequent "sense of inadequacy" overturns and defeats them. Some students simply "become disillusioned with the system," which has absolutely "no meaning" for them; because graduate study in English and American Literature "is irrelevant to modern problems." There are, of course, "the departmental myths of terror," and their prevalence begets "graduate student trauma." Many students discover to their dismay that "you can't buy a hammer in a grocery store;" and, we assume, it is hammers not delicatessen that they want. But there are fleshly reasons discovered by the professors besides these spiritual ones. "Good job offers," especially "too big junior college salaries" take many students away from the excitement of proseminars. In these enticing and well-paid places, many of the dropouts undoubtedly learn again (what one professor feels turns them away from the pursuit of the doctorate), that "you cannot cope with professional bureauracy." Finally, for several professors, some graduate students find it impossible to follow the solitary life of the scholar when offered "the lure of a metropolitan environment."

Although the chairmen of departments with doctoral programs and their professors are not unanimous as pathologists, they are no more agreed as diagnosticians. There is no academic encephalographic device that enables the admissions officials to forecast graduate success from undergraduate excellence; but once the graduate students are wards in the upper division of a university, both the chairmen and the professors have some skill at discerning the moment of academic crisis. Over 50 percent of the chairmen or directors of graduate study can predict a student's prospects for earning a Ph.D. at the end of his first graduate year. In this ability, the leaders of graduate study in English are more proficient than their 1170 colleagues, who are only one third sure of their premonstrative powers at this time. The moment of the preliminary examination or the final test before the candidate is unleashed to do research is another poignant moment in prognosis. About 20 percent of the chairmen know he will not make it, and they are joined in this solemn decision by something over 20 percent of the graduate teachers. When he fails this examination, a conservative twenty of the chairmen and 327 of the graduate professors can detect the falling pulse rate and the filming over of the retina (Tables 4.27, 4.28). But there are a few cheerful graduate professors who can still hope for recovery and reach only for the funeral wreath when the first draft of the dissertation comes in. There is also a small number of respondents, far more pessimistic than their fellows, who notice the burden of mortality at the M.A. oral, at the end of the first term, at the qualifying examination, or when the courses are almost completed. We can assume that they quietly inform the patient or the next-of-kin as soon as they know.

But all of this descriptive material is only the prolegomena to the beginning of the graduate program. The student admitted, fellowshipped, given a file number and a schedule of courses, is now ready to wrestle with the champions for the guerdon of the doctorate. What will he do, or better, what will they do to him?

CHAPTER 5

The Initial Training
of Doctoral
Candidates

———————◆•••◆———————

I We would like to think, now that the candidate for the
doctorate in English and American Literature has
been received into the temple of learning, that the
ritual he must follow and revere is as faithfully accepted as rituals
are intended to be. The credos should be the same in all branches of
the church. We know that he will take courses and debate in seminars,
but we also know that the number and nature of these elementary
obligations will differ from province to province. In some regions he
will be forced to take specific courses; in others he will be allowed
a slight savouring of free will. With the exception of two graduate
departments, he will have to prove his alleged competence in the
reading of one, two, or three languages besides the one he proposes to
profess. Some departments will give him a choice of tongues; in others
they will be prescribed. In all departments he will be liable for a
streak of examinations, qualifying and/or preliminary ordeals, which
may be written, oral, or both. Purified by these ventures, he is ready
for his dissertation, a work that differs in intellectual and gross weight
depending on local standards. Enlightened by this exercise, he arrives
at the moment of unity, "defends" his thesis, and is joined in oneness

54

with his former teachers and examiners. This chapter will discuss everything anterior to the final outcome and will begin with the courses, the *fiat lux* of the graduate departments.

II   The chairmen of departments or directors of graduate study have instructed us about their required courses.

About 16 percent of them claim to have nothing of the sort (Table 5.1), but numerous recent recipients of the doctorate confess that "while there are no required courses at X university, you had better have taken _____ before you risk your orals." More than two thirds of the reporting departments are not so lenient and see to it that their doctoral students pass from one to three such courses. There are also some seven departments with much more rigor where four to six courses cannot be avoided. Departments vary in their insistences; but 69 percent (Table 5.2) of them demand work in Old English, that massive keystone of the nineteenth-century curriculum. That language (if it is one) is of the most simple nature, and it is incredible that people who manage to pass reading tests in French and German are disturbed by it; nevertheless, it seems to be a matter of anguish not only to the students who are imprisoned in it but also to the people who teach it. When the graduate professors were asked about it and its handmaiden, Middle English, they voted to the extent of 51 percent for Old English and 68 percent for Middle English. Their interest in Modern English Grammar squeezes between these two figures (Table 5.3). The reasons offered by the faculties of the graduate departments for their requirements of antique dialects are worth mention.

The commonest opinion is simply "they should know it all;" but many answerers point out that these required dialects enable a student to "see a text as language before they interpret it" and are, hence, especially useful for "close literary analysis." "To teach Joyce and Lawrence," writes one supporter, "you must know *Beowulf* and Chaucer." Another puts the same idea musically: "Could you hear Debussy and Wagner if you had never heard Hadyn and Palestrina?" Most of the professors argue that it is impossible to know the present if one is ignorant of the past. "To understand modern irony, we must know Langland and Chaucer." A somewhat cynical member of the profession writes that "most students go into modern fields, not only for their intrinsic value, but to escape the discipline required to master an older area."

But in the contention about Old and Middle English and other required subjects, such as bibliography and "philology" (it is usually put in quotes by the recent graduates), there is naturally a left as vociferous as the right. A center appears to be wanting. "The older forms of the language," states one member of the opposition, "take up too much student time, are never mastered, and soon forgotten." "Old English," another graduate professor tells us, "is a foreign language useful only to specialists." "Only *Beowulf*," says a third, "is worth reading and to learn Old English for this is a dubious effort." Several critics of the system feel that the way in which Old and Middle English are taught instills a habit of superficiality in the student, and a number of marginalists come down hard on the pedagogical methods of the linguists who teach these courses. "*Beowulf* as a poem and not as 'philology.'" "These languages," another remarks vehemently, "are taught simple-mindedly—sheer rote drill—and they are used to eliminate, not educate, graduate students." To these negative responses, we may oppose the opinion of a professional medievalist: "I feel that scholarship and teaching in the earlier periods will be improved by removing the requirements and making the field competitive."

The knowledge of historical and modern grammars is more highly thought of by graduate teachers than a knowledge of Old English. Although there are opinions to the contrary, such as "philology as it is taught today is plain drudgery, memorization, and translation," many professors recognize that "grammar is today's weak spot." One respondent states that all graduate students "should be trained in linguistics, semantics, rhetoric, and critical theories"; and another doubts that "without an understanding of twentieth-century synchronic linguistics" a student is "more than half prepared to teach." "Grammatical concerns," we are reminded, "have the habit of announcing themselves in class." The judgment of several professors, who are taking aim at the very modern student, are summed up by one, who says, "No literary critic can be without linguistic training."

Although none of them agrees with the graduate professor who concluded that "hacks and nonproductive scholars control required courses," the recent recipients supplied us with striking information about their experience with required courses. Over 75 percent of them took such courses although many had thought, once the sophomore year was ended, they might elect work at their pleasure (Table 5.4). Of this group 1124, or 78.9 percent, studied Old English, whereas almost half took a course in Bibliography or the History of the Language. Fewer than 10 percent were required to absorb the philosophy of modern English and the various fashionable grammars, and almost none had any training in pedagogical methods (Table 5.5). Some of them complain about all their courses both required and elective, and we shall hear their outcries in due season; but at least half of them found their classroom work useful in passing their preliminaries or in their current teaching (Table 5.6).

Since almost 20 percent of the newer Ph.D.'s had words to utter about their courses other than those suggested by our inquisition, their comments should be recalled. Many of their statements should warm the hearts of their former teachers. "My course work trained my mind," "widened my awareness of literary matters," "fed my private needs," "confirmed and ennobled my character." Many students enjoyed courses which gave them "a grip on their subject" or "provided an interest in a speciality." In taking them, they learned "the meaning of professionalism," "improved their style," "sharpened their critical awareness," "filled in gaps," and "had to read *Beowulf*, which otherwise I would not have read." One man states that his courses "helped me discover what men and the world are like," and another describes all of them as of "true but mysterious value." The courses provided some of these students with an understanding of their professors, "scholarly and exemplary men," or with the stimulating competition of "excellent classmates."

In some instances the value of courses was more practical than intellectually or spiritually hedonistic. They "paid off in teaching" and "provided nine tenths of the iceberg." One man reports that his courses caused him to write a number of papers that have since been printed in *PMLA* and other learned journals. The mimeographed bibliographies passed out by professors were a great aid to others in their subsequent studies; whereas several respondents learned to teach by watching and hearing the great instructors at whose feet they sat. Some of the younger members of the profession admit that they also learned to teach by bad example. "My courses illustrated how bad teaching could be"; "they taught me to be a good teacher by showing me how not to be a bad one." But there are other reasons besides pedagogical ones for being on the wrong side.

A certain number of autodidacts found their courses an enormous waste of human time. "Many courses simply repeat undergraduate courses." "They were all boring except for research papers which I worked out on my own." The milder critics say that the courses had value only "to show me how to squeeze through the prelims" or "to provide guidelines for my own private study." Others are by no means so charitable. "I had ninety course hours—most of them next to use-less—independent study would have been better." "I certainly learned nothing about teaching nor was I prepared for anything I now teach." As a penultimate comment, we can quote a desperate academic sigh: "The courses were generally valueless. I had to relearn what I had learned. But this is education!" One objector found the ultimate solution and writes that since attendance was voluntary, "I was able to use my time more valuably."

III   Since the institution of American doctoral programs, it has always been assumed that graduate students were able to read some languages other than English. In the last century, it was taken for granted that everyone knew Latin and had mastered French and German, the tongues of elegance and of learning. The acquisition of these two languages enabled the *étranger* or *Ausländer* to follow the scientific discoveries and the sophisticated wisdom of Europeans. If he was an embryo mathematician, he needed no more than a handful of conjunctions and a few verbs; but if he was entering the serious study of literature, he would need more of a language than his scientific classmates to read the fine essays in *La Parole* or *Anglia Beiblatt*.

The reasons for the retention of this venerable requirement are being currently scrutinized by graduate departments of English and American Literature, and many of them have not only agreed to allow the student a choice of languages but also have reduced the prerequisite to that of one language more than adequately mastered. The greatest number of recent recipients of the doctorate demonstrated their skill by passing reading examinations in two languages, almost always French and German; but a third of them were faced with testing in three languages (Table 5.7). Some 1338, or over 70 percent, had to learn their languages after they became graduate students (Table 5.8); but, fortunately, most had only to put their minds on one of them (Table 5.9). It almost goes without saying that the missing language was usually German, which was ingested for examination purposes in some fashion or other by 939 students or 55 percent of all recently made English Ph.D.'s (Table 5.10). Few of these late learners got round to reading a paper in the *Archiv für das Studium der neuren Sprachen*, because only half of them were ever asked to use one of the necessary languages in a preparation for a graduate course (Table 5.11) or in their dissertation (Table 5.12). About half of the 1880 respondents state that they have used their reading ability in French or German in their subsequent researches as anyone who reads the footnotes in scholarly journals knows (Table 5.13); but about a quarter of the newer Ph.D.'s confess that they have not tried their memories of these essential scholarly implements since they received their degrees. They must be now as monolingual as they were when they began graduate study.

The heads of departments and directors of graduate studies are nearly unanimous in their belief that the language requirements are sound (Table 5.14), but they defend this conviction on the ground that languages are the service stripes of education and not of utility (Table 5.15). They are joined for cultural reasons in this assumption by 1115 of the graduate professors (Table 5.16), but 804, or 72 percent, of these men and women see utilitarian values, too (Table 5.17). It is interesting to discover that 735, or 66 percent, of the graduate professors have not, during the academic year 1965–1966, asked their own graduate students to read anything in either French or German or any other strange tongue (Table 5.18); nor have half of them heard a seminar report or read a term paper with a quotation or reference in one of these essentially scholarly languages (Table 5.19). Two members of this group have employed their knowledge of alien languages more than a thousand times during the year; but over 20 percent have not used them at all, and about 76 percent have read in them on fewer than twelve occasions (Table 5.20). All of this piles up to what might be called a demi-spes or the half evidence of things not seen. But some have seen it and the chairmen (Table 5.21) and their colleagues in the graduate department (Table 5.22) divided almost equally into "yeas" and "nays" when they were asked if they would accept one foreign language in somewhat better control than the normally demanded two languages.

The attitude of the recent recipients—at least the complaining ones—will be reported in Chapter 6; here we shall make a record of only the graduate professors' views on the language problem. "Languages," we are told, "separate the scholars from the pseudo scholars" and are "the mark of the doctorate." They are necessary not only for utility but are the best antidote to the provincialism of English studies. Some of these seasoned teachers readily agree that one foreign language is enough if it also means a knowledge of a second literature. One professor puts it very trenchantly, "German is justified when the student reads *Faust* and the *Duino Elegies* not just scholarly books and articles." Another very hopeful professor would like to have his students read, write, and speak two foreign languages; but others contend that such a requirement for only one language would slow down the procession to the doctorate beyond reason. This opinion could be very exact, because a sampling of the questionnaires filled out by the recent recipients shows that those who had to learn at least one language were stayed on the course to the degree by a year longer than those who did not.

IV   Although the double requirement in foreign languages is a source of sorrow and anger among graduate students in general, the so-called preliminary examination, which qualifies the successful student to begin the composition of his dissertation, is traditionally the greatest producer of infernal wails and purgatorial suffering. Doubtful candidates for the doctorate are presumed not to arrive at this station, but many wait there for the train that never comes. The reports of sixty-three departments able to produce exact figures shows that they eliminate more than 200 students a year at these ordeals (Table 5.23). These people never get elected to the "Ph.D. Club," but become members of the "Dropout auxiliary," the membership roster of which is known only to the angels.

The customary procedures for this salient moment in the graduate student's ascent vary from department to department. There is no such thing as a standard preliminary test. In 10 percent of the eighty-eight graduate departments, the whole examination is oral; in one third of them, it is written; and in the remaining departments, it is both oral and written (Table 5.24). The hours allotted to the examination are quantitatively as diverse as the methods of examination. The purely oral examinations may be one to three hours of questioning (Table 5.25); the purely written examinations may run from three to forty-eight hours (Table 5.26). When the preliminaries are both talk and ink, the average length of the oral part is two hours and the student writes for about ten hours (Table 5.27). A clever student should very sensibly do a little window-shopping before he enters a graduate department to buy a degree, because he might not always have enough nervous energy on deposit.

The areas of acquired knowledge investigated in these examinations are similarly uneven in both number and quantity. If we assume that the full scope of English and American Literature is contained in nine fields, then one third of all departments subscribe, as one respondent says, to "the whole damn mess." About 12 percent of all departments are willing to settle for one third as much learning or for about three fields. The remaining departments oscillate between four and eight fields (Table 5.28). The successful eluders of this academic deadfall, to the extent of one third of them, stood in nine fields and answered questions on everything from the "Finnsburg Fight" to the Ginsberg "Howl" (Table 5.29). These people were denied any liberty of choice, as they are in some other departments where the student selects fields, and threw their tough memories against the iron will of their professors' demands (Table 5.30).

One of the central problems about the preliminary examination, which was probably easier a quarter of a century ago when Browning and Tennyson were considered contemporary poets and hence too recent to consider, is that the graduate student is uncertain about how to prepare for it. He hardly knows what it will be like until he undergoes it. Many humane departments where the examination is written have a file of former tests, and in about 15 percent of the reporting departments there is a syllabus (Table 5.31). Many of the recent recipients had the use of these "crutches" before they limped into the examination (Table 5.32). Nonetheless, the "grapevine," the advice of professors, and the autobiographies of other men and women who had endured and triumphed plus "read! read! read"! are the regular means of attempting to pass.

The uncertainty about the nature of the examination is enhanced by the fact that the examinee is sometimes faced with a sea of strange faces when he enters the chamber of interrogation. He encounters professors whom he scarcely knows by sight and whose mental quirks and intellectual standards are unknown to him. Too much of the questioning is based on a "guess what I have in mind" philosophy, which only the clairvoyant can manage. In 40 percent of the graduate departments replying, the nightmare of an ocean of strange voices and manners is there to haunt the examinee (Table 5.33). In most instances, men and women aspirants are granted two opportunities to pass, but in nineteen departments there seems to be a third chance (Table 5.34). But the chairmen of departments think well of this examination; they are not inclined to throw it out although almost a third of them stand ready to reduce it in scope (Table 5.35). About one half of their colleagues in the graduate divisions believe it should be reduced to fewer fields; on the other hand, a third of them feel that it is too simple and should be enlarged (Table 5.36). The chairmen, in the main, offered clarifications of their reactions, but their suggestions are not very significant (Table 5.37); the graduate professors by letter and marginal comment were more vocal and, therefore, more specific.

Among the graduate professors are some who stand firmly for the full-scale nine-field examination and would add to it. They advise us that a candidate should be responsible for "everything" plus some further special fields, that departments which allow some choice of areas or authors should abandon this timid and relaxed idea. One respondent, aged thirty-seven, writes, "I am old-fashioned, the more comprehensive and demanding the examination, the better they are for the student." Some of his older academic companions would reduce the examination to three, four, or five areas. "Test breadth in courses," says one man, "and limit the prelim to the field of specialization." With this view others agree, because "the present system merely encourages mindless memorization."

The notion that the examination should try "capabilities and not crammed information" is approved by a few graduate professors. "Why not," asks one, "make a section of the oral a piece of research," or as another suggests, "replace it with a lecture on a specific topic allowing the student a fixed amount of time in which to gather and organize his material"? A number of the graduate professors are well aware of the confusion that attends this examination. "You are told to study everything and get tested on anything." The student should be provided, some believe, with "a modest reading list that he knows thoroughly," and "the criteria for passing should be more clearly expressed." Graduate professors are not loath to concede that the preliminaries are unfair, and sometimes do not take the concerns of the student very much into account. "He prepares for it for years, has a bad day, flunks, and quits—that's the way we lose lots of good teachers." Like the procurator of Judea, one graduate professor asks a question and does not stay for an answer. "Examinations of this nature," he states, "are partly given as a mechanical screening device and partly for the sake of tradition. Whom are we examining and what is the purpose?"

This sardonic question which might be answered in the first phrase by "the professors on the committee" and in the second by "an exhibition of learned oneupmanship" carries us to the reactions to the test of the recent recipients of the doctorate, all of whom survived this great interrogatory festival and 86 percent of whom made it on the first try (Table 5.38). As a consequence of their triumph, 82 percent voted it a valuable procedure for the examinee (Table 5.39). Survivors always view a catastrophe as not too fearsome; in fact, after some time, they see something salutary in it. Now "they can write their dissertations in peace," and, as they look back on it, "they realize now that at one time they knew something."

When they decorate their survival with virtues, many of the recent recipients recall that the preliminary made them read madly and fill in the gaps between courses. "In the absence of articulated courses, it helped to pull things together." In expressing this nearly universal opinion, those who made it to the life rafts use significant verbs, "it forces," "it compels," "it makes." There is a faint requiem of coercion in these terms. A great deal of praise is also accorded to the test for its psychological benefits although it is also described as "a psychological bad dream." It is "a heck of a lot of satisfaction for the student who passes" and "gives him a dim sense of strength." We are told that it aids "in self-evaluation," that it induces "a pleasant feeling of intellectual intensity," and "a sense of progress." It "tests native ability," "forestalls complacency," "indicates real weaknesses," "requires one to ask himself whether he has a vocation," "measures moral muscle," "teaches the meaning of *hubris*," "puts steel in the soul and measures what steel is there," and determines whether or not the body "is ulcerproof." To one former graduate student it was "like being circumcised or castrated—a significant event in life"; and to another, it brought home Kurtz's last words, "The horror! The horror!"

For the recent recipients, the preliminary examinations have certain practical merits. The examination "makes you aware of professional levels" and "shows you whether you can speak out before your future peers." It is "an introduction to standards," which, we gather, the attesting professor did not learn in his courses or seminars. Besides these intrinsic values, the examination "puts your hands on the ropes," and "teaches you how to master material in a hurry." On occasion, the examinees learned "that there is no such thing as a right answer," as well as "the value of good, cold facts, a necessity in our discipline." It is a fine indication of "future professional success and failure," in that, perhaps, it "teaches the student to be articulate under stress," or to describe it more succinctly, "it instructs him in glibness and gamesmanship." Finally, it not only gives the examinee an intimation "of the level at which he will work for life," but better still, "it is worth $5000 a year."

Some of our former students are not so cheerful as others when they recollect their experiences at this examination. "It is no learning experience but a bore!" This weary utterance is not very common, but it is paralleled by the remark of one recipient who held that the test was not frightening, because "the professors asked the same questions every year." Its effect on other students was anything but mild. "It teaches one to despise the institution of sadism"; nonetheless, "many who survive it remain sane for years." This "anxiety-ridden, humiliating, valueless experience" is properly summed up by one of the successful, who writes, "It scares the hell out of him, delays him unduly, leaves him with a lasting feeling of stupidity."

Although the preliminary "forces the student to uncork his notes" and is sometimes "the most worthwhile" or "single most important experience of my life" without which "I wouldn't know so much," many recipients find it of only transitory value and the passing of it chiefly "governed by Fortune." "For a week I knew a hell of a lot," "a delightful but temporary illusion of knowing," "a once-in-a-lifetime synthesis," "a momentary conviction that one has a coherent view of literature," "ephemeral knowledge of a vast field," or to express it with some finality, "You will never again know so much."

A certain number of answerers praise the examination as a means of eliminating professional competition and "protecting the university." It is a high barrier against "dilettantes," assuring the successful student that "total fools will be excluded from the degree." In a kinder way, "it warns off students with no chance of success," "weeding out those incapable of writing a dissertation and so saving time for everyone." These opinions supporting the screening nature of the examination may exonerate the graduate faculty as well as the younger Ph.D.'s who hope in time to be part of it. But the tone of the examination, "a form of academic hazing," "which often degenerates into a recital of facts and dates," and "can endanger one's interest in reading for life," is the subject of various serious criticisms. "If it cannot be eliminated," one recent recipient inquires, "if it is a necessary evil, can it not be humanized?" Some of the suggestions tending in this direction have already been related, but there are respondents who urge that courses and seminars provide a more adequate estimation of a graduate student's talents than a qualifying examination, and that the preliminary, if there must be one, should be shaped more to suit the examinee's recognized abilities than the vanity of the examiners. "It could be done more beautifully!"

CHAPTER 6

The Doctoral
Dissertation
and Beyond

I   The real value of passing the preliminary examinations, one Ph.D. in English announces, is that "it frees
one from taking courses which are fantastically bad,
mechanical, dull, arbitrary, boring, anxiety-arousing but not intellectually challenging or emotionally satisfying and allows one to plunge
into the independent life of the research scholar." The recent recipients,
having sailed into this snug harbor, sat down on the wharf and in
about three years' time wrote 1880 theses of which 85 percent were
between 150 and 500 pages in length (Table 6.1). Some 78 percent
of them selected a research area which was personally attractive to
them, but by "attractive" they mean a number of things.

For some of them the topic of study was "an old interest"; in fact,
for a few it was the continuation of their master's degree thesis or
the expansion of a seminar paper. Others decided on a subject that
"had not been beaten to death" or on a major author "who was not
yet trampled into the ground." Often it was something either suitable
to their own abilities or lack of them, to "individual tastes and talents."
For these reasons one student who "wanted to avoid language prob-

lems," consequently, "wrote on Shelley." The reason is not infrequently pragmatic: "it seemed an easy topic"; "it was easy to shape and limit"; or more sadly, "I thought it was a problem I could understand; later I realized I did not." Still more realistic is the response of one professor who selected his thesis area "with special reference to the market's demands."

In the choice of dissertation topics there is a certain axiom not widely enough known: "Do what no professor wants to do!" The professor's character and scholarly peccadilloes are often taken into calm consideration; hence, a few men chose areas they were not too keen about, because the director in the one they preferred "was an impossible to please scholar," or "the area in which I wanted to work was directed by a nincompoop." Most of the recent respondents seem to have found shady and convenient spots on the research terrain, but a number of them were influenced in their choice of country by the lodestone that attracted one clear-sighted respondent, "The good health of my professor, the unlikelihood of his leaving for another university, his high opinion of my course work" (Table 6.2).

More than half of the dissertation writers either found the problem they went on to investigate by themselves or with the aid and comfort of their supervisors. Only about 12 percent of them were assigned a topic (Table 6.3). One of them acknowledges the inspiring advice of a fellow student, and a woman scholar says with justifiable pride, "My husband suggested it." About 83 percent of all recent recipients carried their original design for a dissertation to ultimate success on the first try, but 315 of them did not and almost everyone of them told a tale (Table 6.4).

The reason for initial failure can be symbolized by four esses: the Student, the Subject, the Supervisor, and the Surprise. We should like to expound this enigma by a series of sentences after the manner of an anthology of familiar quotations.

A. The Student
  1. "I got scared of the Renaissance; it was too big for me and I had no Latin and hardly any German."
  2. "I got even more bored than my director said I would."
  3. "I lost interest."
  4. "I needed classical and romance languages to carry on."
  5. "I was not competent to bring a diffuse subject into form."
  6. "I floundered."
  7. "I chased too many dead ends."
  8. "My undergraduate enthusiasm turned sour."

9. "I was too ambitious."
10. "It was beyond me."

B. The Subject
1. "It would have taken thirty years."
2. "I began to read Spenser looking for a topic, but I didn't like Spenser."
3. "My professor urged me to write on H. G. Wells, but I couldn't care less."
4. "I decided after a time that Wallace Stevens was not talking about something I wanted to think about no matter how attractively he expressed it."
5. The project required mountainous reading of very dull material."
6. "I did some research on Victorian verse satire; then I decided to look for a fruitful topic."
7. "The necessary documents were unavailable until the death of a man aged fifty."

C. The Supervisor
1. "I wanted to work on a major figure, but the department head said, 'No, work on a minor one.' So I did."
2. "The first director was too vague to trust; the second thought my author only worth an essay."
3. "The professor who encouraged the topic retired; his successor discouraged it after I had worked on it for three years."
4. "Succeeded the third time; the second topic had been more thoroughly treated than my professor or I knew."
5. "After three tries I had nothing. The fourth time my director objected, I changed to another professor."
6. "Powers-that-be thought it too challenging; that is, they didn't understand it."
7. "After three topics *he* was satisfied."
8. "My professor wasn't interested in my results, and I wasn't interested in his topics."
9. "It was directed by two badly coordinated professors."
10. "After two years my director went on leave, and the new and more experienced professor advised me to abandon the whole thing."

D. The Surprise
1. "The whole dissertation had to be rewritten to suit *one man's* specifications."
2. "Half-way through a book appeared—the archetypal story."
3. "My professor refused to accept my conclusions."

4. "Someone else finished before I could."
5. "There was a Yale dissertation on the same subject."
6. "An authority on the subject pointed out to my professor that the subject had been done."
7. "After my advisor was called to another university, it was discovered that the subject had been used."
8. "Another student working under my professor turned out to be writing on the same topic."
9. "My director approved, but the committee regarded my dissertation as too narrow."

Some of these mournful dumps would suggest that the directors of dissertations were consistently standing very flat-footed in some cases and at other times were not very much on their toes. An arbitrary firm stand is probably as distressing to a dissertation student as the discovery that his professor is not *au courant* in his special fields. In general, the recent recipients of the doctorate felt that their supervisors had helped them as much as could be expected (Table 6.5). Some of them are grateful, indeed, to the men who first guided them through the labyrinth of professional research. "He was tactful and opened things up for me." "He gave me more of his time and energy than I had any reason to expect." "He was a model of restraint and good sense," and "he limited his help to wise and necessary revisions." One student describes an "ideal director," who took time out from his own study abroad to search the archives and "send me notes." Praise goes to directors because "they left me alone," "did not get in my way," "gave encouragement when it was needed," or "helped me lick it into shape." The praise is occasionally a trifle damp. "He knew nothing, but he was helpful." Now and then there is a stain of damnation. "He helped too much; I would have profited by less;" but this objection is balanced by an account of a "distinguished man who was too busy to oversee my project adequately." Here and there, a student found himself sitting on the fulcrum: "What help was given was counteracted by what was not given; it was a bitter and unnecessary trauma." A last recent recipient can be permitted to close this glorious yet gory history; he wrote under the third choice on this question, "Why not a box on hindrance?"

The contrary views on the directors are ameliorated by the fact that 68 percent of the recent recipients found their dissertation requirement both "exciting and absorbing" (Table 6.6), but many of them had suggestions for reforms, and we should like to extract some of these more fully. One thoughtful respondent, who encountered no grave difficulties in attaining the degree, provides the following advice.

In the first place, the problem often lies in the limitations on acceptable dissertation subjects and approaches, so that a student who could do a splendid job on some subject for which there is no precedent, or through some approach where the scholarly demands are great but not obvious, will be turned down and will end up grinding out one more edition of one more tenth-rate play. Secondly, the dissertation writer is often disheartened by the non-research problems he encounters: drafts which are not returned for months; dissertation advisors who disappear on leaves or accept positions at other schools; demands for drastic revisions in chapters which had earlier been praised; and assorted rivalries and politics which infect so many graduate committees. Finally, many candidates attempt to complete the dissertation after they have left graduate school and have assumed full-time positions where very little energy remains for research and writing.

We would find it impossible to enlarge on this description of a state of things which most of us recognize only too acutely.

When the current graduate professors of English and American Literature were asked in their questionnaire to estimate the real value of most of the dissertations they had read, they more or less rushed to the safety of the middle. The greater number of them felt that perhaps 10 percent of the theses they knew were substantial and probably worthy contributions to literary scholarship and criticism. An equally large number of them thought half of all dissertations were adequate to their purpose. Fewer than 10 percent of the whole group marked them all as almost of no value (Table 6.7). If the majority of these men and women are right, about fifty books should appear every year that are substantial and worthy contributions to scholarship and literary knowledge and undoubtedly this surmise is proved to be true as year follows year.

The time spent on all dissertations, an average of three years, and the accumulated comments by successful dissertation writers on the problems involved in this traditional requirement may indicate that some thought should be given to an alternative to the thesis. Some respondents propose that a literary work of some nature is just as solid a demand as a thesis, provided that its author has pursued the regular doctoral course up to that point. One of the recent recipients makes the following proposal.

> Most second and even third year graduate students badly need to do a lot more reading. Few are ready to undertake a book-length research project. I think an artful combination of shorter studies, designed to train the candidate in different scholarly and

critical problems and methods and to familiarize him with several major figures or areas would be more efficient as a scholarly discipline.

This innovator asterisks the fact that we not only force a graduate student to write a book before he has learned to write a chapter, but that we also send a relative amateur to work on a grand topic, to find his way through a rain forest of scholarship where experienced feet would fear to slog. The majority of departmental chairmen and a still larger company of graduate professors indicate partial agreement with this conviction when they affirm their faith in a shorter type of dissertation than we have been accustomed to request. The chairmen, to the number of thirty, do not object to the acceptance of several publishable papers—provided that "publishable" can be sensibly defined—in lieu of the old-line, bulky thesis (Table 6.8). With this opinion 55 percent of the graduate professors (Table 6.9) and 66 percent of the recent recipients of the doctorate are in agreement (Table 6.10).

II   The roughhewn dissertation annotated, punctuated, and tentatively approved by the directing professor or the departmental thesis committee is typed on the proper paper with correct margins and spacing, bound in some style or other, and deposited by its author with some dignitary of the graduate school. The end now draws near, and the candidate begins to feel feathers on his shoulders and to glimpse an incandescent glow above his eyebrows. Only the final oral, still humorously called "the defense of the dissertation," stands between him and the terminal string of letters that will magically change him from *indoctus* to *doctus*. A few graduate departments have forsaken this final stage of the process; nonetheless, 85 percent of the recent recipients sustained it (Table 6.11), and, much to our amazement, a third of them regard it as "a real defense" (Table 6.12). Our private suspicion is that most of them enjoyed the whole affair. They knew more about their subject than anyone at the meeting; they felt safe now "because no one ever fails"; in fact, "no one had flunked at X University in the memory of man." The amusing comments that the invitation to talk about this examination elicited from the recent recipients of the doctorate are, even when they are enameled with violence, the observations of reasonably relaxed people.

To some respondents, however, it was a final round of pure agony. The examination "enables some professors to show the candidate he's still a hack," but it is also "one last bearbaiting session," with "overtones of ritual humiliation." It is "the final emotional ordeal." In a lighter vein "it permits the committee to display finesse, erudition, and ingenuity in the application of intellectual fraternity paddles." The whimsical creak of the rack that is heard in these remembrances is silenced by a certain gaiety that hints at a modest occasion of festivity. For many of the newer Ph.D.'s the final oral was "painless," "a joke," "light conversation," "a lark," "a farce," "a tribal welcoming," "an academic civility," "group therapy," "frosting on the cake," "a nice little chatter," "a gesture for the records," "an amicable discussion," "a pleasant get-together," "general good humor," "a congratulatory picnic," and "a chance for the professors to shake hands with me." A few of those who commented on this moment felt it to be more solemn. One of them describes the examination as "very meaningful," and another names it "the most pleasant of my academic experiences." Several respondents enjoyed "defending" their theses before an "interested and friendly group." "It was marvelous," exclaims one of the emancipated, "I was treated as a fellow teacher."

The characters of the examiners and their preparation for and conduct of the final oral was microscopically observed by both elated and depressed thesis-bearers. The student, they noticed, is asked "uninformed questions," "foolish questions," "superficial questions," or questions "either too vague or too specific to indicate anything but my ability to maintain my poise." The questions are also marked "petty," "precise," "irrelevant," "peripheral," and, as one replier states it, "the one serious question asked was answered by my thesis director." Too often, we gather, the examination seemed a pompous trapeze act, because no one "asked a proper question, since only the director had read the dissertation." "The deplorable unpreparedness" of the committee members or the fact that "most of the committee did not know what the thesis was about" and "did not seem competent to criticize it" converted the final oral for several recent recipients into "a formal test of what the examiners knew best"; or, to express it another way, "they were more interested in their questions than in my answers." "The examiners were not interested in my thesis," says one bored professor, "nor by that time was I." As one observer walked out of the examining room, he knew that "one examiner, fortunately not my director, had miserably failed my oral."

The final oral, dull or exciting as it proved to the examined, is clearly not without drama. "Those who had read my thesis quibbled over the footnotes; those who had not quarreled about the title." The duel between the student and his professors was sometimes second to the saber play among the professors themselves. "My examiners got into a fight and I watched from the sidelines"; or "since the committee know nothing about my field or my thesis topic, several members of the committee got into an argument." The drama was, of course, more comic than tragic, but on occasion it had elements of both. "There was a fight between factions in the department which Pirandello would have loved, but it nearly killed me." There were episodes that Ibsen also would have adored: "Professor X was so embarrassed by his general ignorance that he made my oral into a personal dispute." To these epic interludes of less than Homeric proportions, we can conclude with one recollection worthy of Lucian: "The Dean of the Graduate School took up most of the time berating modern poetry."

For many of these newer Ph.D.'s the whole oral was a "waste of time." "No one is ever refused the degree at this point, because nobody on the committee will risk offending a colleague by failing his student." The students who regard the whole examination as a hollow mockery are also aware how the faculty of the graduate department values these tests. "It was of no real interest to the professors. We had to pull the Head off the golf course, and one member of the committee had to leave before the examination was over to meet a train." The examination has a certain social merit, because it not only "enables the junior members of the committee to show off before the Head," but it also gives them "a chance to meet me because I had been away from the campus for so long." The overtones of wasted time and money pervade a great many of the responses and are underscored by those students who were employed on distant campuses and were forced to make a long and expensive journey "to have a perfunctory conversation with a few men who asked very little because they wanted to get home." One complaint quoted in full can state the case for this critical minority: "It cost $125 to hear a discussion of how many uses of the word 'quite' a thesis should contain and of the respective merits of Arabic or Roman numerals for section headings."

III   It is almost all over. Sustained and supported by *x* number of courses, *x* number of foreign languages, *x* number of examinations, and a buckram-bound dissertation of *x* number of pages, the successful candidate for the doctor's degree in English and American Literature is ready to receive the blessings of the President or Chancellor, resplendent in his doctorates *honoris causae,* and have his first glimpse of the Board of Regents or Trustees, each of whom is a Litt.D. at least once. While a man too old to be immoral lectures the incipient A.B.'s and B.S.'s on the virtues of morality, the new doctor of philosophy, impervious by long custom to orotundity, may lick his wounds and meditate on what we have done to him.

It is pleasant for those of us who have staggered along in the academic procession too many time to discover that 563 or 30 percent, of all the 1880 recent recipients of the doctorate have no charges against us (Table 6.13). Of this group, 32 percent, in spite of the lurid remarks of some of them, voted the courses we administered as the finest aspect of the whole doctoral program. "I wish that I could have had more courses," writes one, and others speak kindly of "the broadening experience" of course-taking. But after they applaud the courses, it is their own independence that they are most likely to clap. "Freedom" is the impressive noun that is used again and again, and it is statistically represented by the nearly 1000 votes for "independent study" and the more than 1100 votes for the dissertation, the written proof of each student's "independent study" (Table 6.14). Nevertheless, nearly 70 percent of the recent recipients are unhappy about one or more phase of the doctoral program, and they enforce their bills of complaint in statements separate from their questionnaire. The language requirements and the courses, which now seem only the least of many evils, lead the list of charges (Table 6.15). Old English, Middle English, "philology," the preliminary examinations, and the dissertation clump secondly. The inscribed criticisms constantly re-echo those we have heard in the sectional accounts of the program, but we shall preserve some further objurgations for the sake of emphasis if not for that of unity and coherence.

The courses, according to some of the 1307 objectors, "seldom live up to their titles," "rehashed what could be read," "concentrated on minutiae in order to make literature scientific," or were "based on books which the professors had written." The true villains are the professors. Some of them "lectured from notes compiled twenty to thirty years ago," and "much of the material mastered could have been learned if the professors had stayed at home." "The lecturers at X University," one former student recalls, "some of them quite distinguished men, made literary scholarship so unattractive that I was tempted many times to forget the whole thing." More than once, recent Ph.D.'s inform us, they learned what they learned "in spite of the professors." The disinterested or lazy professor was the subject of a somewhat extensive and vituperative literature, but this gray account of graduate courses can be adjourned with a final marginal note: "Most of the graduate faculty were poor teachers—dull, harried, nervous, in a rat race to publish with the dehumanizing result that to them the garnering of critical opinions from books and articles was more important than enjoying and developing some individual approach to literature."

The general objection to the language requirements, though sometimes virulently expressed as in the case of the German or Old English requirements, are less varied in their gruffness than the comments on the courses' contents and the professors who furnished them. One common complaint is that the language tests give a sense of value to superficiality. "It took me three years to pass German, and I still can't read it," or "it is possible to pass them without knowing them at all." There are those who think it is a foolish waste of time to learn a language unless one is shown how to use it. This view leads into criticisms of the obstinate demands of certain departments for two traditional languages. "I learned German, but I need Latin and Italian." The extension of this sort of comment is found among those recent recipients who are specialists in American Literature or Modern Literature. "French has some value for people in recent areas; German has no worth at all." The phrase, "one good one is better," is repeated many times, and the respondents state that the one language "should be aimed at reading literature and not monographs." The general grumble is that one of the required languages is never really learned at all; or if it is mastered well enough to pass the test, is quickly lost. "Languages quickly acquired, quickly forgotten."

Although some of the recent recipients are disturbed by their failure to be granted any guidance as they wandered through the dark wood of the department's demands and write "no contact in my university between the professor and the graduate student," many, we gather, must have profited from the isolation begotten by professorial aloofness. The professors were "patronizing," "lofty in attitude," "fake professionals," "filled with academic hocus pocus," but, also, "too paternalistic." There was, as one man reports, "an aura of omniscience and pretension, but the encouraging of unrealistic expectations in students naive enough to take a professor literally was the worst feature." One cloud in the bad air of the departments seen by a new Ph.D. was "the implied opinion that anyone who was not going to be a full-time high-powered scholar was of little value." This atmosphere was not only thick in the Department of English and American Literature, but it also drifted in through the transom, and was breathed in other chambers of the university. "No college or university treats its undergraduates as most universities treat their graduate students. . . . A graduate student who wants an answer to a question or an appointment with a dean can wait, and he had better do his waiting humbly."

We wonder, however, whether or not these complaints are as seriously felt as they are voiced, because 1707, or 90 percent, of all the 1955 to 1965 group of doctors when they considered their expenditure of time and money on their training were inclined to say, "It was worth it" (Table 6.16). We must hasten to admit that many qualify this choice of response with a "maybe," a "yes and no," an "ask me in ten years," or "I really can't say." Some waver in their conclusions, "I don't always think so" or find the question "too disturbing to answer." Of course, a large number who think "it was worth it" add that it was not so in a material sense of the word. "A skilled laborer earns more." Others are dubious about the temporal waste involved in taking the doctorate, but many are very precise in their exact reasons for earning the degree. "I wanted to be promoted"; "I needed the degree for tenure"; "I preferred studying to a 9-to-5 job." But commencement is over and with his or her hood untidily distributed down the back and round the neck, the new doctors enter the brave, new world of academic existence. They have won the rat race of the graduate school, now they enter that of the professional world. How do they get their start in the maze, and how will they run it?

CHAPTER 7

The Professional Career and Its Problems

———◆•◆◆———

I   Proud of his new designation as "doctor" which in many American colleges is a higher title than "professor," nine out of ten of the new Ph.D.'s in English and American Literature will enter the teaching profession. With the coming of September, they will appear before classes in a variety of educational institutions; and their professional career, freed of all its former lets and hindrances, will truly start. The degree of doctor, as we know only too well, guarantees at best a basic minimum. One thing it does not signify is that its possessor can teach at all; nonetheless, 43 percent of the chairmen of departments or directors of graduate study are of the opinion that only a Ph.D. is competent to instruct upperclassmen (Table 7.1), and almost the same percentage of graduate professors concur with them in this conviction (Table 7.2). The recent recipients of the degree, who have just left the greenhouses of the graduate department for the stony fields of undergraduate teaching, are somewhat less converted to this belief (Table 7.3). Very few members of any of the three groups think that a doctorate is the prime essential for a teacher of freshmen and sophomores, and it is just as well they hold to this idea. An underclassman, unless he finds himself in a large lecture class, is not likely to see or hear a Ph.D.

76

Among the recent recipients of the doctorate (the men and women who live at the grass roots), there are numerous vigorous reactions to the doctorate as an essential teaching requirement. Most of them accept the notion that the Ph.D. should be held by teachers of upperclassmen and, especially, of graduate students. "A Ph.D. improves the odds that a man will be a better teacher," writes one man, and another reports that he has "seen much well-intentioned but bad teaching by unprepared M.A.'s." A third correspondent adopts this theory about the pedagogical skill of Ph.D.'s "as a general principle, but I don't see much evidence in the results." Some recent recipients point out that there is a difference between transmitting and discovering knowledge and "that's where a Ph.D. scores." Those who want merely to teach are advised by some of their contemporaries to "go to a college where that is all that will be asked of you," whereas, college chairmen are informed by one replier that "if they want teachers, why don't they hire teachers?"

Those who take a negative view of the principle that a doctorate is the admission ticket to the teaching profession can usually recall various fine teachers to whom they sat or with whom they were associated who did not have doctorates. G. L. Kittredge is often summoned from beyond to testify to the virtues of the nondoctored savant. One of the respondents admits he was a far better teacher before he had his degree than he has ever been since, and his confession enforces the opinion of a second that "an enthusiastic doctoral candidate is always better than an established, unmotivated Ph.D. reading stale notes." The truism that it is the person not the training that makes the professor, or "that Shakespeare without a Ph.D. could teach drama" returns to greet the reader of these questionnaires again and again.

Light is shed on the division of opinion on this controversial point by the steady observation that there is practically no connection between graduate training and the lifetime task of teaching generation after generation of undergraduates. One critic takes as his theme the "absurdity of training men to teach at a large university with a vast library in order to send him out to teach at a small college with almost no library at all." The examples set by the graduate teachers themselves are regularly repeated in some version or other, but we cannot overlook the understatement in the question, "How much teaching is done in the graduate courses?"

The relation between graduate training and college teaching is a moot yet rather trite speculation. A teacher, like a first baseman, is probably born; but men and women can be led to a wide and deep knowledge of intellectual matters provided they have this desire to be taught. One cannot imagine a graduate student, much less a Ph.D., without a devouring hunger for knowledge. But granted the eagerness of appetite, is it properly nourished? The graduate professors believe they have given their students "a broad training" (Table 7.4), which has prepared them equally for both teaching and research (Table 7.5). The recent recipients are probably in full accord with this ambidextrous hypothesis because they assume that a Ph.D. will prove to be a finer teacher than someone without the degree (Table 7.6)— provided his research interests continue without slackening. Although they give their students broad intellectual training, one third of the graduate departments do not insist that all their doctoral candidates have teacher training of some sort; hence, when they recommend them to colleges, they must have little on which to base their judgments except their impression of the student's character and his record in courses (Table 7.7). The blame for this curious oversight rests either with the advisors or with the students themselves, since seventy-two of the replying graduate departments have supervised teaching in their gift and twenty-seven have a definite course in the methods of teaching English (Table 7.8). Instruction and evaluation in this most important aspect of the profession will seem more worthwhile than the sorrows of Hrothgar to some but probably not to all. More than half the graduate departments, aware that their Ph.D.'s will be confronted with problems as college teachers that are unknown to university men, claim that they make some attempt to brief their outgoing students in these matters (Table 7.9), but in only thirteen departments is the briefing anything but informal (Table 7.10). The effectiveness of anything but a well-organized effort in this area of ignorance is very dubious.

II   John Doctissimus or Jane Doctissima frames the diploma and prepares to transmit the learning garnered in the graduate department to undergraduates somewhere else. We know from our earlier account some of these new Ph.D.'s have full-time posts and have simply returned to the home departments for their final orals. The immediate future of this group is, in a sense, assured; but the majority of the new Ph.D.'s have been dispersing their spare time on the writing of the dissertation, the preparation for that "pleasant bull session on a warm afternoon," and a search for an initial position with a low teaching schedule, a fine location, a good library, a superb salary, and excellent fringe benefits. In general, the chairmen of their departments have left the search for this never-never land to the student himself and to his thesis director (Table 7.11), but the graduate professors are more inclined to leave it entirely up to the student (Table 7.12) although we assume that they stand ready to advise him if need be. Both groups, when they scan their students' placement records for the past five years, have reason to congratulate themselves on their efforts, because, in the main, their protégés are rather well settled in posts that well betoken their training and abilities (Tables 7.13, 7.14). There is no doubt from what we are told, that the graduate departments are better at suiting their Ph.D.'s to teaching positions than are the college chairmen at fitting their seniors to graduate departments.

When we consider that most of these young teachers will begin by instructing undergraduates at four-year liberal arts colleges and state colleges, we view the whole group with a cheerful eye. They have come under the scrutiny of a mature group of experts who live a multilife and who are not easily bewitched. Fewer than 20 percent of them, for example, give preference to one of their former majors who has gone to some congenial graduate department and earned a degree (Table 7.15). It is possible that they know their graduates too well or that they want fresh minds on their campuses. To search for new talent, they depend, as does the graduating Ph.D., on direct applications; to a lesser degree, they write letters of inquiry to the old-line graduate departments (Table 7.16). When they make an appointment, it is teaching skill that is uppermost in their minds, but how they measure it at an interview or on the authority of letters from professors is a higher mystery. Next they are impressed by the applicant's knowledge of his subject, another intangible (Table 7.17). We do not want to second the ancient philosophers of Cyrene, but we cannot help but imagine that personal attractiveness plus the name of the graduate department and the field of specialization are the elementary decision makers.

The doctoral program the applicant has been put through must also come into the mind of the chairmen with vacancies to fill; yet most of them have no serious complaints about these programs, beyond suggesting that they be somewhat improved. The chairmen of college departments who still have to finish their Ph.D.'s are naturally more critical of graduate programs in English and American Literature than those who have seen the degree through (Table 7.18). Many of them wish that the universities would emphasize teaching as much as they do research in the training of graduate students, and for this reason about half of them stand ready to subscribe to a degree between the M.A. and the Ph.D. or for a revitalization of the old-fashioned M.A. (Table 7.19). But their opinions can be enlarged by those of all college chairmen.

When the college chairmen made specific recommendations about the doctoral program, they moved for more pedagogical training (not the kind provided by the educationists), for field training, and for a greater breadth in knowledge, not only of English and American Literature, but of various other cultural areas. "The Ph.D. training," writes one chairman, "should have teaching requirements and those who show no ability as teachers should be denied the degree." Another college man states that "narrowly trained literary pedants who cannot also teach writing and who do not enjoy teaching skills and have information outside their fields are of little use." The narrowness of young Ph.D.'s, who know everything about Alfred Austin and nothing more, causes wide consternation among college chairmen. "Often intensive graduate specialization leads to a distressing unworldliness, a narrowness that betrays the professor before his students." The inability, or unwillingness, of young Ph.D.'s to teach composition courses is also widely lamented. If they are willing, they almost never have a knowledge of modern linguistics in their academic saddlebags. Too often, however, they feel above any kind of elementary work. One chairman regrets that the doctorate is no "badge of qualification for college teaching as it pretends to be, but a fraud on the students." To help remove the tarnish and make the badge sparkle a bit, another chairman offers a four-point program: (1) offer better initial counseling of graduate students about courses, prospects, and problems; (2) make learning, not competition, the graduate school ambience; (3) think of the profession of English teacher more in terms of service; and (4) abolish or de-emphasize the "star system" in the universities.

Although the products they buy are not very well packaged, the college chairmen find it very difficult to make purchases. About 76 percent found it very difficult to persuade Ph.D.'s to come to them (Table 7.20). Most lay the blame at the door of scarcity, but there were other reasons, some of them financial, geographical, or basically academic (Table 7.21). We have always supposed that the accrediting agencies with their demands for "fully trained teachers" were the principal persuaders of college presidents and deans about the virtue of the doctoral degree; and that, relieved of this pressure, the liberal arts colleges would be content with inspiring and conscientious teachers, one of whose main qualities was, not a Ph.D., but self-sacrifice. The vote of the college chairmen proves us wrong in that 295 of the 363 of them would employ as many Ph.D.'s as they now do if the accreditation demands were removed. About 10 percent would employ even more than their current number (Table 7.22).

The colleges and the state colleges are growing, as their larger brothers and sisters, like mushrooms, but they are far more durable plants. The falling birth rate has caused some experts to prophesy that the registration in institutions of higher learning will stagnate in the next two decades. This prediction is probably not worrisome unless the national income falls more rapidly than the desire to breed. Colleges are as variable as equities, and there will always be many of them, as now there are some, whose aim—regardless of their inspiring mottoes—will be to provide custodial care for the offspring of tuition payers until they are ready for the paternal front office or the domestic duties of marriage. We have no estimate really of what the future personnel demands of higher education will be, but we know that the three hundred and sixty-three colleges made at least 4500 appointments to their teaching staff in English and American Literature between the years 1960 and 1965 (Table 7.23). Some of these appointments were, of course, replacements, but most of them were necessary in order to handle augmented student enrollments. Almost 18 percent of these new appointees were Ph.D.'s, and 17 percent were ABD's (Table 7.24). In other words, 35 percent of them had finished their dissertations or expected shortly to do so. Within the next five years (by 1971) these same colleges hope to engage almost 1800 Ph.D.'s and almost 1900 other teachers with lesser degrees (Table 7.25). When we remember that we have heard from fewer than 20 percent of all colleges, the number of instructors required becomes very impressive. Student increases undoubtedly impel much of this past and future instructional increase, but the college chairmen are also ambitious to enlarge their undergraduate programs to take care of the steadily growing number of majors in English and American Literature. Many of them do not consider their course offerings comprehensive enough (Table 7.26), and they carefully specified the fields and areas in which they should like to expand (Table 7.27). We can assume that many of them have thought of these extensions of their course offerings in their plans for the next four years, and their revealed ambitions should provide the graduate departments with a relatively reliable prognosis.

The publication virus, so infectious in the universities, has also invaded the colleges. We had always thought that only 2 percent of all American institutions of higher learning had this plague sign on them, but 75 percent of all reporting colleges attach "great or some importance to publication" when they think in terms of promotion or tenure for members of their English staff (Table 7.28). To make this yardstick more agreeable to their teachers, more than half of the colleges have made or are planning to make provisions of some sort—grants, paid sabbaticals, released time—to aid and encourage their scholars who are interested in advanced literary study and writing (Tables 7.29, 7.30). The fact that the colleges' English chairmen are agreeable to this requirement does not necessarily represent the full assent of the staff.

There are also heretics in the colleges who feel that there is some sort of pedagogical correlation between the publishing and the non-publishing college teacher. The publication requirement is coped with by one respondent, who exclaims, "When the administration puts emphasis on publication, it is done at the expense of teaching; when it does otherwise, there is no concomitant increase in good teaching." Some agree that "research makes a better teacher provided he has time to teach," or that a good teacher "gets better with research." One teacher probably puts his finger on the vital spot when he concludes "a man who grubs about in the latest literature in his field is bound to be a better teacher of upperclassmen, but the grubbing itself is of no benefit to his teaching."

The college men are, in general, on the orthodox side. They widely believe, with a few exceptions, that good scholars are either poor or lackadaisical teachers. "The greater the publication record, the poorer the teacher." Several admit that their own publications were done at the expense of their classroom preparations; whereas others are confirmed in their notions that the best teachers are creative writers, non-Ph.D.'s, or people with other than "Ph.D. interests." A teacher who rethinks texts rather than one "who meanders through class talking about or thinking of his articles" is the preferred man, because "the writing teacher usually just can't manage to give enough energy to both teaching and writing." One man, like the Roman god, Janus, succeeds in looking two ways. "If all those who find serious research distasteful were suddenly released to positions (with same pay) in which they could teach (from ancient class notes); and if all those who are consecrated to the quest for truth were relieved from the piddling chores that now waste their time, the educational system would be vastly improved."

We know from Chapter 3 that in most colleges a teacher without a doctorate cannot expect to become a full professor, no matter how long his service nor how conscientious and fruitful it has been. We also know that the majority of college teachers are ABD's or below that modest level. Of the 363 responding colleges, 306 have an average of one to three ABD's (Table 7.31), and the chairmen, confident as minor prophets, believe that two thirds of them will complete their degrees (Table 7.32). They hope to keep about 90 percent of them on their staffs, an expectation that suggests these people are reasonably successful teachers (Table 7.33). To this end, many colleges have devised means to enable their ABD's to finish their dissertations (Table 7.34). Nonetheless, more could be done in bringing this desired situation about, and 84 percent of the college chairmen would welcome some sort of federal aid to effect it (Table 7.35).

The graduate professors are not so convinced as the college chairmen that quite so many ABD's will finish. About 68 percent of the professors estimate that fewer than 25 percent of their students who have been working toward a doctorate for eight or more years will ever be done with it. There is a more optimistic 10 percent who believe about half of these delayed ones will earn the doctorate (Table 7.36), but half of all graduate professors agreed there is a close relationship between the time a student takes to earn his Ph.D. and his ultimate success in the profession (Table 7.37). The shorter the time, they say, the surer the success. We have made no study that confirms this axiomatic conclusion; but if it should chance to be true, the prosperity of the masses described in Chapter 3 who take far longer than eight years is seriously threatened.

What is as plain as an elephant in a patio is that the colleges depend for their teaching staffs on ABD's and teachers not yet that far advanced; yet the chance that at least half of these teachers will achieve the conventional respectability of the oh-so-necessary Ph.D. is slight. Unless some means can be found to transform these half-dressed teachers into full regalia professors, none of the colleges will be able to come within miles of their 1971 goals. We could always increase the number of students whom we admit to graduate work (and so, perhaps, increase the ABD population), but even here the prospects rub thin given the limited number of graduate departments. When the chairmen of graduate departments were asked whether they could comfortably increase their enrollments, most of them confessed that an enlargement could not take place without a concomitant increase in teaching staff (Table 7.38) and a large outlay of money (*see* Supplement to Questionnaire A).

III   The answer to the scarcity of Ph.D.'s in English and
             American Literature, a scarcity which we face on all
             levels, may be "no answer." There is a limit to the
number of people in any generation who are interested in, and capable
of, undergoing the training and completing the requirements in any
enterprise demanding better than average intelligence and perseverance. Each year an enormous number of horses are foaled, but not
many of them ever run in the Kentucky Derby. Animals are animals,
and we may already have reached an intellectual supersaturation
point beyond which we can expect no more worthy doctoral candidates
than we have now. Few of the departments functioning as Ph.D. makers have a student quota; but, should we find there are more candidates for the degree than we can manage, the remedy is, perhaps, a
further proliferation of graduate departments. Since 1900 the number
of doctoral departments has increased fourfold; but when the chairmen of the current departments were required to give their opinion
about the merits of this increment, more than half of them decided it
had had a bad effect on the doctoral degree itself (Table 7.39). To
a somewhat lesser extent, the graduate professors concurred in this
view, but those of them who had earned the degree in the last decade
were not so sure of the deteriorating result of the multiplication of
departments as their elders (Table 7.40). The opinion of the graduate
professors was shared by the recent recipients of the doctorate (Table
7.41). The older one is, the more sure he is that the status quo of
1930 was the proper status quo, but the majority of all English teachers
subscribe to the notion that ivy means excellence.

     The boomerang of tradition thrown by so many professors in
newer graduate departments richochets on the throwers. When the
chairmen of these departments search for a young colleague, they tell
us they look carefully at the source of the candidate's degree (Table
7.42). They are, however, more relaxed in their decisions than their
predecessors, and this relaxation is demonstrated by the fact that the
state universities are now ready to employ a Ph.D. from another state
university, an action almost unthinkable a generation ago. The graduate professors are, probably, the mitigating force behind this new
direction because they are not so stiff in attitudes when it is a matter
of a tenure appointment (Table 7.43). On the other hand, and it is
difficult to comprehend, the chairmen are still somewhat standoffish
when the appointment must be made at even this higher level. At
that late date the character of the prospective professor is well known
and his scholarly impedimenta can be carefully sorted through (Table

7.44). They may really be hesitating to ask a man to join a club to which he obviously was not born. The graduate professors, who are more liberal in appointments at the top, are just as straight-backed when they judge junior appointments as their chairmen (Table 7.45). We are pushed to ponder whether or not the practice really squares with these ideals. Although both these groups consider the source of a man's doctorate when considering his appointment, there is, fortunately, no way to weigh the merits of respective departments. However, in almost every decade someone with a handsome grant has conducted a kind of popularity poll of graduate departments in all subjects. These appraising affairs are never so well organized as the Miss America Contest, because the departments are not required to parade in the aisles in full academic costumes or to give public exhibitions of their talents or lack of them. The decisions reached by the judges are based on a ballot not unlike those arranged by the television analysts who determine whether the "Beverley Hillbillies" are greater artistes than Red Skelton. Departments win either according to the quantity of their production or according to the fame of a few prominent professors—some of whom are either dead or retired. The great imponderables—such as the rationale of the department's program or the proportional relation between the failures and successes on its staff and among its alumni—are shunned, and the ballots are cast by a selected and limited list of voters who are moved by personal disinterest, irritation, sentiment, hostility, or a bad breakfast.

The most recent of these plebescites, conducted by Chancellor Cartter, furnished us with a list of twenty first runners among the graduate departments of English and American Literature. Using this group of medalists as a norm, we asked the respondents to indicate whether or not they thought a Ph.D. produced by some member of the prime group was likely to be "better on the average in ability and training" than one graduated by the long string of back runners. The results of our ballot may demonstrate the value of these decennial competitions because almost 85 percent of the graduate professors agree with Chancellor Cartter's findings (Table 7.46). The recent recipients are a little more chary and not so impressively influenced; fewer than 50 percent of them are swayed in their views by these results (Table 7.47). A very limited percentage of both groups, however, can look with unprejudiced eyes on a Ph.D. from one of the newer graduate departments. The alumni of the departments which failed to show in the Cartter report have a sorry sense of their own inferiority and are inclined to agree with their betters that they themselves are neither so well trained nor so able as they (Table 7.48). Of course, sounder decisions about the status of a graduate department of English could be made by an accrediting commission that had objective standards, could talk to members of the department, compare records, and take a census of tombstones of long-gone professionals, but both the chairmen of graduate departments and their professors (Table 7.49) show no delight in the idea of accreditation. But the moment has come to abandon data and to harken to the sound of some still, small voices.

The commonest reaction of the members of the profession to the proliferation in recent years of graduate departments is that it has created "more Ph.D.'s." This is, of course, a false assumption, because it is the older department that have upped their output and the newer departments which lag behind. Such an opinion probably controls the conservative view that the spread of doctoral programs while "it serves the market" and "has made it possible for a poor student to get a degree somewhere" has resulted in "a watering down," "a deterioration," and "poor standards." It "has debased the hell out of the doctorate," and consequently "made a questionnaire like this one necessary." It is further supposed that "the original purpose of the degree has been obscured" by the multiplication of departments, and that the degree has become "less reliable," "nebulous," and simply "a threshold requirement." We need only study the roster of English Ph.D.'s produced prior to 1918 to see how just these views are. Were there, indeed, great men before Dr. Agamemnon? The social value of the degree, we are informed, has also been lessened. "It is no longer an elite degree but a professional one"; "it is a commodity not a symbol of dedication," and hence, "it is a degree no longer taken seriously by the general public." There is a reverse to this medallion, and some respondents rejoice in the democratization of the doctorate and praise "the loss of snobbishness." "Let us give up our European elitist notions," exclaims one replier, "after all we live in America"!

Here and there, a somewhat weary observer considers the whole doctoral process, regardless of time and place, as "merely the perpetuation of Original Sin;" but many smell redemption and sniff in the proliferation of graduate departments the pollen of improvement. The degree has been "liberalized and made more dynamic," "more reasonable in its requirements," and "more pedagogical in its purpose." "Many of the older men in my department," writes a younger teacher, "are hardly credits to the older systems." The increase in the number of departments may have "produced a race of Ph.D.'s unknown to their professors," but it has resulted in "more clear-sighted training." Now "we look more carefully at the source of a man's degree," but the numerical increase in departments granting it has "produced a variety of candidates," "a variety of programs," and all of this has "improved the advanced study of literature." The competition of the new departments, some respondents believe, keeps the old departments up to snuff, but "essentially it has destroyed the Establishment— a good thing." After observing this monkey wrench land in the teacup, we may read what the marginalists and composers of epistles have to remark on the grandeur of the departments anointed by Chancellor Cartter's report.

Not all the commentary on life and letters in the leading twenty departments came from irate graduates of the other departments, because graduate alumni, as we have pointed out, sometimes sing the "old college ode" through clenched teeth. The general reaction of most of the correspondents is that the favored departments may give better training of some sort or another, but the real truth is that they work with better human material. "These schools get good students, whether they produce anything is another matter." There is a strong doubt among some graduate professors and recent recipients of the doctorate about the superiority of the training provided by the top twenty. Some writers notice that the newer departments are far more rigorous and discriminating than their elder brethern. "My own degree," states a modest graduate of one of the select old ones, "is a case in point." The "theory" behind the "folk belief" that the discipline in these superior departments is of a higher grade rests on the conviction that the professors at the newer schools are "more poorly educated, but who educated them?" "The people I have seen from these places," says one objector to the theory that the top twenty produce the best men, "give me pause." Another doubting Thomas puts it very succinctly, "Some of the most ineffective teachers and scholars come from the best places. They are the only ones who have the courage to give degrees to such people."

But if we are going to liberalize the doctorate and if we are going to attempt to meet the demand for better trained professors of English and American Literature, we must stand ready to admit every properly qualified group of English professors to the society of doctoral departments. The established and flourishing departments with their excellent clienteles of supposedly superior students are generally disinclined to augmenting their registrants unless they have an equivalent increase in teaching personnel. The recent benefactions of great foundations toward improving the production of the great producers (a sound business principle) may enable these departments to keep their promises. But these promises are likely to remain just that unless the degree itself is adjusted to the needs of the twentieth century. The solution may be contained in something other than venerable procedures—in a streamlined doctorate that reduces the whole course to three or four years of full-time work or in a degree intermediate to the M.A. and Ph.D. The first plan would see the student through the graduate school in less than the average decade; the second would dignify the impossible professional status of the hundreds of ABD's who now carry the major burden of underclass teaching.

CHAPTER 8

The Purpose of Doctoral Training and Some Proposals

—————————◆•◆—————————

I   There is little doubt, and this survey supports it, that the time has come to not only define the doctorate in English and American Literature, but also to make the training that leads to it more rational, more attuned to our century and its demands. To use a metaphor, we live in a Victorian house encumbered with excessive and useless decorations, filled with crooks, turns, and bad plumbing. It is a comfortable house inherited from our fathers, but it wastes space and, hence, time. It could be torn down and made into a shopping center, but it also could be modernized and made efficient. If it is not refurbished, it is likely to become little more than a museum stored with artifacts imported from nineteenth-century Europe, no longer cherished in the lands whence they came.

Professors of English and American Literature should face the fact that society has always supported them because they are teachers.

To be better teachers and to be more honored as teachers, they should be competent scholars. While the modern scholar should have a ready "memory bank," he no longer need be the ambulatory encyclopedia once celebrated in Leipzig. The book is his memory. Originality in synthesis and analysis has replaced the older ideal, and the modern literary interpreter uses learning to stimulate and correct his imagination. Unless he is psychopathically modest, he will want to offer what he—and he alone—hears in a text to those who have interests like his. It will be a "fit audience but few" which attends to what he says in print. Society as a whole cannot be very much interested in his speculations, nor should it be. His endeavors as a scholar keep him intellectually alive, but he should never forget that society keeps him physically alive because he is a teacher. The first sort of aliveness depends rather fully on the second.

In emphasizing the duty to teach, we are not denigrating scholarly and critical writing (which temperately pursued for its own sake and not for necessity is the mark of the original teacher). Those who see, or think they see, the magic finger writing "publish or perish" invariably complain that a teacher who is a writer cheats his students. This is probably the "good reason." The "real reason" behind the objection is the belief that a teacher's outlay of printed paper is somehow or other directly proportional to his inlay of salary. No doubt this is sometimes the case; but when administrators measure a teacher by his length of wit in print, they use as sorry a yardstick as when they do not measure him by his skill in stimulating an excitement for literature in his colleagues, his students, and his immediate community. The truth is that the slogan "publish or perish" is an untruth. It is a rigorous administrative war cry in only the great universities, and is, unfortunately, used on occasion as a cover for more damning faults, even in these institutions where those who "perish" have often other "moles in nature" besides a short bibliography. In the lesser universities and in liberal arts colleges, the shout drops to a whisper, and in many institutions it is not audible at all. It is more accurate to say that in many colleges a man who publishes a book will be made a professor a few years before his nonwriting coevals; but if everything else is equal, they never perish but join him at the top.

We must have the scholar whose writings are clever, original, sensitive, and well expressed, but we should also distinguish between him and the "publisher." In well-regulated institutions, these distinctions are really made. Where they are not made, scholars in the true meaning of the word are hardly ever found. But even where the best scholarship is admired and courted, the publication of learned and critical work should be the by-products of, and ancillary to, teaching. The other learned professions long ago recognized that their debt to the public was to transmit their knowledge and experience to those who had less of both. The hundreds of physicians, lawyers, and clergymen who leave their professional schools each year, go forth ideally to assist a public that is unskilled in these arts. Only a few of them remain inside to hold the inner keep of medicine, law, and theology. We should observe the rules of social duty, like other professionals who are supported by society. If we do not, we are kept people; and, like courtesans in all times, we can hardly complain that we are not respected or that our work is not commonly approved.

Our unfortunate conviction that we are a race set apart by some special ordinance has too much influenced our attitude toward doctoral training. We feel that our postulants must crawl to the altar of the Ph.D. in order that their ultimate sanctification will be a proof of their worthiness. Each one of our graduate students must be subjected to rigors and deprivations so that he may in time become an archbishop, and yet what we produce in quantities, and what in all honesty we should produce, are curates. The average amount of time expended by the average student wandering through the litter of a conglomeration of irrational academic demands is a scandal. To make him a better "curate" faster, it has been proposed (and it is now implemented by grants from the Ford Foundation), that the whole process be reduced to three or four years (twelve-month years) of full-time study. This proposal will bring our training more closely in line with that of the other learned professions. Some 70 percent of the interrogated graduate professors think that syncopation could occur without the lowering of standards (Table 8.1), but the recent recipients of the doctorate, who took on the average three to four times as long to earn their degrees, are not even half convinced (Table 8.2); nonetheless, by a larger majority, they are conscious that the Ph.D. points toward classroom teaching and should involve a reasonable internship in that art (Table 8.3).

When we inquired about the practicality of a four-year degree, we used the medical degree as a comparative example. Perhaps it was an unlucky choice, because we were asked why we used "the least knowledgeable of degrees as our model," and we were told that we should not consider "medicine a learned profession." One recent recipient feels that "nibbling away at a degree for ten years has a good deal to say for it"; whereas another is glad that he was a teaching fellow for ten years and doubts whether or not we can make faster and better Ph.D.'s by "watering down the program and supplying everyone with fellowships." A member of the same group thinks that "only lazy and uncommitted students would take this easy way out," and expounds his opinion with the observation that "many of those now swelling the college ranks do not deserve to be there." To these contrary views on the four-year doctorate, we can join the statement of an exponent of the indefinite Ph.D. program.

> I think that the Ph.D. should not be awarded after four years (or any other period) of graduate work. It should be awarded after the accomplishment of some piece of research following a period of disciplined training in one's field in which one has the opportunity to organize and integrate the knowledge contained therein.

The comments of the graduate professors on a four-year in-course doctorate can begin with the recorded regrets of one of them who earned his degree in only four years. Had the time been longer, the statement runs, there could have been more talk about ideas and a beneficial trip to Great Britain. This slice of autobiography can be annotated by the admonition of his contemporary, who writes, "The question is not how quickly but how slowly we can get the candidates through." Setting aside occasional objectors, most of the graduate professors who bothered to comment support the notion of a four-year degree. "Those who take forever," one of them notes, "are no better prepared than those who take four years." Some of the favorers of the faster degree see it as a goad, because "most graduate students are time wasters;" but others approve of it since the doctorate "certifies competence not endurance" and believe that a "lessening in the quantity of required work does not lessen the quality of the work." "Changing standards," says one, "does not mean lowering standards." It is also held that "not all present standards are legitimate," and that "somebody's standards do not determine the qualities of another person's mind." Actually "one ought to know all that is needed about a student within four years." With this remark we are in harmony.

Some of the graduate professors suggest ways to bring about a four-year doctoral process, which they think should replace "the older busywork program which did not promote higher qualities of attainment, just more sterile skills." To effect such a program, they advise the elimination of "traditional courses," and "a reduction in the language requirements, the scope of the orals, and the length of the dissertation." "If we removed the mammoth dissertation," one predicts, "we would have fewer burned-out ABD's." All the requirements are for one professor "so much formalistic nonsense." The contemporary doctoral program is thought by a few of the graduate professors to be too slanted in the direction of original specialization, and "hence our discipline ceases to be human, since English teachers talk only to English teachers." This view is endorsed by other people, who hope that a change in the whole technique of the doctoral procedure will shorten the course. "We need education, not indoctrination."

II   The alternative to a streamlined Ph.D., obtainable through the pruning of augmented excrescencies in four years, is an intermediate degree. Such a degree, properly fitted for teaching, has been suggested for many years and has recently taken flesh in the Yale M.Phil. or the University of Michigan Ph.C., a degree now being solemnly considered in other graduate departments. Both degrees guarantee that the possessor has finished his courses, passed his language requirements, and survived the examination that permits him to devote all his time to the dissertation. Only this last chore stands between him and the Ph.D. The intermediate degree is to be thought of as both interim and terminal. As a terminal degree it is intended for anyone who has no desire to publish or to be a member of a graduate department; hence, it appears to be ideally suited for college teaching. As an interim degree, it is a kind of amulet for someone who must seek a full-time teaching position while he composes his dissertation in that it distinguishes him in the eyes of the administration from his colleagues who have yet to progress thus far.

We expected that the intermediate degree would be attractive to college chairmen, and our survey shows they would be very happy about it. Almost all of them would employ an M.Phil. or Ph.C.; two thirds of them would retain him on their staff even though he never took a doctorate; and one fourth would promote him to full rank if he turned out to be a satisfactory teacher and colleague (Table 8.4). The chairmen of college departments think this degree would be "fine for college teaching" although some demur in favor of "a more economically handled Ph.D. program" and predict that both the employing college and the man with the intermediate degree "would feel apologetic." A few of them unconsciously speak of it as "an ABD"; and, thinking of it as primarily a teaching degree, have doubts about the students who accept it. One of them illustrates his fears by recalling an interview with a candidate who had "a teaching degree." The man was an experienced teacher of the Victorian novel, but "he placed Scott's novels in the eighteenth century, referred repeatedly to Hardy's *Far from the Maddening Crowd*, owned to having yet to read anything by Meredith or James, betrayed ignorance of the term 'Gothic novel,' confused William Godwin and Samuel Butler."

The recent recipients of the doctorate concur with the college chairmen by a vote of almost four to one in approving an intermediate degree for teachers in state colleges and liberal arts colleges. They disapprove of the degree for university teachers by almost the same ballot (Table 8.5). One of them asks "why all this hysteria about the word 'doctor'?" Another man in this group thinks an intermediate degree "would be less destructive of people" and opines that "most Ph.D.'s are zombies—intellectually dead—secure in their tenure and in their certificate of respectability, the Ph.D. degree." On the other hand, it is recommended that everyone should be urged to acquire this degree and that no one should be given a Ph.D. until he presents "a body of respectable published work." The intermediate degree is further favored because the Ph.D. "does not represent ability, only perseverance and experience." In keeping with these attitudes, one recent recipient asserts that no one should write a dissertation until he is ready; so the intermediate degree should qualify him "to teach for a decent salary in a decent school." A full-scale comment on the subject is probably worth reproduction:

> I believe that colleges and universities should accept those with a Doctor of Arts degree (the designation I prefer) with the understanding that they would have equal privileges with the Ph.D. insofar as rank and salary are concerned, and that such teachers would not be barred from any level of instruction (though they would have to prove themselves exceptionally good to be accepted as teachers at the Ph.D. level). However, it would be understood that those with the Ph.D. would have priority for any encouragement of research which the university or outside foundations could give. The Ph.D. should be recognized as a research man first and a teacher second.

The vast majority of the recent recipients of the doctorate approve of an intermediate degree, but 72 percent would have avoided taking it even if it provided them with the same post and prospects that they now have as full-fledged Ph.D.'s (Table 8.6). Those who confess they might have been tempted to take such a degree in lieu of a doctorate sometimes admit their reasons are not "healthy," and they are pleased such a degree was not available to them. One of them reminds us that he now holds with his doctorate a post for which he was turned down years before when he had "only the intermediate degree of ABD." The ambiguity of the recent recipients who approve the intermediate degree—but not for themselves—is undoubtedly expressed when they explain why they would have avoided the degree if it had been beguilingly set in their way.

"Who would work," asks one, "for a halfway degree?" and "be patronized by every Ph.D. in the place," adds another. The true prestige of the doctorate is emphasized by many. An intermediate degree signifies "a doctoral loser," "a second-class citizen," "a cadre of drudges," "a debasement of 'doctor'," "a sub-Ph.D.," "equal but separate." The in-between degree is "simply the old M.A. writ large," "a complication of the whole system," "a title with no snob appeal," and "a proliferation of the caste system." Although the intermediate degree is thought to be "more respectable than a watered down Ph.D.," one is prone to think that "hanging a title on a guy will not change him." Other recent recipients see the intermediate degree as merely a means of supplying a demand for teachers and disapprove of the whole idea because "universities are not service institutions" and are not intended to "turn out technicians." One recent recipient puts on yellow lenses and tells us what he sees:

> Every field has its charlatans . . . but where there are requirements to be met the number of them is diminished. An in-between degree or a reduction of doctoral requirements will have at least one effect—the charlatans will finish the course.

The members of graduate departments are far more conservative in their estimate of the intermediate degree than the college chairmen or the recent recipients of the doctorate. Slightly more than 60 percent of the graduate professors endorse the proposed degree (Table 8.7), yet a somewhat larger number of them stand ready to accept it as both an interim and terminal degree should it catch on (Table 8.8). For its interim phase they are moved to set a time limit on its convertibility into a full-scale Ph.D. (Table 8.9). They vote in the main for a period of between three and five years (Table 8.10). This is, of course, the time limit that is generally established for the completion of the dissertation. The new M.Phil., Ph.C., or D.A. (a title widely opposed by the recent recipients) will, consequently, have just about the same number of years to put the thesis together as the current ABD. Such a time limit vitiates to some extent the virtues of the degree, which unlike other degrees, the A.B. or M.A., appears to grow flabby after its possessor accompanies it for a while.

Although there is a tendency for the respondents in all groups to speak of the intermediate degree as "an ABD," they should be aware that the ABD has no papers and the intermediate degree is an academic Nansen passport. It entitles the man or woman who has it to enter Ph.D.-land when they have a dissertation in their luggage. The land he enters will in this case be the one he left, and in the fact of limited migration there may be a problem. Many departments of English lacking adequate libraries and full competent staffs are unable to qualify themselves in good conscience as granters of the doctorate; yet these same departments might be very capable of training a graduate student up to the limits set by the intermediate degree. It is quite comprehensible that departments now doing work toward the M.A. but hesitating to push beyond this will grasp the opportunity to establish a program for the M.Phil. or Ph.C. If they do, there is nothing to stop them. The imbroglio that then can arise when a Ph.C. from a nondoctoral program appears at a department with a doctoral program and offers his dissertation as fulfilling all the requirements for a doctorate is one that we can imagine but do not care to ponder. To refuse him the Ph.D. means that the doctoral department declares the intermediate degree earned in the other department totally invalid. By an extension of the same logic, they should strike down all the lesser degrees earned in the nondoctoral department. Almost two thirds of the responding graduate professors take the position that an intermediate degree must be converted at the place of issue; hence, we foresee a beam to trouble the mind's eye (Table 8.11).

We have assumed the intermediate degree will provide the liberal arts colleges with more adequately trained teachers of English and American Literature than they are now able to procure. The chairmen assure us they are ready to appoint and promote people who have these degrees; but though the graduate professors approve of the intermediate degree and stand ready to award it, the majority of them are very wary about adding a M.Phil. or Ph.C. to their staffs. Three fourths of the chairmen of graduate departments would make one of them an instructor; one fourth of them would advance him to an assistant professorship (Table 8.12); but only one ninth of them would grant him tenure (Table 8.13). The chairmen's colleagues on the graduate staff who were willing to venture an opinion generally agree with their heads that an M.Phil. or Ph.C. could be appointed to the lowest rank, but they back away from a tenure appointment with an overwhelming vote of "no confidence" (Table 8.14). The reaction of the academic uppercrust is possibly summed up by the answer of a dean of a graduate school where the M.Phil. is given when he was asked whether or not his university had yet employed a teacher with an intermediate degree. "We haven't yet," he said, "but we might."

The reluctance of university professors to accept the intermediate degrees as valid conducts to university teaching breaks out in the comments of members of the graduate departments. One of them points to the disinfecting fact that the intermediate degree "would eliminate those who are now given the Ph.D. because there is nothing in between." His fellows often feel that the M.A. or "a beefed-up M.A." would solve the college teaching problem just as easily. Others gladly vote for the M.Phil. or Ph.C. provided the degree is given by the "top twenty departments," or requires "double the work for an M.A." Many of the graduate professors agree with one of them who insists there must be a "better reason for intermediate degrees than the teacher shortage." There are those who think "even a floundering student will settle for nothing less than a Ph.D." and, as seems clearly to be the case, "most departments will hire nothing less." Several observers recall the death of the Ed.D. as an ominous widower's warning to those who espouse an intermediate degree. The real question, one respondent suggests, "is how astute should the bird be before the cage is opened"?

III   Many respondents, through marginalia or letters, have urged us to invent a totally new way of preparing teachers of English and American Literature. They would like some sort of individualized degree or, on more possible bases, a degree similar to the one given in Germany or Scandinavia: a license to teach in the present while the results of time and talent are awaited. One graduate professor proposes a D.A. for teachers, a Ph.D. of the status quo sort, and a D.Lett. to be given anyone, regardless of his preparation, who submits to the university a fine piece of research. Unaccustomed as we are to turning loaves into fishes, we cannot at this stage in academic history produce any miracles beyond revisions and emendations in the formal text, but we should like now to make a transition to a new movement toward postdoctoral study, and we shall make our pirouette on a quotation from a recent recipient of the doctorate.

I would like to see a degree established *beyond* the Ph.D. to make up for the quality we are losing through "easy" Ph.D. programs. The easier we make it, the lower the value—that seems to me an elementary equation.

Postdoctoral study is the invention of our scientific confreres, who have been using it as a means of identifying the best investigative ability among their Ph.D.'s for more than a decade. About half of the current Ph.D.'s in the sciences do not go into teaching immediately but to another institution's laboratory where they become levers and cogs in the enormous manipulations of some happily endowed project. After due service and efficient performance, they are touched by the wand of the master who has assigned and supervised their efforts and are transformed into university teaching positions, which are usually associate professorships. This transmogrification marks them indelibly as "men to be watched." The Humanities are not agreed on this procedure, and all discussions of postdoctoral work in English and American Literature are dreadfully inchoate; nonetheless, work of this nature has already been instituted in several English departments. The policies, *laus Deo*, are quite different from those of the sciences, because it is assumed that what the English postdoctoral appointee (always a man with an "honors" Ph.D.) needs is free time, a library adequate to his research, and the advice of experienced—even distinguished— seniors in his chosen area of scholarship. It has been generally assumed he will spend his postdoctoral year converting his dissertation into a worthwhile book, pursuing with the help of skillful associates a new line of thought, or filling in some gaps that he has come to perceive in his education. There is no reason for the "or" because he might want to do all of it. To enable him to lose this year from teaching, it has been proposed he be given a stipend equivalent to, or almost equivalent to, what he would earn in a full-time teaching post.

The theory of the postdoctoral appointment in English and American Literature presumes that it will be made either for the year immediately after the doctorate is completed or within a comparatively short time after that. Like the intermediate degree, the postdoctoral is thought to be something between a fellowship for the dissertation year and the sort of grants that the NEH, the ACLS, and the Guggenheim Foundation make to young but more advanced applicants. One of the recent recipients praised the prospect of the postdoctoral because it "would enable a new Ph.D. to take a place at a small college with high hopes." The college chairmen are 90 percent in favor of the idea (Table 8.15), although they might sometimes suffer through it. They would, for instance, be forced to find substitutes for their best young teachers while they were on a postdoctoral year; moreover, if one of them was a very good man, they might discover that the university that had entertained him for a year was trying to keep him permanently. The graduate professors, most of whom ought to have been competitors for postdoctoral fellowships had these opportunities been available in their day, are almost 60 percent opposed to the idea (Table 8.16); nevertheless, if the plan were widely taken up, they stand ready to nominate between 5 and 25 percent of their thesis students as worthy of postdoctoral fellowships (Table 8.17). The recent recipients, who are closer to their dissertations than most of the graduate professors, were not asked to express opinions either for or against postdoctoral study because it was assumed that many of them could still hope to benefit from it. They were, however, invited to express ideas about its conditions; and they voted, as we had hoped, for a year of total intellectual freedom (Table 8.18).

The negative vote of the graduate professors is impossible to interpret, but the marginalia supplied by some of them may help the understanding. They are afraid that a postdoctoral year "would keep them dependent too long," and are often convinced "a good man can go along on his own." They reason that "if graduate study was improved, postdoctorals would not be needed," and see in the proposal the creation of "a superclass that will destroy the Ph.D." Many of them are familiar with the postdoctoral methods of the scientists and coldly observe that students of literature have nothing in common with chemists and physicists. We also wonder whether or not, though no one expressed it, the graduate professors fear a postdoctoral program in their own departments would add another weight to their burden. Their reaction deserves careful study when and if the plans for postdoctoral study in the Humanities come more fully into being.

We have now finished counting the votes and sorting out the opinions of our colleagues in English and American Literature, and we should probably set down some recommendations of our own making. But before we write the final chapter, we shall read in the best priestly manner a text from the First Book of Recent Recipients, Chapter D, verse 42, so we may also in the best priestly manner write a sermon which has almost nothing to do with our reading.

> Unless we get away from the tired questions about whether to require one or two languages, three, four, or five areas for the preliminary exams, we shall continue to discourage and to lose

bright, vital students who are interested in other questions. So far as I'm concerned, the important questions about the Ph.D. concern the curriculum and the kind of teacher and program needed for the next twenty-five years.

CHAPTER 9

Some Suggestions
by Way
of a Conclusion

———————◆•◆———————

(1) The standards of a profession are maintained or improved by the intellectual quality of the people who enter it; hence, the teaching and study of American and English Literature depend entirely on the talents and energy of the men and women who teach and study this subject. With proper machinery sows' ears may be transformed into silk purses, but no engine has yet been invented that turns a large amount of postgraduate quantity into even a small amount of academic quality. The graduate departments of American and English Literature may heap requirements on requirements, supply the training course with hurdles as tall as Goliath, stretch the temporal demands out to Judgment Day, but none of these requisites will make their doctoral graduates more industrious or intellectually talented than they were in the beginning. The first duty of the profession is, then, the enlistment of the finest minds in our regiment.

(2) To achieve the recruitment of the best men and women is our major task. Very few of our recent Ph.D.'s decided on their careers before they entered college, and only one third of them foresaw an academic future by the time of their baccalaureate degrees. The other

two thirds made their decision at a much later date. This slowness of choice is mirrored throughout the Humanities in general, and is, in some respects, also true of the Sciences and Social Sciences. Nonacademic professions fare better because their practitioners often select their lots in adolescence.

(3) Unfortunately, the academic life is for many students an invisible one until they are in college. The profession is really publicly unknown. The physician is a familiar figure even to children; the lawyer and the journalist are always in the newspaper; the clergyman stands over years of Sundays; the engineer and scientific technician dominate advertisements and live across the street. The professor is seldom seen. The other professionals are not only known to high-school students but even better known to their parents, whose common-sense admonitions to their young, or material and social ambitions provide the second reason why young men and women come so late to opt for the academic life.

(4) One probably can do very little to encourage a precollege student to think about a college or university career. But once he is matriculated and seated in the classroom, more can be done. The seasoned teacher of American and English Literature—in fact, the seasoning need not be too extensive—should find (with a little effort) volunteers for the profession in his freshman and sophomore classes. First-year undergraduates often stand out from their associates in their enthusiasm for literature, their natural skill in the use of language, their inborn good taste, and their better than average love of learning. These gifts are sometimes made manifest by the undergraduate's participation in campus literary affairs and by his ability to infect his classmates with his excitement about literature. Underclassmen of this type are not rare, and they should be carefully watched and pointed toward the professional study of letters as a lifework. The scientific departments of universities are rather good at spotting scientific ability; the Departments of English are sometimes very high nosed about the literary undergraduate: It must be remembered that many of our superior professors are poets and novelists *manqué*.

(5) An underclassman, just as rightly as an upperclassman, who has the personal and intellectual traits demanded by the profession should be made the ward of the whole department and should be given a wise and enthusiastic professor as his advisor—almost his intellectual valet—for his undergraduate years. In universities with a graduate school, this advising should be a prime function of the graduate dean's office. The office of the graduate dean is sometimes the most coldly

formidable bureau in the university and is presided over by a severe dragon of many years service whose aim in life is to protect the dean from contact with students. In a liberal arts college without a doctoral program, the councilors of potential professors of American and English Literature should be men and women who have friendly connections with members of graduate departments elsewhere and who are well informed about graduate practices, admission requirements, changes in graduate methods, and trends in literary study. It would be a splendid idea if more colleges arranged cooperative scholarships with graduate departments in their immediate geographical areas. The chairman of a college department should keep in close touch with alumni and alumnae who are pursuing graduate study, and it would be sensible if one of these graduates were brought each year to consult with the departmental graduate advisors and talk with promising English majors. Perhaps these visits might encourage more undergraduates to enter the profession and properly prepare them for the course ahead. The requirements of advanced study too often come as a surprise.

(6) Colleges without graduate programs outnumber the graduate schools by a ratio of more than twenty to one. As state programs proliferate and junior and community colleges burgeon, the ratio will be multiplied. It is these institutions that now feel the pinch of the short supply of teachers; and feeling the pinch, they cry out. More than 300 of them have reported a general increase in the interest of their students in obtaining advanced degrees. During the last decade they think they have sent about 400 students a year to the graduate departments, but during the next five years they expect to employ as many people with the doctorate as they now send. The group of colleges reporting is a very small one, only 363 in number, and one wonders whether or not this forecast equality of outgo and intake is the common case. One also wonders whether or not all the college students sent to the graduate departments succeed in obtaining a doctorate, or, if they do, obtain it in a reasonable amount of time.

(7) The colleges themselves could help more in this problem if they provided their majors planning to do advanced work in English and American Literature with a predoctoral program similar to the prelegal or premedical programs. Much of the delay in graduate education is a direct result of poor preparation and mediocre standards. A pre-English doctoral program that emphasized a good grasp of the history of English and American Literature, that put stress on the history and canons of criticism, that gave instruction in the princi-

ples of bibliography and method, that insisted on a sound knowledge of one literary language, either ancient or modern, and that saw to it that the student wrote his own language clearly and accurately would unquestionably be of enormous aid to the graduate departments and to the students entering them. The undergraduate once he is both confident and chosen should clearly be given sound professional preparation.

(8) The profession, and that word is used advisedly, welcomes talented people to its fold. The serene humanist at home in his own world because he is familiar with the past is the ideal. It is, as many other ideals, infrequently achieved; yet the profession manages to reach its limited ends. In this it is no different from other professions. Solons are uncommon in courtrooms; hospitals are not overrun by Galens. The cultured humanist can be perfected, but he has to be born. We should, consequently, stop thinking of the Ph.D. in American and English Literature as a person with a cultural degree. They are as professional professionals as physicians, engineers, and public accountants. The false emphasis on the doctorate as an indication of a wide ranging and learned enlightenment is one of the roots of our problem. The notion that the Ph.D. is a symbol of intellectual excellence (historically it never was) has resulted in our tolerance of the long course to its attainment. We have talked about the necessity of enormous reading though we really never test it, of eons of contemplation about this reading, and of the necessity for "maturity." "Maturity" is the bothersome word. Most of us never mature; those of us who almost mature take about sixty years in the process. Actually the word is best applied in connection with vegetables; for human beings maturity is only a matter of degree.

(9) Of the 1880 recipients of the doctorate between 1955 and 1965 some 1522, or 81 percent, had from one to four years of uninterrupted study for the Ph.D. in American and English Literature. The median time for the whole group is two years. In spite of this length of free time, which flies against the notion that all doctoral candidates are on part-time, only eleven members of the whole group had their doctorates in hand at the end of three years and only fifty-five secured the degree in four years. When the facts about the current graduate teachers (presumably the more talented members of the profession) are scanned, it is discovered that the average age at which they took the doctorate (the median is the same) was slightly over thirty-two or ten to eleven years after the bachelor's degree, and yet almost half of this group had between one and four years of uninterrupted

study. One third of the male members of the recent recipient group did military service, although almost none of them were in either World War II or the Korean War. There is, consequently, something wrong with a system that keeps 90 percent of the males and 92 percent of the females in pupil status so long.

(10) When one contrasts this situation with that of other professions, one is seriously distressed. It is true that the young M.D. must intern before he is allowed to practice, but the Ph.D. in American and English Literature can be described as an intern until he is a full professor. It is also true that the more promising young physicians and lawyers are often delayed while they receive special training, a condition similar to the proposed postdoctoral training in the Humanities, but the average physician or lawyer is in full practice five or more years before our Ph.D.'s can call their souls their own.

(11) The prime recommendation, now blessed by the Ford and Danforth Foundations, is that the Ph.D. in English be regarded as a four-year [in-course] degree. The consecutive nature of such a program should go a long way toward preserving a candidate's enthusiasm for his profession, which the current in-and-out delaying process often destroys. Such a process would certainly help to eliminate the dreary ABD predicament of the more than 1000 teachers now in the 363 reporting colleges. Actually the true count of these Iolanthe-like professors must be four or five times this number. Better than all these advantages would be the fact that each Ph.D. could anticipate a longer professional life. More than one third of the recent recipients of the doctorate were thirty-five or older when they took their degrees. They were "mature" no doubt, but their professional prospects are clearly 25 percent less prosperous than those who took their degree a decade earlier.

(12) In order to lessen the time for the degree, we must see to it that the candidates are almost completely supported for the whole four-year course. Too many graduate departments are at fault in exploiting their graduate students as teaching assistants. In some cases the necessity of placing cheap instructors before Composition sections has outweighed the moral importance of carrying them to a degree as rapidly as possible. This material practise is the result of a badly developed sense of economy. The sour effects of the custom on the student are obvious, but it is equally obvious that when a decent pay scale exists, the teaching assistants required to instruct three freshman sections are almost as expensive, perhaps more so, than a full-time assistant professor.

(13) The blame for this situation does not, of course, fall entirely on the departments. The students must share the burden of criticism. One does not want to thwart nature's simple plans, but too many graduate students begin their training as married men; and as the tabulations show over half of the recent recipients were fathers with infants on their hands before they had their doctorate in hand. There should also be more family support (and by this we do no mean the secretarial wife) for students seeking the doctorate in American and English Literature. Thirty years ago when college teaching was an untonsured branch of the Franciscan Order, parents and relatives who gladly paid the way of a son training for a more lucrative profession, assumed that charity should take care of their charitable child. The profession is no longer financially straitened. Successful professors of English do as well financially as moderately successful physicians and lawyers. The fringe benefit has also become a regular inducement in most colleges and universities. The professor of thirty years ago who taught until he dropped (because pension plans were generally unknown) is seldom encountered in our time. Students who cannot secure family aid and who are unable to secure an NDEA grant or a Wilson or Danforth Fellowship should think more about borrowing funds than they do now. The average doctoral candidate who borrows enough to enable him to get a degree in four years will retire with a higher life earning than the student who spends a dozen years as a teacher without a Ph.D.

(14) It is clear that within the next decade, doctoral programs will be introduced in many newly established universities. The department that begins to grant the doctorate must want to give the degree as a service to American education, and not for the sake of competitive vanity, or for the securing of what so many respondents to the questionnaires call "slave labor." To do it properly, the supporting institution must look toward a complete graduate program in all university areas, although it may righly begin by granting the degree in its strongest departments. The first requirement is trained and active personnel. In some current departments too much of the graduate teaching is done by people who have not had the experience of earning a doctorate, by people too fresh from their own doctorates, and by professors who have never sullied their amateur standing by writing other essays or books once their own dissertation was microfilmed and shelved. These people hardly know what the scholarly or critical process is and their lack of reputation inspires their students with little confidence. Their own lack of confidence is often evidenced in

the inordinate demands they make of the students; in fact, the doctorate in English is often harder to earn in a weak department than in a strong one.

(15) Another important requirement for granting a Ph.D. in American or English Literature is the actual physical presence of a good library with sufficient holdings and proper study facilities for faculty and students. Unless the library has a balanced collection of more than 500,000 titles, it is doubtful that a successful doctoral program can be launched. In modern times xeroxing, microfilming, and microcards can be readily and inexpensively obtained. The presence of a large collection of rare books and manuscripts is generally unnecessary, but ordinary study will always be done from books and it is the ordinary reading for courses that we have in mind. The dissertation can often be done from photographic reproductions, but a sound graduate department will have grants enabling both students and professors to spend time at proper material centers. The necessity for adequate study space for both students and faculty goes without saying. A scientific professor or doctoral candidate does not do his work at his kitchen sink, and a professor or student of English Literature should not be asked to do his research on a workbench in his basement or at his dining-room table. A university that cannot provide study space in its library for students and faculty should not embark on a doctoral program.

(16) The extant graduate departments of English and American Literature are fantastically distinguished by their failure to communicate with each other. They are uniform in their lack of uniform requirements for admission, in their general standards, and in their methods of instruction. One does not ask for a 1984 totalitarian system, but some common requisites should be widely understood and accepted. Some departments have no decisive voice in the admission of candidates. The graduate dean is in charge of admissions although the department is sometimes permitted a veto. In other departments the student is admitted by the divine right of the chairman, who is sometimes assisted by the director of graduate studies—if there is one—and sometimes by a committee of elder departmental statesmen. The more eyes that scan the application and the undergraduate record, the wider the share of responsibility; likewise, the more the interest evinced in the future of the admitted candidates, probably the better luck the candidate will have.

(17) Principles of admission should be more efficiently thought out than they are now, and it can be hoped that, given the great stu-

dent surge toward graduate departments, they will be. At the moment, grade ranges for admission to graduate studies in English and American Literature vary from a "C" average to a "B+." The very fact that these alphabetical units are stated in printed brochures shows a certain lack of sense, because everyone knows that grading standards shift enormously from college to college. Some departments state that they are influenced only by the grades in English; some by only the general average; some by both. A very few departments look "only at the man." The demand for testimonial letters is also irregular. Many departments require letters from undergraduate teachers; others do not. In addition to grade transcripts and letters of recommendation, other departments require a specimen of the student's work—a term paper or an essay published in the *Literary Magazine of X College.* The GRE tests are widely required, but not by all graduate departments. Very few departments ask for a personal interview. In other words, admission requirements on which so much of the success and failure of the graduate student depends have not been discussed at all, and this failure to establish entrance standards may be a major crux of the whole problem. Any graduate professor knows how haphazard is student selection, and sometimes even the *summa cum laude* graduate turns out to be unequal to graduate discipline; whereas an occasional student with an undistinguished undergraduate record turns out to be superb.

(18) The general requirements for the doctoral program, though becoming more uniform than they were several years ago, are still far from uniform. If one asked an assembled group of departmental chairmen when they allowed a candidate to take the examinations that permitted him to be recognized as an authentic doctoral candidate and proceed to the composition of his dissertation, one would get many responses: "at the end of the second year," "at the end of the third year," "after he has accumulated 20, 21, 30, 36, 48, 54, 60, 60 to 70, 70 to 80, 75, or 90 units of course work." The same group of chairmen would exclaim that a reading knowledge of one, or two, or three languages was to be regularly expected, although in two departments the language requirement has been completely abolished. In some departments there are no course requirements beyond the accumulation of units, credits, or residential time; in other departments there are one to four required courses. When the student appears for his preliminary examination (which qualifies him to begin work on his dissertation), he can be examined (depending on the department) in anywhere from three fields of literature to "the whole damn works,"

and his examination may vary in length from one hour to five solid days. In a very few departments he has only one chance to pass this examination; in most he gets two tries; but in more lenient departments (about 20 percent) he has a third chance. When his thesis is done, he is no longer required to publish it, but two thirds of the graduate departments require him to provide a printed abstract. In these very simple matters, we are in general disagreement.

(19) We cannot be certain that agreement—a general university compact of some type—would solve all our problems, but it might make a beginning. The discussion of graduate procedures in American and English Literature is hardly a duty of the Association of Departments of English, but it would be reasonable for the chairmen of graduate departments or the directors of graduate program (since the chairman is usually fully engaged in staffing problems) to meet for a half-day at the Modern Language Association meetings to discuss and unify their graduate requirements and methods. Representatives of departments planning to do doctoral work should also be invited because they have much to learn. The members of these incipient graduate departments usually have never been actively associated with a department providing doctoral study and have only their own experience as graduate students to guide them; they are generally eager to learn about the pitfalls before them and the *modus operandi* of a doctoral program.

(20) But the lack of uniformity in graduate programs is greatly surpassed by our persistent avoidance of self-criticism. The whole system brought across the Atlantic by Americans of the last century has become fossilized, and like all fossils is dead and stone cold. We have only infrequently asked ourselves what we are doing or why we are doing it. The heroes who taught the heroes who taught us invented an American version of the methods they learned at Leipzig or Berlin. They endured it; we endured it; and, by all that's holy, our students shall endure it! In primitive societies a youth starved, stuck himself with bone needles, held fire in his hand, and after forty days had a vision from which he took his name; but it is not recorded that any of these initiates called himself "Doctor of Philosophy in English Literature." We have unquestioningly followed these primitive customs, but we regard them as high acts of civility. In reconsidering our polished *rites de passage,* we may begin with our graduate courses.

(21) Some wit has noticed that there is a realistic way to determine student composition of a class. If the students say, "Good morning" when the professor addresses them, they are undergraduates; if

they write his greeting in their notebooks, they are graduate students. The average graduate student is convinced that everything uttered by a professor must be preserved, and yet the professor must ask himself how much of what he says is not already preserved and how much of that is worth preserving. A few of the recent recipients of the doctorate state that they have lectured to their classes from their graduate notes for years, and though the majority of them regard the courses as the best aspect of their graduate training, more than 10 percent of them describe the professors as "tired," "preoccupied," "dull," "pedantic," "riding his own hobbyhorse," "talking from outlines made twenty years earlier," and "unable to answer a question unless he could find the answer in his crumbling notes." In spite of what seems to be approval, we must ask what can be done to improve graduate courses and whether or not there should be courses for graduate students at all.

(22) The best argument in favor of many graduate courses is that they instruct the student in "how not to teach." Even when they have this real pedagogical value, they cannot be too helpful because students have been observing teaching methods since they were six years old and should be pedagogical specialists by the time they leave college. It is possible that the courses as such make the transition from undergraduate to graduate work a bit smoother; and since there is often little difference between undergraduate and graduate courses, this may be their real merit. But the best graduate student hardly needs courses at all—certainly not the kind presented to the vast lecture groups that are assembled in some universities. A proper graduate student stands on the edge of self-education. As an intending teacher and scholar, he must continue to educate himself for the remainder of his life. It would, perhaps, be better to provide him with a syllabus or a reading list and to permit him to confer from time to time with the professional expert in whose area he was reading. The fearful compulsion that now impels the graduate student to put down a book he finds engrossing so that he can attend and take notes on a lecture that he can hardly endure would in this way be alleviated.

(23) But if courses must be given so that graduate professors can justify their existence and sleep well at night, they should be properly articulated with the graduate program in general. In the scurry to attain graduate teaching status, to belong to what is curiously regarded as the university's elite corps, too many specialized and unrelated courses are recorded in most graduate catalogues. When Professor U has a course in Victorian Poetry, Professor V a course in

Victorian Prose, Professor W a course in Tennyson, Professor X a course in Dickens and Thackeray, Professor Y a course in Arnold, Professor Z's course in the Corn Law Rimers is a little too much. This illustration is not invented but drawn from life; nonetheless, one can grant that some courses are essential. A student may easily learn a simple dialect like Old English by himself, but it is easier and wiser to learn languages by sitting to a master.

(24) Perhaps the most wasteful aspect of the ordinary graduate courses is that they do not often allow the student to work independently and to show early evidence of his promise as a scholar or critic. Seminars do just this, and departments would do well to stress them. The younger Ph.D.'s sometimes complain bitterly about their seminars. They were "too narrow," "too contentious," "too time consuming." But these complaints, which must sometimes be valid, are not frequent. A properly conducted seminar with a true expert at the head of the table is the best means of graduate training. If the seminar, in keeping with its history, is kept small and if the topic is liberal and exciting, it is here that the graduate student will learn his trade and demonstrate the powers that will decide his future. Seminars should be, as the name implies, meetings where the seeds of a humanistic understanding of literature are sown. They should never be—as unfortunately they sometimes are—congregations of research assistants who gather material for the director's next paper or book. The fact that a Professor of English or American Literature does not use his students to do his scut work is what distinguishes him from his scientific colleagues. It is why he is called a humanist.

(25) A true seminar is a small club of enthusiastic people presided over by an expert; instructing each other, and very often instructing the expert. Hence a true seminar leads to something other than the performance of exercises. The seminar in which each student reads in turn an annotated bibliography or lists all the variants between two manuscripts or follows some similar clerical occupation is beyond apology. A good seminar should result in an interesting final essay that all liberal students of the topic will want to read. It produces at its best a dissertation in embryo or a chapter or two of what eventually will be the dissertation.

(26) The seminar, besides testing the inborn talents of the graduate student through significant independent work, should also be the place where he exhibits his ancillary skills. It is here, rather than in the tests given all graduate students in the university by the department of foreign languages, that the student should be made to use his read-

ing knowledge of languages other than English. The foreign language requirements, in vogue in all departments, are a principal source of complaint; and it is right that they should be criticised. A student working in an early period of English Literature cannot expect to be a competent scholar unless he knows many languages, both ancient and modern. If he is truly interested in his area, he will learn these languages without any stimulus other than his own intellectual needs. On the other hand, a student whose interests are directed toward the later periods of English Literature or to American Literature can become a very accomplished professional without any other languages than his own. He will lose some of the pleasures of the intellectual life without Greek, Latin, French, or Italian, but these languages have no practical value for him.

(27) If there is anything that this study makes clear, it is that many students begin graduate work in the Department of English with at least one of the expected languages unlearned. Most students have to learn one language—and many two—after they have begun graduate work. This very fact is responsible for an average delay of one year in achieving the doctorate. The recent recipients of the doctorate, almost each of whom learned at least one language (usually German) after entering graduate school, inform us that fewer than half of them used a foreign language in any graduate course or seminar or in the preparation of their dissertation. Since taking the degree, a fourth of them have never looked at a line in any language they were required to learn. The teachers of graduate students to the number of 735 out of 1059 confess that during 1965–1966 they gave no reading assignments in foreign languages, and 470 of them cannot recall that they received a student paper during the same period with a foreign language reference or quotation. More than half of this number used their knowledge of a foreign language less often than once a week during the immediate year, and 178 of them never turned to look at a foreign text. This is startling information when one realizes that they all are in more than ninety-seven instances out of a hundred supporters of a religion that requires its neophytes to pass reading examinations in two tongues and sometimes in three.

(28) A knowledge of other languages is beyond doubt the mark of a cultured man but not necessarily of a professional man; and since our recommendations are posited on the basis of professionalism, we should look with a grave eye on this antique requirement. One knows to begin with that in many universities the foreign language tests are pure farces. The examined student reads a childish text and is passed

if he can assemble a rude English version of a few sentences. The graduate student who spends a month in the study of German and passes his test is as well known a figure in graduate departments as the student who fails German twenty times. When the tests are widely given by the foreign language departments to chemists, biologists, historians, and all other aspiring young doctoral candidates, the test and the grading are likely to be easy and perfunctory, because the Department of French is certainly not eager to incur the wrath of the entire graduate staff of a great university by failing the best mathematician since Reimann or the finest physicist since Maxwell. Until a satisfactory national language test can be supplied, the language examinations, if they must be given, should be administered by the Department of English to their students and should measure up to the standards of proficiency that an English professor should possess. In any graduate department of English there ought to be scholars capable of testing students in at least two ancient languages (Greek and Latin) and in five modern languages (French, German, Italian, Spanish, and Russian). If people capable of giving these tests are not to be found in the department, it should, perhaps, do a little soul searching about its demands on the graduate students' language knowledge.

(29) Although it is definitely out of date, some departments still cling to two required languages, French and German. These two languages are encysted in the tradition, and we, as scholars, have a blind love of the past. A more modern sort of graduate department, while still asking for a knowledge of two languages, will allow a reasonable choice among the literary languages of Europe. No department seems ready as yet to accept a knowledge of an oriental tongue as satisfying a language requirement. The insistence on two languages is probably impractical if we are to think in terms of a four-year doctorate; and we recommend—what is already the practice in some departments—that this requirement be changed to at least one language "well learned." By "well learned" we can mean many things. An ability to speak and write the language with fluency would be the ideal, but it is an ideal not likely to be generally achieved; hence, we can define "well learned" as the equivalent of four years of undergraduate study. At the end of such a term, a better student will be able not only to read the language with relative ease but also to have a fair familiarity with its literature.

(30) The examination which qualifies the graduate student to devote his full attention to his dissertation must be as carefully scrutinized as the course and language requirements. The quantification

of this test varies widely from department to department. In addition to the discrepancies in length of time and number of knowledgeable fields, it is sometimes written, sometimes oral, and sometimes both written and oral. Graduate departments have also experimented with its nature, and examinees have been asked to stand for it on the basis of a given number of authors, on major authors and genres, on seventy-five or a hundred set texts, on fixed specialized areas like Medieval Studies or American Studies. Interesting as some of these deviations from the older universal methods are, they indicate that the departments differing have strong doubts about the nature and purpose of the examination.

(31) The recent recipients of the degree are in accord to the extent of almost 1500 votes about the value that the examination has for the student involved. This is a surprising agreement, because the preliminary is widely feared and is a firm begetter of nervous tension. The vote represents, however, the reactions of those who successfully sustained the ordeal, although 13 percent of these yea-sayers did not pass the first time. We have no way of knowing how many students' professional hopes were terminated by the preliminary. But even if we have no news of disaster, decency suggests that no unqualified student should be allowed to face this inquisition. The examination should seldom be used to eliminate weak students, because when a graduate student is allowed to reach this stage of his training and fails, his professors fail with him.

(32) The successful students approve of this examination for strange and wonderful reasons. The optimists regard it as the exact moment they knew they were true members of the profession. The students who draw these satisfying breaths are as much in the minority as those who are cheered because the test "eliminates the clods from the profession." A much larger group found the preparation for the examination more useful than the examination. They read heavily for it. They read material they might never otherwise have read. They assembled a knowledge of English Literature in chronological and categorical fashion such as their courses had never done for them. And they did it all by themselves!

(33) If the student is wisely guided and prepared by his courses, there is no reason to abandon this examination. Actually we cannot imagine a student who has done well in his seminars ever being disqualified by it. It should, however, be made more uniform, perhaps more limited, in both time and scope, and it should be realistically related to the student's previous work. He should not be asked out-of-bound questions; in fact, he probably should be asked no questions

that most of the members of the examining board are unable to answer. It would be fairer if no examiner asked questions about his own special field. The problem of whether the examination should be oral, written, or both is a moot one. Prior to this examination, students—unless they have been in an honors program—have never been orally tested and this novel experience must be a psychological handicap for many; nevertheless, the oral examination can suggest something about the student's classroom ability if this skill has not been ascertained by more practical means.

(34) The dissertation used to be considered the ultimate proof of the doctoral student's competence. The dissertations written during the early days of the American graduate programs do not all support this opinion. The almost 1900 dissertations written between 1955 and 1965 on which we have information were plainly not all "original contributions to knowledge." Only 40 percent of them have been divulged to us in whole or part; yet 83.2 percent of them were judged acceptable upon first submission. The performance of the research required and the putting together of the researched material has not exactly stimulated all of the younger doctors to further effort. Of the recent recipients, 726 teachers of undergraduates and 41 teachers who now conduct graduate courses have yet to write anything that did not depend directly on their dissertation work.

(35) The dissertations composed by this same group were in eight instances out of ten between 150 and 500 pages in length. Some were still longer. This mass of typed paper—much of which is now a mute, inglorious accession number in the home library—represents an enormous amount of foot pounds in physical effort and an immeasurable quantity of cerebral vibrations. The time involved is 1880×2.9 years. We ask ourselves whether the results justify all of this. If not, it is undoubtedly time for graduate departments to agree on something more limited. Most dissertations have a few worthwhile points to make that can be expressed in lesser space. Probably a short study is all that should be asked of the student. A few talented students succeed in having a paper accepted for publication by respected journals before they embark on their dissertations. This evidence of ability could certainly be received in lieu of a thesis. If good sense suggests that the thesis should be greatly shortened and made more to the point, does not good sense also suggest that something other than the traditional dissertation is sufficient evidence of a candidate's literary ability? Many theses are now of a so-called critical nature and would have been turned down coldly before 1935. May we not go further and, granting that the student follows the usual doctoral pro-

gram, accept an original work of literary merit? We cannot say we are unable to judge this merit. If we do, we should give up our profession.

(36) There is one more disturbing feature about the current dissertation requirement. Too many students, one sixth to be exact, report that their first effort was a failure, and they give certain uniform reasons. They discovered after some labor that the subject had been written up or the topic approved by their director would not work out. The finger of blame in these instances points at the director. Any professor who permits this to happen to a student is incompetent to direct graduate research. In the replies to Questionnaire D there is a definite indication that some dissertation directors are lackadaisical in their guidance of student research. It is assumed by the students that they are too busy with their own careers to sacrifice themselves. No one is forced to direct dissertations; and if the professor finds the work burdensome, he should withdraw. In some instances, we are informed, the director took months or longer to read and return the dissertation drafts. Time may have meant nothing to him, but it is of inestimable worth to the student. Theses drafts should be read, criticized, and returned promptly.

(37) Once the dissertation has been accepted, its author—according to old tradition—defends it before a final committee. There are occasions, few indeed, when the student is failed. When this occurs, the director of the dissertation usually never speaks to his colleagues again. But the old Germanic custom is passé. Nobody defends anything, because usually there is nothing to defend, and no one on the committee has enough knowledge to attack. The responding students enjoy this final moment, but they all regard it as fake. Those who are teaching elsewhere and have to make a trip to the home campus for these hours of emptiness find the cost in money and time objectionable. It is, of course, a ceremony comparable only to the laying on of hands in Christian ordination, and it should be regarded as nothing more. The problem of the final oral is one for the whole graduate school to consider; but now that many departments in the sciences have abandoned it, it should be given some thought by the English Department. Perhaps, the student should be asked, if it is convenient to give a talk either about his research work or to present a lecture arising from his special field. The latter practice already obtains in some universities. Probably the hooding of the young doctor is ceremony enough.

(38) The Ph.D. in English and American Literature is assumed to possess a broad knowledge of his subject and the ability to explore

and interpret it in a humanistic manner. Too often the emphasis is on exploring it and interpreting it in a way sufficient to himself and to like-minded specialists when, if we may say it again, his honest professional duty is to the undergraduate student. We must consequently see to it that our doctoral students are better than mediocre teachers, and we should make more than ordinary effort to train them as teachers and measure their teaching skill.

(39) Too great a percentage of our recent Ph.D.'s have had no teaching experience when they assumed their first posts. This may be an unfortunate situation and we should give more thought to it. Many young Ph.D.'s are, of course, inherently gifted as teachers and have enough passive experience with teaching to do well enough on their initial day in the classroom; but no matter what the gifts and the experiences are, active effort always brings improvement. Anyone can profit from some sort of teacher education before he enters the profession fully armed with learning; and by teacher education we do not mean the thin and redundant instruction provided by colleges of education. We have something more simple and probably more effective in mind. Each graduate student should have classroom experience, directed and criticized by a senior teacher of merit.

The recommendation that each graduate student be required to do practice teaching is not a commendation of the long drawn-out teaching assistantship already denounced; it springs from the realization that it is unfair to society to send out pedagogically ignorant Ph.D.'s whose teaching powers are unknown and cannot be described. Hence, a part of the regular doctoral course should be required supervised teaching for one or two years. The student should teach no more than two or three hours a week, but he should meet with his fellow apprentices in a seminar under the direction of a senior professor to discuss and plan each week's program. He should be visited in his classroom by the same professor, who can then inform his colleagues about the student's talents in the profession's principal art. Each student should be given the same credit for this work as he received for his other required courses like "Philology"; in fact, this course, so often the cause of complaint, might be better justified were it considered as a preparation for the teaching of Freshman Composition, a subject that will engage the energies of many young Ph.D.'s for quite a while.

(40) This recommendation of a teaching requirement arises from the comments of college chairmen who appear very unhappy because the Ph.D.'s they engage are unskilled in teaching and have no knowledge of college problems. The first complaint might be erased were the graduate departments to demand teacher training of their students

and be completely truthful in their appraisals of their graduates' ability. The second complaint cannot be removed at the university level. The colleges should see to it that each newly employed teacher be given a short course in this matter during his first term of residence by one of the college's veteran professors.

(41) The colleges themselves are the constant hosts of the largest body of graduate students who have not yet finished their Ph.D.'s. Any graduate student whose financial needs exceed the usual university fellowship's stipend finds his way to a college that can employ him full time at a fair living wage while he moves slowly *in absentia* toward the doctorate. Many of these people are eventually frustrated in their doctoral hopes and fail to continue their studies. At the moment there are more than 1800 teachers in the 363 reporting colleges who occupy one of the three professorial ranks and who lack a doctorate. Of this number 1011 have only the dissertation to write. A fully supported four-year doctoral program in the universities would go a long way toward eliminating this difficulty; but the intermediate degree, proposed for so many years, may be another solution.

(42) A graduate student who has really finished all of his doctorate except the dissertation should be given formal recognition. If he has written one or two substantial research papers in his seminars, he has already satisfied the requirements for a doctorate in Switzerland, Austria, and some German universities. The British universities, as it is well known, ask only a substantial dissertation for the D.Phil. In the United States, the student in this curious condition is really a dignified person without academic dignity. To signify his status, he probably should be given a lesser doctorate which could be considered both as an interim stage to the Ph.D. and as a terminal degree. Such a degree would also assure employers he was what he was said to be, and one suspects that a large number of current ABD's lack more than the dissertation. Over three hundred college chairmen say they approve the issuing of an intermediate degree; over two hundred of them say they would appoint the holder of such a degree to their staffs and would be generally inclined, all else being equal, to promote him.

(43) The institution of an intermediate degree for graduate students who still have a dissertation to compose suggests that there should be further opportunities of a postdoctoral nature for the particularly talented young Ph.D. whose graduate work and dissertation indicate that he is likely to become one of the leaders of the profession. About one out of ten new Ph.D.'s would annually make up this

group. They are as yet too young and unknown to win one of the national awards from the Guggenheim Foundation, the National Endowment for the Humanities, or the American Council of Learned Societies. Many of them may not want to make use of any postdoctoral facilities, but those who do could spent a year shortly after they had earned their degree either in transforming their dissertations into valuable books, in following out an idea or investigation, or in mastering a different field or technique. They would then be able to either go to a new post or to return to an old one better prepared as scholars and more seasoned.

(44) Postdoctoral study in English and American Literature should in no way be like postdoctoral study in the sciences where almost half of each year's Ph.D.'s are taken into an apparatus directed by an eminent scientist. The postdoctoral student in our profession must not be made a cog in some senior scholar's enormous research project. He must be attached to a distinguished professor who will advise and help him but never use him. In addition, postdoctoral institutes can only be established at universities that are now important scholarly centers. One can imagine, though we do not like the prospect, that although many universities now without a doctoral program in English will grant the intermediate degree, very few universities can justifiably do postdoctoral work. Since such work will be accompanied by the highest standards, it would be wise—perhaps, it is only visionary—if the federal government or one of the great foundations would establish a few institutes to set the tone.

APPENDIX 1

Footnotes
for Chapters
1 and 2

—————————◆•◆————————

Footnotes for Chapter 1

[1] S. E. Morison, *The Founding of Harvard College* (Cambridge, 1935), p. 168.

[2] C. F. Thwing, *A History of Higher Education in America,* New York, 1906; D. G. Tweksbury, *The Founding of American Colleges and Universities before the Civil War,* New York, 1932; R. F. Butts, *The College Charts Its Course* (New York, 1939), pp. 1–250; G. P. Schmidt, *The Liberal Arts College,* New Brunswick, N. J., 1957. Almost every college is the subject of at least one historical volume and a good bibliography can be found in Schmidt.

[3] See, for example, Herbert and Carol Schneider, *Samuel Johnson, President of Kings College,* New York, 1929, 3 vols.; P. Dorf, *The Builder: A Biography of Ezra Cornell,* New York, 1952; C. M. Perry, *H. P. Tappan,* Ann Arbor, Mich., 1933.

[4] W. C. Ryan, *Studies in Early Graduate Education* (Carnegie Foundation for the advancement of Teaching, Bulletin 30), New York, 1939; B. J. Horton, *The Graduate School,* New York, 1940; Richard J. Storr, *The Beginnings of Graduate Education in America,* Chicago, 1953. Most university histories (and there are a few histories of individual graduate schools) will be found to be rather vague on all of this matter.

[5] E. M. W. Tillyard, *The Muse Unchained*, London, 1958.

[6] My information is usually drawn in statements of this nature from the catalogues and announcements of the universities under discussion.

[7] R. Hofstadter and W. Smith, *American Higher Education* (Chicago, 1961), I, 274–275.

[8] *The American Journal of Science and Arts*, XV (1829), 329. The complete report, which precedes an essay on sea serpents, occupies pages 297–350. An abridged text is found in Hofstadter and Smith, I, 275–291. For the effect of this report on American education see the speculations of Butts, pp. 118–125; Schmidt, pp. 55–58; and R. Hofstadter and C. De Witt Hardy, *The Development and Scope of Higher Education in the United States* (New York, 1952), pp. 15–17.

[9] *Autobiography* (New York, 1905), I, 27.

[10] Schmidt, p. 60.

[11] Josiah Quincy, *The History of Harvard University* (Boston, 1840), I, 517.

[12] Storr, pp. 16–58. This historian gives a fine account of the attempts at establishing advanced work at Western Reserve, Union College, the University of New York, and Columbia.

[13] *The Launching of a University* (New York, 1906), pp. 8–9.

[14] C. F. Thwing, *The American and the German University* (New York, 1928), p. 25.

[15] W. C. Eells and Harold Haswell, *Academic Degrees* (Washington, 1960), p. 45; W. C. John, *Graduate Study in Universities and Colleges in the United States* (Washington, 1935), pp. 20–22.

[16] R. H. Chittenden, *History of the Sheffield School of Yale University, 1846–1922* (New Haven, 1928), I, 87–89.

[17] Ralph P. Rosenberg, "The First American Doctor of Philosophy Degree," *Journal of Higher Education*, XXXII (1961), 387–394; and "Eugene Schuyler's Degree," JHE, XXXIII (1962), 381–386.

[18] I have used the *DAB* for my data on Child.

[19] See Royce's biography in the *DAB*. Morris is described as a teacher of modern languages in the University of Michigan catalogue for this date, but within a few years he is a professor of philosophy. The subject of Royce's dissertation in "literature" was "The Interdependence of the Principles of Knowledge."

[20] For a precise statement of Gilman's intents *see* Fabian Franklin, *The Life of Daniel Coit Gilman* (New York, 1910), p. 196.

[21] I am grateful for much of this information to Professor George Stewart of California, Professor Thomas Moser of Stanford, Professor Walter Rideout of Wisconsin, Professor Warner Rice of Michigan, Professor John W. Clark of Minnesota, Mrs. Janet Miller of Princeton, Professor Robert Lumiansky of Pennsylvania, Professor David Greene of New York University, Professor Edgar H. Duncan of Vanderbilt, Professor Ephim Fogel of Cornell, and Professor John Schroeder of Brown. The only good account of an English department is O. J. Campbell's "The Department of English and Comparative Literature," in *A History of the Faculty of Philosophy, Columbia University*, New York, 1957.

[22] W. C. John, pp. 20–22; E. C. Eells, "Honorary Ph.Ds. in the Twentieth Century," *School and Society*, LXXXV (1957), 74–75. The American Philological Association and the AAAS directed resolutions against the custom in 1881 and were seconded by other learned organizations; nevertheless, fifty honorary Ph.D.'s were handed out in 1889 when Professor C. S. Smith of Vanderbilt denounced the practice before the NEA. In 1939 Gonzaga University gave a Ph.D. to Bing Crosby. The last of such degrees seems to have been given at Providence College in 1958.

Footnotes for Chapter 2

[1] S. W. Rudy, *The College of the City of New York* (New York, 1949), pp. 285–286; Allan Nevins, *Illinois* (New York, 1917), p. 141.

[2] Material for this sort of statistical evidence is always drawn from two publications of the United States Office of Education: Wayne Tolliver, *Enrollment for Advanced Degrees*, Fall 19—, and Tolliver or Patricia Wright, *Earned Degrees Conferred*, 19—.

[3] For this information the biennial research report of the NEA, *Teacher Supply and Demand in Universities, Colleges, and Junior Colleges* is the source.

[4] Hans Rosenhaupt, "Report of Woodrow Wilson National Fellowship Foundation," *Journal of Proceedings and Addresses*, AGS (1958), pp. 60–63; in the same publication for 1960, the Ad Hoc committee on the fellowships presented the following pertinent statistic on the number of awards before that date and the institution chosen by the student.

Brown—26	Illinois—44	North Carolina—57
Californias—190	Indiana—32	Northwestern—50
Chicago—198	Iowa—25	Pennsylvania—58
Columbia—222	Johns Hopkins—69	Princeton—233
Cornell—93	Michigan—101	Stanford—96
Duke—47	Minnesota—52	Washington—28
Harvard—393	N. Y. U.—25	Wisconsin—104
	Yale—238	

[5] J. L. Chase, *Doctoral Study: Fellowships and Capacity of Graduate Schools* (Washington, 1961), pp. 23–41.

[6] *Graduate Students Experience at Columbia University, 1940–1956* (New York, 1958), pp. 84–85, 125.

[7] *Graduate Education in the United States* (New York, 1960), p. 158.

[8] *NEA, Teacher Supply Bulletins.*

[9] *USOE, Degrees Conferred.*

[10] In 1955, McGrath had suggested in *The Graduate School Today and Tomorrow* that (1) a different Ph.D. program be established for the intending undergraduate teacher than is now found in the research-emphasizing graduate schools. He thought (2) that graduate faculties should define what they mean by the research requirements and (3) broaden the training of intending undergraduate teachers on both the pregraduate and postgraduate levels. He stated that (4) the teacher candidate should be introduced to research in seminars and be given a teaching apprenticeship before he has his degree.

[11] *Saturday Review* (January 15, 1966), pp. 62 ff.

[12] *Harper's Magazine* (March 1966), pp. 51 ff.

[13] Deans Elder, Barzun, Gordon, and Hobbs, who looked into this matter and reported at the Fifty-Eighth Annual Conference of the AGS, deplore the fact that the road to the Ph.D. is not so brilliantly marked as that to the M.D. or LL.B. They are persuaded that the insistence on the discovery of new knowledge makes the Ph.D. less a professional degree and is mainly responsible not only for a time lag, but also for eventual academic malaise and intellectual revulsion. "We see many a man less mature, less self-poised, and less confident after two years in a graduate school than he was as an inspired college senior." To remedy the disease, it is suggested that the following program be viewed with general favor.

1. The total time required for obtaining the degree should be no more than three years.
2. Before the student begins his course, he should prove by examination that he can write English prose and that he knows one foreign language.
3. In the first year, the student should take a proseminar and seminar; in his second year a seminar. He should have an advisor who discovers the gaps in his knowledge.
4. The qualifying examination should be based on depth not breadth and the examinee should be informed well in advance what his department considers a demonstration of competence.
5. The thesis should be of such a modest character that there is no difficulty in getting it written within a year.
6. The final oral should be a real defence of the thesis.

An account of the CGS "Present Status of Accreditation of Graduate Work" presided over by Dean Nichols is found in the records of the 1964 meeting (pp. 185–229).

[14] The discussion of the Ph.D. as a research degree, a teaching degree, or both began in the last century and has not yet concluded. In 1946, Howard M. Jones proposed in *Education and World Tragedy* (Cambridge, 1946), pp. 151–154, that there be a Graduate College and a Research Training Institute. The students in the former would be broadly educated men and women able to administer genuine education maturely, richly, and with a high sense of its importance. The staff would not be departmentalized but organized into broad groups—Humanities, Social Sciences, and so forth—and be all of the same rank. The college would not have linguists qua linguists, or those "who have discovered a new system" or are famous for "rarefied research work." This latter group would staff the Research Training Institute. Professor Jones subsequently gave up this idea, but other men have taken it up in one way or other. Eugen Weber, a precursor of Arrowsmith, complained in "The Shirt of Nessus," *JHE*, XXVIII (1957), that as American educational standards go down, the value of the Ph.D. improves. All the degree means is "increasing earnestness," "minds working on . . . safe . . . unexciting lines. The man who generalizes, the man who takes too many accepted values in vain, the man who risks too many cute unscholarly ideas . . . is not really serious, or reliable, or one of us." There is a subsequent response, "Keep Your Shirt on Nessus." In the *Graduate Journal*, I (1958), 144–154, H. E. Spivey in "The Role of the Graduate School in the Promotion of Scholarship" makes fifteen suggestions for the restoration of scholarship in the curricula for the M.A. and Ph.D. The problem is realistically discussed by Berelson in "What Should Be the Direction of Graduate Study," *Current Issues in Higher Education*, NEA (Washington, 1959), pp. 150–154, but a year later Hans Rosenhaupt in "House of Pedantry," *National Catholic Education Association Bulletin*, LVII, 193–197, talks about the fragmentation of knowledge in the graduate school, its pedantry, and lack of freedom. Kind words in support of the conventional Ph.D. are to be found in Stuart Tave, "A Word on Behalf of the Ph.D.," *The Journal of Teacher Education*, XIII (1962), 444–447. Some recent attitudes are found in Moody Prior's essay in Everett Walters, *Graduate Education Today* (Washington, 1965), 30–61, and the remarks of Logan Wilson in the *Journal of the AGS*, XVII (1965), 22–23.

[15] The problems of time lag and attrition have long been pondered by the experts and one will find extensive sections on the necessity for acceleration in D. Perkins and J. L. Snell, *The Education of Historians in the United States* (New York, 1962), pp. 176–188, 193–199, 203–207, and in Berelson, *Graduate Education*, pp. 156–167. In his *Preliminary Report on an Inquiry into the Length of the Doctoral Program: Survey of Recent Doctoral Graduates*, (n.p., 1960), Kenneth Wilson indicates (p. 17) that it takes 9.7 years to get a doctorate in English at a graduate university in the South. This average figure was supported in 1963 when Alexander Heard, Chancellor of Vanderbilt, noticed in *The Lost Years in Graduate Education* that the Eng-

lish Ph.D. took the most time. His tabulations indicate that the fastest 10 percent of English graduates takes 5.4 years and the slowest 10 percent require almost 21 years. The median elapsed time is 9.7 years, a figure close to the national average. The "Report of the Committee on Expediting the Ph.D. Degree" made to the AGS in 1964 shows that the time lag has increased for every discipline since 1920 by about 50 percent. English Ph.D. candidates required about 8.4 years in 1920 and now require 12 years. Berelson has a general account of attrition (pp. 167–172), and it is discussed popularly by President F. W. Ness in "The Case of the Lingering Degree," *Saturday Review* (Jan. 15, 1966), pp. 64 ff. The most recent full-scale study is A. Tucker, G. Gottleib, and J. Pease, *Attrition of Graduate Students at the Ph.D. Level in Arts and Sciences* (East Lansing, Mich., 1964).

[16] *Graduate Education* (New York, 1965), p. 10. The author states (p. 18) that more doctorates were given between 1953–1965 than between 1861–1953. A somewhat older study of the same confusion is found in Ernest V. Hollis, *Toward Improving Ph.D. Programs* (Washington, 1945), pp. 172–204.

[17] J. P. Elder, "Reviving the Master's Degree for the Prospective College Teacher," *JHE*, XXX (1959), 133–136.

[18] *Graduate Education* (New York, 1961), p. 162, suggests that talented and properly motivated sophomores could be selected to enter a three-year Master's program at the beginning of their junior year. They would receive an A.B. or B.S. at the end of the fourth year, and an A.M., M.S., or M.Phil. at the end of the fifth year. By this time they would have satisfied the usual language requirements. The M.Phil., which would lead to the D.Phil., would be considered a sufficient degree for college teaching. The D.Phil. is a similar degree but more advanced and is to be distinguished from the Ph.D., a research and professional degree. A not unsimilar solution is offered by Eugene Arden, "A Solution to the Crisis in College Teaching," *Liberal Education*, LI (1965), 1–8.

[19] Conference of the Division of Graduate Programs, USOE, September 19, 1966.

[20] "Intermediate Degrees: Some Possibilities and Problems" read at the Conference of September 19, 1966.

[21] "Candidate's Degree." Statement adopted at the CIC Graduate Deans and Faculty Representatives Meeting, University of Chicago Center for Continuing Education . . . April 19, 1965; Stephen Spurr, "The Candidate's Degree" Conference of September 19, 1966.

[22] J. L. Chase, p. 31.

[23] Chase, 138.

²⁴ Professor Fredson Bowers, whose active study of the whole situation is well known, should be surely consulted on many of these points; see his article in *College English*, XXVII (1965), 123–128, and his "What Can We Do About the Ph.D.?" delivered at the CEA of Ohio on April 1, 1966.

²⁵ *ADE* Bulletin, No. 6 (January 1966), 2–4.

²⁶ The notion of an individualized doctoral program adjusted to the talents and needs of each student has been talked about by various experts. T. S. Painter in "The Selection and Recruitment of Graduate Students," *Graduate Journal* I (1958), 41–50, proposes a "practitioner's rank" and a more flexible "honors rank." L. B. Beach, "Freedom and Discipline in Graduate Programs," *JHE* XXX (1959), 120–123, and R. H. Eckelberry, "Graduate Degrees vs Professional Degrees," *JHE* XXX, pp. 172–173, both recommend letting the students pursue his own interest, making the Ph.D. constructive rather than disciplinary, and enabling the aspirant to fulfill the needs of his professional objectives.

APPENDIX 2

Tabulations
for Chapters
3 to 8

Tabulations for Chapter 3

(In this series of tables, as in those that follow for succeeding chapters, a key letter and number refers the reader to the questionnaire and the section of the questionnaire from which the information is derived. A = Questionnaire for Departmental Chairmen or Directors of Graduate Study. B = Questionnaire for Teachers of Graduate Courses in English. C = Questionnaire for Chairmen of Departments without a Doctoral Program. D = Questionnaire for Recent Recipients of the Ph.D. in English and American Literature.)

Table 3.1.   *Responses to Questionnaire D*

Mailed	3623 Questionnaires
Returned by PO	219
Assumed received	3404
Received	1977
Too late	74
	1903 or 55.9%
Unusable	23
Usable	1880 or 55.2%

$$N^* = 3404$$

* In all tabular material, N = the number of people counted in making up the percentage.

Table 3.2.   *Sex of respondents to Questionnaire D*
(D.3)

Male	1564	83.2%
Female	316	16.8%
	1880	

Table 3.3.   *Undergraduate major of recent recipients*
(D.4)

	NUMBER OF RESPONDENTS	PERCENT
English	1535	82.7
Not English	320	17.3
No answer	14	
Not applicable	11	
	1880	

$$N = 1855$$

Table 3.4.   *Sources of recent recipients' undergraduate degree*
(D.4)

	NUMBER OF RESPONDENTS	PERCENT
Private university	506	27.2
State university	577	31.0
State college	61	3.3
College of 1000+	388	20.8
College of −999	225	12.1
Other	104	5.6
No answer	10	
Not applicable	9	
	1880	

$N = 1861$

Table 3.5.   *When the recent recipients decided*
(D.8)   *to work for a Ph.D.*

	NUMBER OF RESPONDENTS	PERCENT
Before entering college	63	3.4
By the junior year	253	13.5
By graduation	384	20.4
After graduation	54	2.9
While working for M.A.	631	33.6
After M.A.	475	25.3
Another time	20	1.1
	1880	

$N = 1880$

Table 3.6.   *Major subject of the recent recipients*
(D.4)   *for the M.A.*

	NUMBER OF RESPONDENTS	PERCENT
English	1719	96.0
Not English	71	4.0
No answer	7	
Not applicable	83	
	1880	

$N = 1790$

Table 3.7. *Most important reason(s) for the recent recipients*
(D.9)   *to select the graduate department they chose*

	NUMBER OF RESPONDENTS	PERCENT
Academic	1019	54.2
Financial	480	25.5
Geographical	459	24.4
Others	25	1.3

N = 1880

Table 3.8. *The academic reason indicated by recent recipients*
(D.10)   *some of whom marked two reasons*

	NUMBER OF RESPONDENTS	PERCENT
Reputation of the university	588	57.7
Reputation of the department	500	49.1
Reputation of the major professor	257	25.2
Special program	157	15.4
Other reasons	156	15.3

N = 1019

Table 3.9. *Sources of all degrees possessed*
(D.4)   *by recent recipients*

CATEGORY	NUMBER OF RESPONDENTS	PERCENT
No M.A.	90	4.7

N = 1880

M.A. and Ph.D. at same university	934	52.2
M.A. and Ph.D. at different university	856	47.8
M.A. and A.B. at same university	290	16.2
A.B. and Ph.D. at same university	58	3.2
All degrees at same university	203	11.3

N = 1790

Table 3.10.   *Ages at which the Ph. D. was earned*
(D.4)   *by the recent recipients*

(a) MEN

   1955–1960 Average age: 33.8
   1961–1965 Average age: 33.1   Average age for all males: 33.4

   1955–1960 Median age: 33
   1961–1965 Median age: 32   Median age for all males: 32

   1955–1960 Range: 24–58
   1961–1965 Range: 24–58

(b) WOMEN

   1955–1960 Average age: 35.3
   1961–1965 Average age: 36.3   Average age for all females: 35.9

   1955–1960 Median age: 38
   1961–1965 Median age: 34   Median age for all females: 35

   1955–1960 Range: 25–63
   1961–1965 Range: 23–68

(c) TOTALS

AGE	FREQUENCY	AGE	FREQUENCY
23	1	36–40	323
24	8	41–45	149
25	24	46–50	61
26	56	51–55	26
27	90	56–60	5
28	125	61–65	2
29	144	66 or older	1
30	137	Do not know	96
31	151		1880
32	155		
33	126		
34	109	Average age:	33.9
35	91	Median age:	33

N = 1784

Table 3.11.　　*Elapsed time for both sexes of recent recipients*
(D.4)　　　　　*between the A.B. and Ph.D.*

| | MALES | | | FEMALES | | | |
YEARS	1955–1960	1961–1965	TOTAL	1955–1960	1961–1965	TOTAL	ALL
2	0	0	0	0	0	0	0
3	3	6	9	0	2	2	11
4	18	35	53	0	2	2	55
5	28	73	101	6	14	20	121
6	46	86	132	8	15	23	155
7	70	89	159	5	12	17	176
8	72	81	153	5	15	20	173
9	88	85	173	6	13	19	192
10	57	87	144	12	11	23	167
11	38	75	113	4	14	18	131
12	29	77	106	8	13	21	127
13	25	62	87	8	10	18	105
14	23	51	74	3	5	8	82
15	23	25	48	6	7	13	61
16–20	72	46	118	19	33	52	170
21–25	18	30	48	12	24	36	84
26–30	10	12	22	3	6	9	31
31–35	5	4	9	7	4	11	20
36–40	0	0	0	1	0	1	1
41–45	0	0	0	0	0	0	0
46 or over	0	0	0	0	1	1	1
Don't know	2	2	4	0	0	0	4
Not applicable	7	4	11	1	1	2	13
Totals	634	930	1564	114	202	316	1880

Table 3.12. *Years spent by recent recipients in full-time study*
(D.15)

YEARS	MALE	FEMALE	TOTAL
0	219	65	284
1	300	74	374
2	484	97	581
3	362	53	415
4	134	18	152
5	36	2	38
6	8	2	10
7	3	2	5
8	4	0	4
9	1	0	1
Don't know	13	3	16
Totals	1564	316	1880*

Over-all average time: 1.9 years
Median time: 2.0 years

$$N = 1880$$

* It is apparent that 1580 or 84.0 percent had one or more years of full-time study.

Table 3.13. *Source of support for full-time study*
(D.18)

SOURCE	MALE	FEMALE	TOTAL	PERCENT
Parents/relatives	316	60	376	23.8
Wife/husband	339	46	385	24.4
Grant/fellowship	841	172	1013	64.1
Loan	114	16	130	8.2
Savings	448	79	527	33.4
Others	31	47	78	4.9

$$N = 1580$$

Table 3.14.   *Elapsed time for recent recipients between beginning*
(D.14)   *graduate study and passing preliminary examinations*

YEARS	MALE	FEMALE	TOTAL
1	55	12	67
2	260	65	325
3	391	81	472
4	284	45	329
5	178	33	211
6	124	13	137
7	80	14	94
8	56	7	63
9	21	5	26
10	27	7	34
11	14	0	14
12	11	5	16
13	8	4	12
14	3	1	4
15 or more	21	10	31
No answer	31	14	45
	1564	316	1880

Over-all average time: 4.4 years
Median time: 4 years

Table 3.15.   *Elapsed time for recent recipients between passing*
(D.16)   *preliminary examinations and completing dissertation*

YEARS	MALE	FEMALE	TOTAL
1	386	104	490
2	469	87	556
3	240	45	285
4	158	31	189
5	126	14	140
6	56	19	75
7	41	4	45
8	21	2	23
9	21	1	22
10	14	3	17
11 or more	16	2	18
No answer	16	4	20
Totals	1564	316	1880

Average time: 2.9 years
Median time: 2 years

Table 3.16.   *Time spent by recent recipients between A.B. and*
(D.17)   *Ph.D. degrees as teaching fellows*

YEARS	MALE	FEMALE	TOTAL
0	524	165	689
1	180	28	208
2	273	47	320
3	229	31	260
4	189	19	208
5	83	21	104
6	46	2	48
7	19	2	21
8	5	0	5
9	5	0	5
10 and over	4	1	5
No answer	7	0	7
Totals	1564	316	1880

Average time: 2.9 years
Median time: 3 years

Table 3.17.   *Time spent by recent recipients between A.B. and*
(D.17)   *Ph.D. degrees as full-time teacher*

YEARS	MALE	FEMALE	TOTAL
0	420	81	501
1	163	25	188
2	173	21	194
3	165	25	190
4	131	23	154
5	123	15	138
6	87	19	106
7	57	12	69
8	57	11	68
9	34	9	43
10 or more	154	75	229
Totals	1564	316	1880

Average time: 4.9 years
Median time: 4 years

Table 3.18.   *Attitudes of recent recipients on length of time*
(D.11)   *required to earn doctorate*

ANSWER	MALES	PERCENT	FEMALES	PERCENT	TOTAL	PERCENT
A reasonable time	601	38.9	132	41.9	733	39.4
Too much time	943	61.1	183	58.1	1126	60.6
No answer	20	—	1	—	21	—
	1564		316		1880	

N = 1859

Table 3.19.   *What is "a reasonable amount of time" to spend*
(D.12)   *in earning the doctorate?*

YEARS	MALE	FEMALE	TOTAL
1	1	0	1
2	6	0	6
3	52	5	57
4	270	16	286
5	308	44	352
6	139	27	166
7	58	13	71
8	27	19	46
9	10	5	15
10 or more	33	33	66
No answer	39	21	60
Totals	943	183	1126
Average time: years	5.2	6.8	5.45
Median time: years	5.0	5.0	5.0

Table 3.20.   *Major causes of delay in earning the doctorate*
(D.13)   *reported by recent recipients*

	MALE	FEMALE	TOTAL	PERCENT
Poor graduate guidance	195	18	213	11.3
Military service	369	9	378	20.1
Finances	552	73	625	33.2
Changes of academic interest	150	23	173	9.2
Foreign language exams	105	8	113	6.0
Dissertation	345	37	382	20.3
Other causes	335	126	461	24.5

N = 1880

Table 3.21.   *Number of recent recipients married at time doctorate*
(D.6)   *was conferred*

	MALE	PERCENT	FEMALE	PERCENT	TOTAL	PERCENT
Yes	1169	76.4	112	36.2	1281	69.6
No	362	23.6	197	63.8	559	30.4
No answer	33	—	7	—	40	—
	1564		316		1880	

N = 1531   N = 309   N = 1840

Table 3.22.   *Number of children born to recent recipients by the*
(D.7)   *time doctorate was conferred*

NUMBER OF CHILDREN	MALES	FEMALES	TOTAL NUMBER OF MALES AND FEMALES	TOTAL NUMBER OF CHILDREN
0	329	37	366	0
1	247	31	278	278
2	330	24	354	708
3	148	13	161	483
4	68	5	73	292
5	25	0	25	125
6	6	0	6	36
7	7	0	7	49
No answer	9	2	11	—
Total	1169	112	1281	1971

* Number and percent of respondents with children when Ph.D.
was earned
Males   831 or 52.4% of total males   N = 1564
Females   73 or 23.1% of total females   N = 316
           904 or 47.0% of total respondents   N = 1880

Table 3.23. *Recent recipients who remained as teachers at university*
(D.5)   *from which they earned the doctorate*

	MALE		FEMALE		
	1955–1960	1961–1965	1955–1960	1961–1965	GRAND TOTAL
Remained	53	66	4	16	139
	(8.5%)	(7.2%)	(3.6%)	(8.0%)	(7.5%)
Did not remain	570	854	107	183	1714
	(91.5%)	(92.8%)	(96.4%)	(92.0%)	(92.5%)
No answer	8	7	3	3	21
Not applicable	3	3	0	0	6
	634	930	114	202	1880

N = 123 N = 90 N = 111 N = 199 N = 1853

Table 3.24. *To what institutions do the recent Ph.D.'s first go?*
(D.5)

	MALE		FEMALE		
	1955–1960	1961–1965	1955–1960	1961–1965	GRAND TOTAL
Private university	161	185	7	33	386 (20.8%)
State university	257	417	43	51	768 (41.4%)
State college	51	53	12	23	139 (7.5%)
College 1000+	68	124	24	25	241 (13.0%)
College −999	37	64	20	43	164 (8.9%)
Junior college	3	4	0	1	8 (0.4%)
Others	53	75	4	15	147 (7.9%)
No answer	4	8	4	11	27
	634	930	114	202	1880

N = 1853

Table 3.25a.   **Number of different teaching positions held by**
(D.5)   **recent recipients since earning the Ph.D.**

POSTS	MALES	PERCENT	FEMALES	PERCENT
0	13	.8	4	1.3
1	937	60.3	203	66.1
2	452	29.0	75	24.4
3	127	7.4	16	5.2
4	20	1.2	8	2.6
5	3		0	
6	0		1	
No answer	10		9	
Not applicable	2		0	
	1564		316	

N = 1552   N = 307   N = 1859

Table 3.25b.   **Number of teaching positions held by recent recipients**
(D.5)   **of the doctorate since taking the M.A. and Ph.D.**

	SINCE THE M.A.		SINCE THE PH.D.	
POSTS	RESPONDENTS	PERCENT	RESPONDENTS	PERCENT
0	13	.7	17	.9
1	346	19.6	1140	61.3
2	609	34.5	527	28.3
3	488	27.7	143	7.7
4	259	14.7	28	1.5
5	42	2.4	3	.2
6	5	.3	1	.1
7	2	.1	0	
No answer	10		19	
Not applicable	106		2	
	1880		1880	

N = 1764   N = 1859

Table 3.26. *At what ranks have the recent recipients arrived?*
(D.5)

RANKS	MALES	PERCENT	FEMALES	PERCENT	TOTALS	PERCENT
Instructor	29	2.0	30	10.5	59	3.4
Assistant professor	640	43.4	123	43.0	763	43.3
Associate professor	550	37.3	83	29.0	633	35.9
Professor	256	17.4	50	17.5	306	17.4
No answer or not applicable	89		30		119	
Totals	1564		316		1880	

N = 1475   N = 286   N = 1761

Table 3.27. *Attitude of recent recipients as to whether their*
(D.44)   *doctorates were worth earning*

ANSWER	MALES	PERCENT	FEMALES	PERCENT	TOTALS	PERCENT
Yes	1405	89.8	302	95.5	1707	90.7
No	90	5.8	6	1.9	96	5.1
No answer	69	4.4	8	2.5	77	4.0
Totals	1564		316		1880	

N = 1564   N = 316   N = 1880

Table 3.28. *Census of professors engaged in graduate teaching*
(B.3)

CATEGORY	MALE	PERCENT	FEMALE	PERCENT	TOTAL	PERCENT
Ph.D. ante-1955	567	95.0	30	5.0	597	51.0
Ph.D. post-1955	464	94.1	29	5.9	493	42.1
Non-Ph.D.'s	69	86.3	11	13.8	80	6.8
Totals	1100		70		1170	

N = 1170

Table 3.29.   *Current academic status of all graduate professors*
(B.5)
(a) BREAKDOWN BY CATEGORIES

RANK	ANTE-1955	PER-CENT	POST-1955	PER-CENT	NON-PH.D.'S	PER-CENT
Professor	491	82.8	91	18.8	17	21.3
Associate professor	94	15.9	223	46.0	9	11.3
Assistant professor	4	.7	168	34.6	40	50.0
Instructor	0	—	2	.4	14	17.5
Lecturer	2	.3	1	.2	0	—
Other post	2	.1	0	—	0	—
No answer	4	—	8	—	0	—
Totals	597		493		80	

$N = 593$ $N = 485$ $N = 80$

(b) GRAND TOTAL ALL CATEGORIES

RANK	NUMBER	PERCENT
Professor	599	51.7
Associate professor	326	28.2
Assistant professor	212	18.3
Instructor	16	1.4
Lecturer	3	.3
Other post	2	.2
No answer	12	
Total	1170	

$N = 1158$

Table 3.30.   *Elapsed time between the earning of the doctorate and*
(B.6)   *the teaching of a course with graduate credit*

YEARS	ANTE-1955	PERCENT	POST-1955	PERCENT
Same year	58	11.6	105	22.3
First	64	12.8	111	23.6
Second	58	11.6	78	16.6
Third	68	13.6	59	12.6
Fourth	35	7.0	41	8.7
Fifth	43	8.6	28	6.0
Sixth	48	9.6	17	3.6
Seventh	31	6.2	23	4.9
Eighth, ninth, tenth, and eleventh	95	19.0	8	1.7
No answer	65		14	
Not codable	32		9	
	597		493	

N = 500   N = 470

Table 3.31.   *Elapsed time in years between earning the doctorate*
(B.7)   *and directing the first dissertation*

CLASS	AVERAGE TIME	MEDIAN TIME	EXTREMES
Ante-1955*	5.5	7.3	3 to 12
Post-1955†	4.0	5.0	−2 to 11

* Of the 597 respondents, 141 have yet to direct a dissertation; the percentage of directors is 76.3 percent.
† Of the 493 respondents in this class, 216 have already directed or are in the process of directing a dissertation; the percentage here is 43.8 percent. Of the 80 non-Ph.D.'s, 21, or 26 percent, have directed or are directing a doctoral dissertation.

Table 3.32.   *Publication record of dissertations written by recent*
(D.38)   *recipients of the doctorate*

	MALE	PERCENT	FEMALE	PERCENT	TOTAL	PERCENT
Published	686	44.3	82	26.1	768	41.2
Not published	864	55.7	231	73.8	1095	58.8
Not codable	14		3		17	
Total	1564		316		1880	

N = 1550   N = 313   N = 1863

Table 3.33.   *Publications of recent recipients that did not depend*
(D.39)   *on doctoral dissertations*

CATEGORY	NUMBER	PERCENT
Graduate teachers	231	12.3
Nongraduate teachers	1649	87.7
Total	1880	
		N = 1880

1. Recipients now giving graduate courses

(a)
CATEGORY	NUMBER	PERCENT
No publications	41	17.7
Publications	190	82.3
		N = 231

(b)
CATEGORY	NUMBER	AVERAGE
Books	144	.76
Monographs	35	.18
Articles	1246	6.5

2. Recipients not giving graduate courses

(a)
CATEGORY	NUMBER	PERCENT
No publications	726	44.0
Publications	923	56.0
		N = 1649

(b)
CATEGORY	NUMBER	AVERAGE
Books	510	.55
Monographs	104	.11
Articles	3936	4.3

3. Total recipients

(a)
CATEGORY	NUMBER	PERCENT
No publications	767	40.8
Publications	1113	59.2
Total	1880	
		N = 1880

(b) CATEGORY

(PUBLISHERS ONLY)	NUMBER	AVERAGE
Books	654	.59
Monographs	139	.12
Articles	5182	4.6
		N = 1113

(c) CATEGORY

(ALL RECIPIENTS)	NUMBER	AVERAGE
Books	654	.35
Monographs	139	.07
Articles	5182	2.76
		N = 1880

Table 3.34.   *Age of non-Ph.D.'s who are graduate professors*
(B.4)

RANGES	AGE
Average:	52
Median:	58
Extremes	24–71

Table 3.35.   *Degrees earned by non-Ph.D.'s who are*
(B.4)   *graduate professors*

DEGREE	NUMBER	PERCENT
A.B. only	10	12.5
A.B. and M.A.	70	87.5
Total	80	

N = 80

Table 3.36.   *State of progress toward the doctorate by non-Ph.D.*
(B.4)   *graduate professors*

	MALE	FEMALE	TOTAL	PERCENT
Ph.D. (imminent)	45	5	50	62.5
Ph.D. (abandoned)	24	6	30	37.5
Total	69	11	80	

N = 80

Table 3.37.   *Academic ranks of non-Ph.D.'s who are graduate*
(B.5)   *professors*

	PH.D. (IMMINENT)	PH.D. (ABANDONED)	TOTAL	PERCENT
Professor	0	17	17	21.8
Associate professor	1	8	9	11.5
Assistant professor	38	2	40	51.3
Instructor	11	1	12	15.4
No answer	0	2	2	
	50	30	80	

N = 78

Table 3.38.   *Sources of graduate professor's A.B. degrees*
(B.4)

CATEGORY	NUMBER	PERCENT
State university	341	29.8
Private university	351	30.6
College of 1000+	259	22.6
College of −999	106	9.2
State college	26	2.3
Other institutions (foreign, and so on)	63	5.5
Not applicable	11	
No answer	13	
	1170	

N = 1146

Table 3.39.   *Age at which graduate professors earned the doctorate*
(B.4)

CLASS	MALE	FEMALE	TOTAL
Ante-1955			
Average age	32.1	32.8	32.1
Median age	31	34	32
Extremes	24 to 51	23 to 44	
Post-1955			
Average age	32.1	33.9	32.4
Median age	31	32	32
Extremes	20 to 52	25 to 57	

Table 3.40.   *Elapsed time (in years) for graduate professors*
(B.16)   *between A.B. and Ph.D.*

CLASS	AVERAGE TIME	MEDIAN TIME	EXTREMES
Ante-1955	8.9	8	2 to 29
Post-1955	8.9	8	3 to 35

Table 3.41.   *Disposition of elapsed time (in years) between A.B. and*
(B.17)   *Ph.D. by graduate professors*

ANTE-1955 CLASS	AVERAGE TIME	MEDIAN TIME	EXTREMES
Full-time study	2.9	3	0 to 10
Part-time study	3.6	3	0 to 19
Full-time teaching	4.7	4	0 to 28
Part-time teaching	2.9	3	0 to 12
Military service	3.5	4	0 to 7
Other employment	2.0	2	0 to 17
POST-1955 CLASS			
Full-time study	3.0	3	0 to 8
Part-time study	3.7	3	0 to 12
Full-time teaching	3.9	3	0 to 11
Part-time teaching	2.9	3	0 to 11
Military service	2.4	2	0 to 8
Other employment	3.6	2	0 to 19

Table 3.42.   *Number of teaching posts held by graduate professors*
(B.5)   *during the course of their graduate training*

POSTS	NUMBER OF RESPONDENTS	PERCENT
0	216	20.6
1	424	40.3
2	278	26.5
3	106	10.1
4	24	2.3
5	3	.3
No answer	39	
Total	1090*	

N = 1051

* Some 65 of these respondents held positions in secondary schools.

Table 3.43.   Attitude of graduate professors toward the amount
(B.18)   of time spent in securing the doctorate

CATEGORY	ANTE-1955	PERCENT	POST-1955	PERCENT	TOTALS	PERCENT
Reasonable	458	79.1	330	67.3	788	73.7
Unreasonable	121	20.9	160	32.7	281	26.3
No answer	18		3		21	
	597		493		1090	

       N = 579   N = 490   N = 1069

Table 3.44.   Number of teaching posts held by graduate professors
(B.5)   since earning the doctorate

POSTS	NUMBER	PERCENT
1	406	37.6
2	387	35.9
3	205	19.0
4	65	6.0
5	14	1.3
6	2	.2
No answer	11	
Total	1090	

N = 1079

Table 3.45.   Age at which graduate professors attained full
(B.5)   professorships

CATEGORY	AVERAGE AGE	MEDIAN AGE	EXTREMES
Ante-1955	44.3	45	20 to 64
Post-1955	38.5	38	31 to 54
Non-Ph.D.'s	44.4	40	32 to 63

Table 3.46.   *Distribution of graduate professors' time between*
(B.9)   *graduate and undergraduate teaching**

PERCENTAGE OF TIME	UNDERGRADUATE INSTRUCTION NUMBER OF TEACHERS	GRADUATE INSTRUCTION NUMBER OF TEACHERS
Under 10	102	73
10 to 20	26	92
21 to 30	75	113
31 to 40	97	281
41 to 50	307	300
51 to 60	52	27
61 to 70	263	83
71 to 90	179	93
91 to 100	59	98
No answer	10	10
	1170	1170

* Of the professors devoting 100 percent of their time to graduate teaching, 75 are in the ante-1955 class, 18 in the post-1955 class, and 5 are non-Ph.D.'s.

Table 3.47.   *Distribution of graduate professors' student load*
(B.10)

CATEGORY	AVERAGE NUMBER OF STUDENTS	MEDIAN NUMBER OF STUDENTS	EXTREMES
Undergraduate courses	53.6	39	2 to 500
Undergraduate-graduate courses	43.0	35	2 to 300
Graduate courses	21.6	19	1 to 100
Seminars	11.7	12	2 to 33

Table 3.48.
(B.8)

Number of theses either being directed or in the course of direction by graduate professors

CLASS	AVERAGE NUMBER	MEDIAN NUMBER	EXTREMES
Ante-1955*	12.1	5	1 to 165
Post-1955†	4.2	2	1 to 27
Non-Ph.D.'s‡	8.7	3	1 to 92

* More than 2.3% were directed by twenty professors, or 1.7% of all graduate professors.
† Slightly more than 31% of this group have, or are directing, their first dissertation. About 67% have yet to direct more than three dissertations.
‡ Four of these professors have directed 137 theses, or 81%, of all theses directed by this group.

Table 3.49.

Census of chairmen or directors of graduate departments

Mailed	109
Returned and tallied	88
Percent	80.7

Table 3.50.
(A.3)

Sex of chairmen or directors of graduate departments

		PERCENT
Male	86	97.7
Female	2	2.3
Total	88	

N = 88

Table 3.51.
(A.2)

Age of chairmen or directors of graduate study

RANGES	AGE
Average	50.6
Median	50.0
Extremes	34 to 67

Table 3.52.
(A.4)

Earned degrees of chairmen or directors of graduate study

A.B.	87
M.A.	77
Ph.D.	88

Table 3.53.   *Source of the bachelor's degrees of chairmen or*
(A.4)   *directors of graduate study*

		PERCENT
State universities	26	29.5
Private universities	36	40.9
Colleges of 1000+	19	21.6
Colleges of −999	6	6.8
State colleges	1	1.1
	88	

N = 88

Table 3.54.   *Source of the doctors' degrees of chairmen or directors*
(A.4)   *of graduate study*

	NUMBER OF RESPONDENTS	PERCENT
Cartter top twenty	73	83.0
Non-Cartter group	15	17.0
	88	

N = 88

Table 3.55.   *Age at which chairmen or directors of graduate*
(A.4)   *study took Ph.D.'s*

RANGES	AGE
Average	31.9
Median	31.0
Range	20 to 48

Table 3.56.   *Elapsed time (in years) between the degrees of*
(A.4)   *chairmen or directors of graduate study*

	AVERAGE TIME	MEDIAN TIME	EXTREMES
A.B. to M.A.	2.9	2	0 to 13
M.A. to Ph.D.	6.9	5	1 to 20
A.B. to Ph.D.	6.0	7	2 to 8

Table 3.57. *Number of academic posts held by chairmen or directors*
(A.5)   *of graduate study since taking the Ph.D.*

POSTS	RESPONDENTS	PERCENT
1	29	33.0
2	33	37.5
3	18	20.5
4	7	8.0
		———
6	1	1.1
	88	

Average: 2.0
Median: 2.0

$$N = 88$$

Table 3.58. *Years completed in current university by chairmen or*
(A.5)   *directors of graduate study*

RANGES	YEARS
Average service	16.2
Median years of service	12.0
Range	0 to 40

Table 3.59. *Responses to Questionnaire C*

	NUMBER	PERCENT	
Mailed	550		
Returned	365	66.4	$N = 550$
Too late	2		
Tabulated	363	99.5	$N = 365$

Table 3.60.   *Number of M.A. programs (with inaugural dates)*
(C.11)   *at colleges without doctoral programs*

INAUGURAL DATES	INSTITUTIONS	PERCENT
Before 1920	10	8.1
1920–1925	6	4.9
1926–1930	4	3.3
1931–1935	8	6.5
1936–1940	10	8.1
1941–1945	4	3.3
1946–1950	14	11.4
1951–1955	5	4.1
1956–1960	19	15.4
1961–1965	43	35.0
	123	

N = 123

Table 3.61.   *Colleges without doctoral programs that plan the*
(C.13)   *installation of M.A. programs*

CATEGORY	NUMBER OF INSTITUTIONS	PERCENT
Plan to install program	53	23.3
Plan not to install program	174	76.7
No answer	13	
Total	240	

N = 227

Table 3.62.   *Number of M.A.'s either recently granted or in*
(C.12)   *progress in nondoctoral departments*

CATEGORY	NUMBER	AVERAGE
Earned between 1960–1965*	3682	29.9
Now in progress	6208	50.5

* This is an annual average of 736.

Table 3.63.   *Nondoctoral departments giving the M.A. that plan*
(C.13)   *to give the doctorate*

CATEGORY	INSTITUTIONS	PERCENT
Plan to give the doctorate	11	8.9
Do not plan to give the doctorate	112	91.1
	123	

N = 123

Table 3.64.   *Census of chairmen of departments without*
(C.2)   *doctoral programs*

SEX	NUMBER	PERCENT
Male	308	84.8
Female	55	15.2
Total	363	

N = 363

Table 3.65.   *Age of chairmen of departments without doctoral*
(C.3)   *programs*

CATEGORY	MALE	FEMALE
Average age	47.9	52.7
Median age	47.0	53.0

	AVERAGE YEARS IN TEACHING (T.A. TIME INCLUDED)	
Chairmen with Ph.D.	25.5	Extremes 1–48
Chairmen without Ph.D.	16.3	Extremes 1–41

Table 3.66.   *Degrees earned by chairmen of departments that*
(C.4)   *do not have doctoral programs*

DEGREE	MALES	PERCENT	FEMALES	PERCENT	TOTAL	PERCENT
Ph.D.	269	87.3	46	83.6	315	86.8
No. Ph.D.	39	12.7	9	16.4	48	13.2
Totals	308		55		363	

N = 308   N = 55   N = 363

Table 3.67.   Age at which chairmen of departments that do not have
(C.4)   doctoral programs earned doctorates

CATEGORY	MALES	FEMALES
Average age	36.7	37.7
Median age	35.0	36.0
Extremes	24 to 64	27 to 57

Table 3.68.   Elapsed time (in years) between degrees earned by
(C.4)   chairmen of departments without doctoral programs

(A) MALES	A.B. TO M.A.	M.A. TO PH.D.
Average time	3.5	8.9
Median time	2.0	10.0
Extremes	1 to 17	2 to 23
(B) FEMALES		
Average time	5.8	15.8
Median time	5.0	15.0
Extremes	1 to 34	3 to 36
(C) BOTH SEXES		
Average time	3.8	11.8
Median time	4.0	11.0

Table 3.69.   Ranks of chairmen of departments without doctorates
(C.5)

RANK		PERCENT
Professor	17	36.2
Associate	20	42.6
Assistant	7	14.9
Instructor	3	6.4
No answer	1	
Total	48	

N = 47

Table 3.70.   *Ranks of chairmen of departments with doctorates*
(C.5)

RANK (DEGREES BEFORE 1955)	MALE	PERCENT	FEMALE	PERCENT
Professor	143	97.9	27	96.4
Associate professor	3	2.1	0	
Assistant professor	0		1	3.6
	N = 146		N = 28	
(DEGREES 1955–1965)				
Professor	79	64.3	13	72.2
Associate professor	35	28.4	5	27.8
Assistant professor	8	6.5	0	
Instructor	1	.8	0	
Totals	269		46	
	N = 123		N = 18	

Table 3.71.   *Teachers by rank (and degree) on the staffs of*
(C.25)   *departments without doctoral programs*

BREAKDOWN BY DEGREE	NUMBER	PERCENT
With Ph.D.	2707	40.2
Without Ph.D.	4035	59.8
Total	6742	
		N = 6742

BREAKDOWN BY RANKS	PH.D.'S	PERCENT	NO PH.D.'S	PERCENT
Professors	1126	41.6	131	3.2
Associate professors	844	31.2	410	10.2
Assistant professors	693	25.6	1231	30.5
Instructors	44	1.6	2263	56.1
Total	2707		4035	
	N = 2707		N = 4035	

Table 3.72.   *Rank to which a non-Ph.D. may be either appointed or*
(C.35)   *promoted at an institution without a doctoral program*

RANK	NUMBER OF INSTITUTIONS	PERCENT
Professor	28	7.9
Associate professor	142	39.9
Assistant professor	141	39.6
Instructor	45	12.6
No answer	7	
Total	363	

N = 356

Table 3.73.   *Personnel shared with other departments in nondoctoral*
(C.26)   *English program*

(In tabulating this response, it was assumed that the teaching of drama, speech, and journalism are normal functions of many college English teachers. It was also assumed that giving help in the Humanities courses, Comparative Literature courses, and General Education courses came under the same rubric. The same attitude was taken toward teachers of English who doubled in administrative posts. Sharing was accepted when the field was quite diverse and required some additional training.)

(a) STATE OF SHARING	NUMBER OF INSTITUTIONS	PERCENT
Teachers shared with another department	101	27.8
Teachers not shared	262	72.2
Total	363	

N = 363

(b) DEPARTMENTS SHARING PERSONNEL

DEPARTMENT	NUMBER OF INSTITUTIONS	SIGNIFICANT PERCENT
Anthropology*	4	
Art	3	
Education†	29	28.7
Languages		
"Modern languages"	21	20.8
Classics	23	22.8
French	7	
German	8	
Italian	2	
Spanish	4	
Library	3	
History	9	
Music	3	
Natural science	2	
Philosophy	14	13.9
Religion	7	

* Linguistics(?)   † Teaching of English(?)

N = 101

Table 3.74.   *Enrollment in English departments without a*
(C.7)   *doctoral program*

CATEGORY	NUMBER OF INSTITUTIONS	ENROLLMENT
Undergraduate required courses	352	434,271
Advanced undergraduate courses	352	155,799
Total		590,070*

* Since there are 6742 teachers of English reported, these figures suggest a student–faculty ratio of about eighty-seven to
one.

Table 3.75.   *Increase or decrease in English majors as reported by*
(C.9, 10)   *chairmen of departments without doctoral programs*

(a) Total number of majors as reported by 351 chairmen   38,624*

* Assuming that these students would probably be taught by
professors and associate professors, the student–teacher ratio is
about eight to one.

(b) Change in English Majors since 1964

CATEGORY	NUMBER OF INSTITUTIONS	PERCENT
No change	91	31.8
Decrease (average of 14.7% or total of 192 students)	29	10.1
Increase (average of 38.6% or total of 4904 students)	166	58.0
No answer	77	
Total	363	

N = 286

Table 3.76. *Increase or decrease in general English enrollment at*
(C.8)   *institutions without a doctoral program*

CATEGORY	NUMBER OF INSTITUTIONS	PERCENT
No change	90	26.9
Decrease (average of 15%; data on students insufficient)	22	6.6
Increase (percentage data insufficient; number of students 20,322)	223	66.6
No answer	28	
Total	363	

N = 335

Table 3.77. *Weekly teaching schedule of departments without*
(C.22)   *doctoral programs*

HOURS PER WEEK	NUMBER OF INSTITUTIONS	PERCENT
6 to 9	54	15.1
10 to 11	51	14.2
12 to 14	214	59.8
15 to 16	39	10.9
No answer	5	
	363	

N = 358

Tabulations for Chapter 4

Table 4.1.   *Number of college majors who have gone on to study*
(C.15)   *for the Ph.D. since 1961*

Number of institutions responding	265
Number of students sent to graduate school	4131

(This is an average of c.15 students per reporting college)

Table 4.2.   *Attitude of college majors toward earning the*
(C.17)   *Ph.D. in English*

CATEGORY	NUMBER OF INSTITUTIONS	PERCENT
Increasing	229	68.6
Decreasing	9	2.7
Steady	96	28.7
No answer	29	
Total	363	

N = 334

Table 4.3.   *Policies of college chairmen about encouraging majors*
(C.17)   *to earn graduate degrees*

RESPONSE	NUMBER OF INSTITUTIONS	PERCENT
To earn the M.A. but not the Ph.D.	27	7.4
To earn the Ph.D. but not the M.A.	12	3.3
To earn both degrees	317	87.3
To earn neither	1	.3
No answer	6	1.7
	363	

N = 363

Table 4.4.   *Census of colleges that have programs to prepare*
(C.18)   *majors for graduate study in English*

CATEGORY	NUMBER OF INSTITUTIONS	PERCENT
Have a program	256	70.5
Have no program	107	29.5
Total	363	

N = 363

Table 4.5.   *Policy of college chairmen and their colleagues about*
(C.20)   *referring their departmental major to their own*
                 graduate departments

CATEGORY	NUMBER OF INSTITUTIONS	PERCENT
Refer them	68	19.3
Do not refer them	285	80.7
No answer	10	
Total	363	

N = 353

Table 4.6.   *Graduate departments to which college departments have*
(C.14)   *sent at least one student during 1964 and 1965*

INSTITUTION	NUMBER OF COLLEGES REPORTING	INSTITUTION	NUMBER OF COLLEGES REPORTING
Alabama	4	California (Irvine)	2
Arizona	9	California (Los Angeles)	11
Arkansas	25	California (Riverside)	3
Auburn	8	California (Santa Barbara)	2
Boston	8	California (San Diego)	2
Bowling Green	5	California (Southern)	8
Brandeis	5	Catholic University	5
Brown	17	Chicago	33
Bryn Mawr	4	Cincinnati	3
California (Berkeley)	29	Claremont	4
California (Davis)	4	Colorado	5

INSTITUTION	NUMBER OF COLLEGES REPORTING	INSTITUTION	NUMBER OF COLLEGES REPORTING
Columbia	32	Notre Dame	12
Connecticut	7	North Carolina	41
Cornell	13	Northwestern	22
Delaware	1	Occidental	1
Denver	2	Ohio University	8
Duke	21	Ohio State	16
Duquesne	3	Oklahoma	7
Emory	13	Oregon	8
Florida University	13	Pacific	1
Florida State	3	Peabody	3
Fordham	10	Pennsylvania University	26
Georgia	6	Pennsylvania State	10
Harvard	35	Princeton	6
Illinois University	30	Purdue	14
Illinois (Northern)	1	Rice	4
Illinois (Southern)	15	Rochester	8
Indiana	41	Rutgers	7
Iowa	29	St. Louis	3
Johns Hopkins	11	South Carolina	3
Kansas University	28	Stanford	25
Kansas State	3	Syracuse	10
Kent State	5	Temple	6
Kentucky	5	Tennessee	15
Lehigh	4	Texas Christian	7
Louisiana	10	Texas University	16
Loyola (Chicago)	7	Texas Tech.	2
Maryland	13	Tufts	3
Massachusetts	6	Tulane	11
Miami (Ohio)	5	Utah	2
Michigan University	25	Vanderbilt	22
Michigan State	12	Virginia	26
Minnesota	25	Wayne	5
Mississippi	4	Washington University (St. Louis)	1
Missouri	8		
Nebraska	13	Washington University (Seattle)	22
Nevada	1		
New Mexico	5	Western Reserve	6
New York University	27	Wisconsin	57
SUNY (Harpur)	8	Wyoming	2
SUNY (Buffalo)	3	Yale	32
SUNY (Stonybrook)	2		

Table 4.7.   Average and median number of English majors who have
(A.8)   been graduated by departments with doctoral programs in
             1966*

CATEGORY	NUMBER OF MAJORS
Average	105
Median	94
Range	0 to 366

* No answer from ten respondents.

Table 4.8.   Number of English majors who have been graduated by
(A.9)   departments with doctoral programs in 1966, and who are
             continuing graduate study*

CATEGORY	NUMBER OF MAJORS
Average	23.8
Median	24.0
Range	5 to 110

* No answer from 31 respondents.

Table 4.9.   Policy of all graduate professors toward their under-
(B.11)   graduates who express a wish to take a doctorate

RESPONSE	NUMBER OF RESPONDENTS	PERCENT
Urge them to remain with the department	178	15.9
Advise them to go to another department	787	70.5
"Depends"	55	4.9
Other answers*	96	8.6
No answer	54	
	1170	

N = 1116

* "We do not allow them to take three degrees, no policy, both,
I have no contact with undergraduates, should go elsewhere
if they can, give them the facts, and so forth."

Table 4.10.
(A.6)

Source (by approximate percentage) of graduate students in doctoral departments in 1966–1967

SOURCES	AVERAGE PERCENT	MEDIAN PERCENT	RANGE
Home university	18.1	15	0 to 80%
Another university	38.2	38	0 to 95%
College of 1000+	28.0	26	0 to 75%
College of −999	13.8	10	0 to 85%
Foreign institution	3.1	2	0 to 25%

Table 4.11.
(A.7)

Areas (arranged by rank according to effort) in which departments with doctoral programs recruit graduate students

| | RANK | | | |
AREAS	FIRST	SECOND	THIRD	TOTAL
Home university	3	8	36	47
Regionally	15	30	5	50
Nationally	40	10	7	57

Table 4.12.
(A.7)

Means employed for recruiting graduate students

MEANS	NUMBER OF RESPONDENTS	PERCENT
Visit colleges in the vicinity, either personally or with a team	11	12.5
Send out flyers, brochures, and so forth	56	63.6
Depend on the graduate school announcements	3	3.4
Write to regional college chairmen for nominations	11	12.5
Cooperative effort with colleges in the region	1	1.1
Depend on our alumni	5	5.7
Do not recruit	25	28.4

N = 88

Table 4.13.   *Means of selecting applicants for graduate study*
(A.16)

MEANS	NUMBER OF RESPONDENTS	PERCENT
University admissions office	7*	7.9
Graduate dean	11*	12.5
Departmental director of graduate studies or chairman	37†	42.0
Departmental committee	49	55.7
By all graduate teachers in the department	5	5.7
By other means	7	8.0

N = 88

* In all these cases, the chairman or the committee usually has the right of veto.
† In these cases the committee or the graduate teachers sometimes have the right to veto.

Table 4.14.   *Indices (marked in order of preference) considered when the dossier of the graduate applicant is scrutinized*

(a) BY THE CHAIRMAN OR DIRECTOR OF GRADUATE STUDIES (A.17)

GENERAL CATEGORIES	1	2	3	4	5	6	7	8	9	TOTALS
Whole academic record	17	28	18	11	4	3	2	0	0	83
Record in English	61	14	4	6	1	0	0	0	0	86
Record in ancient or modern languages	0	3	6	7	16	12	5	1	0	50
GRE score	6	15	20	14	11	2	4	0	0	72
Letters from professors	5	16	21	20	9	7	1	0	0	79
Students' letters or submitted papers	1	2	2	6	7	5	12	6	0	41
Students' extracurricular honors	0	1	0	2	2	4	7	11	0	27
Source of previous degrees	5	7	12	13	13	12	1	1	0	64
Other factors	0	2	1	0	0	0	0	0	0	3

(b) BY THE GRADUATE PROFESSORS (B.12)

RANKS

GENERAL CATEGORIES	1	2	3	4	5	6	7	8	9	TOTALS
General academic record	304	203	144	93	68	30	4	0	0	846
Record in English	375	234	116	76	45	7	4	1	0	858
Record in ancient and/or modern languages	14	55	76	96	121	130	70	15	4	581
Source of earlier degrees	78	154	191	154	115	60	23	7	1	783
GRE score	77	114	159	153	108	66	38	11	0	726
Letters from former teachers	118	156	196	157	96	58	17	6	3	807
Students' letters or submitted essays	12	19	27	46	46	56	138	54	4	402
Students' extracurricular honors	1	0	6	8	13	33	60	174	10	305
Other factors	14	5	9	2	7	9	2	3	11	62

Table 4.15. *Policy of departments with doctoral programs on*
(A.13) *quotas of graduate students*

CATEGORY	NUMBER OF RESPONDENTS	PERCENT
Have a quota	26	29.9
Do not have a quota	61	70.1
No answer	1	
Total	88	

N = 87

Table 4.16.
(A.14)

Size of quotas in departments limiting graduate enrollment

QUOTA	NUMBER OF RESPONDENTS
25	1
35	2
41	1
45	2
50	3
65	1
85	1
90	1
95	1
100	2
125	2
130	1
140	1
175	1
190	1
200	1
250	1
350	1
	24
No answer	2
Total	26

Table 4.17.
(A.10–12)

Total number of doctoral students as reported by seventy-five graduate departments (no answer or no students from thirteen)

NUMBER	AVERAGE	MEDIAN	RANGE
11,595 students	154.6	111.8	0 to 685

N = 75

Table 4.18.
(A.10)

Total number of full-time doctoral students reported by seventy-five graduate departments (no information from thirteen)

NUMBER	AVERAGE	MEDIAN	RANGE
4548 students*	60.6	38	0 to 325

* 56.3% of all doctoral students.

Table 4.19. (A.11)   *Total number of part-time doctoral students reported by seventy-four graduate departments (no information from fourteen)*

NUMBER	AVERAGE	MEDIAN	RANGE
5875 students*	80.8	56	0 to 685

* 43.7% of all doctoral students.

Table 4.20. (A.12)   *Total number of students not in the above categories who are considered to be doctoral candidates by seventy graduate departments (no information from eighteen)*

NUMBER	AVERAGE	MEDIAN	RANGE
1172 students*	16.1	12	0 to 60

* 10.1% of all doctoral students.

Table 4.21. (B.14)   *Attitude of graduate professors on the quality of the present-day graduate students as compared to those of their own graduate days*

CATEGORY	NUMBER	PERCENT
Superior	208	19.8
Inferior	265	25.2
About the same	577	55.0
No answer	120	
	1170	

N = 1050

Table 4.22.   *Specific estimates of graduate professors about the*
(B.15)   *preparation of current graduate students*

CATEGORY	ANTE-1955		POST-1955		NON-PH.D.'S		TOTALS	
	BETTER	WORSE	BETTER	WORSE	BETTER	WORSE	BETTER	WORSE
Knowledge of English and American Literature	157	94	60	100	15	12	232	206
Classical languages	19	200	3	117	0	28	22	345
Modern languages	106	113	40	77	7	9	153	199
Humanistic areas	148	82	48	93	12	11	208	186
Other* areas	20	15	15	16	0	2	35	33

* Linguistics, critical theory, better; philosophy, music, science, worse.

Table 4.23.   *Specific estimate of graduate professors about the*
(B.15)   *characteristics and skills of current graduate students*

CATEGORY	ANTE-1955		POST-1955		NON-PH.D.'S		TOTALS	
	BETTER	WORSE	BETTER	WORSE	BETTER	WORSE	BETTER	WORSE
Intelligent, careful reading	157	59	59	65	12	9	228	133
Precise, lucid writing	58	137	18	106	4	14	80	257
Intellectual curiosity	114	73	53	75	10	10	177	158
Powers of synthesis or analysis	120	83	41	69	12	6	173	158
Critical taste	127	50	45	54	6	6	178	110
Other qualities*	12	13	4	11	0	0	16	24

* Lack of comprehension, better knowledge of contemporary literature, intellectual sloppiness, knowledge of critical techniques, mathematics, social relations, economics, life and self, great fluency in professional jargon, more ambitious and competitive, no responsibility, conviction, or drive.

Table 4.24. *The approximate attrition rate of departments*
(A.18)   *with a doctoral program*

CATEGORY	NO ATTRITION	UNDER 10%	10% TO 25%	25% TO 50%	OVER 50%
Before the M.A. or its equivalent*	2(2.5%)	39(48.8%)	32(40.0%)	6(7.5%)	1(1.3%)

N = 80

CATEGORY	NO ATTRITION	UNDER 10%	10% TO 25%	25% TO 50%	OVER 50%
After the M.A. or its equivalent†	1(1.3%)	20(26.0%)	31(40.3%)	20(26.0%)	5(6.5%)

N = 77

* No estimate from eight departments.
† No estimate from eleven departments.

Table 4.25. *Important factors that produce the attrition among*
(A.19)   *doctoral candidates, as indicated by chairmen of*
      graduate departments

CATEGORY	NUMBER OF RESPONDENTS	PERCENT
Marriage	21	23.9
Insufficient funds	57	64.8
Domestic problems	20	22.7
Loss of interest	40	45.5
Illness	13	14.8
Poor preparation	32	36.4
No real ability	37	42.0
Other reasons*	16	18.2

N = 88

* Suggestion of the department, moving away, draft, emotional problems, lazy, not enough time, good job offers, and so forth.

Table 4.26. *Important factors, arranged in order of valence by*
(B.13) *graduate professors, resulting in attrition among*
doctoral candidates

CATEGORY	FIRST	SECOND	THIRD	TOTAL
Domestic problems	51	152	93	296
Lack of funds	132	136	92	360
Loss of interest	156	181	97	434
Lack of physical and/or emotional force	225	217	89	531
Poor preparation	86	163	86	335
No ability	242	157	93	492
Other reasons	65	29	19	113

Table 4.27. *Point at which chairmen of graduate departments or*
(A.20) *directors of graduate study become certain that a*
doctoral candidate will not earn a degree

CATEGORY	NUMBER OF RESPONDENTS	PERCENT
At the end of his first year	45	52.9
Before the preliminary	16	18.8
At the preliminary	20	23.5
When he submits the first draft of his thesis	1	1.2
Other answers*	3	3.5
No answer	3	
	88	

N = 88

* At the qualifying examination; when he has almost finished
his courses.

Table 4.28.   *Point at which graduate professors become certain that*
(B.21)   *a doctoral candidate will not earn a degree*

CATEGORY	NUMBER OF RESPONDENTS	PERCENT
At the end of his first year	362	35.5
Before the preliminary	237	23.2
At the preliminary	327	32.0
When he submits the first draft of his dissertation	31	3.0
At some other time*	64	6.3
Not answered	149	
	1170	

$$N = 1021$$

* M.A. oral, first term's end, second year, and so forth.

Tabulations for Chapter 5

Table 5.1.   *Number of required courses for doctoral candidates*
(A.21)

	REQUIRED COURSES							
	0	1	2	3	4	5	6	TOTAL
Number of departments	14	20	29	18	3	3	1	88
Percent	15.9	22.7	33.0	20.5		7.9		

Table 5.2.   *Courses required by graduate departments*
(A.21)

COURSES	NUMBER OF DEPARTMENTS	PERCENT
Criticism	10	13.5
Methods of research, bibliography	46	62.2
Modern English, Linguistics	24	32.4
Old English and Literature	51	68.9
Middle English and Literature	20	27.0
History of the English Language	23	31.1
Methods of Teaching English	5	6.8

$$N = 78$$

Table 5.3.   *Graduate professors who feel that specialized courses*
(B.27)   *in Linguistics and early literature should be required*
                        of students in modern areas

SUBJECT	NUMBER OF RESPONDENTS	PERCENT
Old English Literature	563	51.1
Middle English Literature	751	68.2
Modern English Grammar	649	58.9
None of them	29	2.6
No answer	69	

N = 1101

Table 5.4.   *Required courses taken by recent recipients of the*
(D.19)   *doctorate*

CATEGORY	NUMBER OF RESPONDENTS	PERCENT
No courses required	448	23.9
Courses required	1424	76.1
No answer	8	

N = 1872

Table 5.5.   *Required courses taken by recent recipients*
(D.19)

SUBJECT	NUMBER OF RESPONDENTS	PERCENT
Old English	1124	78.9
Middle English	525	36.9
Modern English	51	3.6
Bibliography	608	42.7
History of the Language	678	47.6
History of Criticism or Critical Methods	103	7.2
Methods of Teaching English	21	1.5

N = 1424

Table 5.6.   *Ultimate value of courses as stated by recent recipients*
(D.20)   *of the doctorate*

| | NUMBER OF RESPONDENTS | | | |
CATEGORY	MALE	FEMALE	TOTAL	PERCENT
In passing the preliminaries	860	182	1042	55.4
Writing the dissertation	206	51	257	13.7
Teaching	850	210	1060	56.4
Other reasons*	303	69	372	19.8

N = 1880

* Most of these reasons arise from some personal satisfaction.

Table 5.7.   *Number of languages required of recent recipients*
(D.21)

NUMBER OF LANGUAGES	NUMBER OF RESPONDENTS	PERCENT
1	27	1.4
2	1216	64.9
3	613	32.7
4	18	1.0
No answer	6	
	1880	

N = 1880

Table 5.8.   *Languages known or learned by recent recipients*
(D.22)

CATEGORY	NUMBER OF RESPONDENTS	PERCENT
Knew required languages	536	28.6
Learned one or more languages	1338	71.4
No answer	6	
Total	1880	

N = 1874

Table 5.9.   *Number of languages learned by recent recipients*
(D.22)   *of the doctorate*

NUMBER OF LANGUAGES LEARNED	NUMBER OF RESPONDENTS	LANGUAGES
1	1007	(1007)
2	295	(590)
3	36	(108)
Total	1338	1705

Table 5.10.   *Languages learned by recent recipients*
(D.22)

LANGUAGE	FREQUENCY	PERCENT
German	939	55.1
French	438	25.7
Latin	210	12.3
Italian	103	6.0
Greek	11	.6
Dutch	1	—
Polish	1	—
Swedish	1	—
Russian	1	—
Total	1705	

N = 1705

Table 5.11.   *Use of learned foreign languages by recent recipients*
(D.23)   *in graduate courses*

	NUMBER OF RESPONDENTS			
CATEGORY	MALE	FEMALE	TOTAL	PERCENT
Used them	766	178	944	50.7
Did not use them	784	135	919	49.3
No answer	14	3	17	
Total	1564	316	1880	

N = 1863

Table 5.12.   *Use of foreign languages in their dissertations*
(D.24)   *by recent recipients*

| | NUMBER OF RESPONDENTS | | | |
CATEGORY	MALE	FEMALE	TOTAL	PERCENT
Used them	718	152	870	47.2
Did not use them	815	158	973	52.8
No answer	31	6	37	
Total	1564	316	1880	

N = 1843

Table 5.13.   *Use of foreign languages by recent recipients since*
(D.25)   *taking the doctorate*

| | NUMBER OF RESPONDENTS | | | |
CATEGORY	MALE	FEMALE	TOTAL	PERCENT
In teaching	536	112	648	34.5
In research	853	150	1003	53.4
For leisure reading	637	142	779	41.4
Not at all	409	80	489	26.0

N = 1880

Table 5.14.   *Attitude of heads of doctoral departments toward*
(A.29)   *foreign language requirement*

CATEGORY	NUMBER OF RESPONDENTS	PERCENT
Favor it	86	98.9
Do not favor it	1	1.1
No answer	1	—
Total	88	

N = 87

Table 5.15.   *Attitude of chairmen on the value of language study*
(A.29)

CATEGORY	NUMBER OF RESPONDENTS	PERCENT
Languages are research tools	64	72.7
Languages are an essential of education	76	86.3

Table 5.16.   *Attitude of graduate professors toward foreign*
(B.26)   *language requirement*

CATEGORY	NUMBER OF RESPONDENTS	PERCENT
Favor it	1115	97.2
Do not favor it	32	2.8
No answer	23	
Total	1170	

N = 1147

Table 5.17.   *Attitude of graduate professors on the value of*
(B.26)   *language study*

CATEGORY	NUMBER OF RESPONDENTS	PERCENT
Languages are research tools	804	72.1
Are essentials of education	876	78.6
Other answers	20	1.8
No answer	13	

N = 1157

Table 5.18.   *Number of times during 1965–1966 that graduate*
(B.29)   *professors gave assignments in foreign language texts*

NUMBER OF TIMES	NUMBER OF RESPONDENTS
0	735
1	75
2	84
3	55
4	29
5	26
6	11
7	1
8	4
9	1
10	12
12	6
15	3
16	1
18	2
20	7
24	1
25	3
30	3
Not codable	26
No answer	85
	1170

Table 5.19.   *Number of times during 1965–1966 that graduate*
(B.29)   *professors either heard a report or read a term paper*
              in which a graduate student used a foreign text

NUMBER OF TIMES	NUMBER OF RESPONDENTS
0	470
1	90
2	123
3	90
4	54
5	51
6	22
7	11
8	13
9	3
10	39
11	1
12	14
13	1
14	1
15	9
16	1
17	2
20	13
25	5
30	1
35	2
50	3
Not codable	74
Not answered	77
	1170

Table 5.20.   *Number of times during 1965–1966 that graduate*
(B.29)   *professors themselves read one of their required*
                 foreign languages

NUMBER OF TIMES	NUMBER OF RESPONDENTS
0	178
1	65
2	87
3	81
4	37
5	59
6	32
7	8
8	5
9	6
10	72
11	4
12	20
13	5
14	1
15	19
17	3
18	2
20	45
22	1
23	2
25	9
28	2
30	12
35	2
40	5
50	22
80	1
88	1
100	22
120	2
130	2
135	7
200	4
250	1
300	1
365	4
550	1
1000	2
Not codable	242
No answer	96
	1170

Table 5.21.   Attitude of chairmen of doctoral departments toward
(A.29)   one language learned well instead of the current
                 two language requirement

CATEGORY	NUMBER OF RESPONDENTS	PERCENT
Favor it	50	58.8
Do not favor it	35	41.2
No answer	3	
Total	88	

N = 85

Table 5.22.   Attitude of graduate professors toward one language
(B.26)   learned well instead of the current two language
                 requirement*

CATEGORY	NUMBER OF RESPONDENTS	PERCENT
Favor it	559	50.7
Do not favor it	543	49.3
Not codable	27	
No answer	41	
Total	1170	

N = 1102

* Here is one of the few real differences between the ante-1955 and post-1955 groups on this issue. The ante-1955 group voted 45.9% "yes" and 54.1% "no"; the post-1955 group voted 56.3% "yes" and 43.7% "no."

Table 5.23. *Percentage of graduate students dropped after failing the*
(A.26) *preliminary, as reported by chairmen of doctoral programs* *

PERCENT	NUMBER OF RESPONDENTS
0	9
1 or fewer	5
5	14
5 to 10	4
10	12
10 to 15	5
20 to 25	5
30	2
50	1
75	1
90 to 100	5
Not codable	3
Not answered	22
	88

* The responding departments indicate about 212 students a year, or an average of 3.4 students for the sixty-three responding departments. The actual number is probably greater.

Table 5.24. *Nature of the preliminary examination in reporting*
(A.22) *departments*

CATEGORY	NUMBER OF RESPONDENTS	PERCENT
Oral	9	10.5
Written	29	33.7
Both	48	55.8
No answer	2	
	88	

N = 86

Table 5.25.   *Length of the oral examinations*
(A.22)

HOURS	NUMBER OF RESPONDENTS
1	1
1½	1
2	4
2½	1
3	2
	9

Table 5.26.   *Length of the written examinations*
(A.22)

HOURS	NUMBER OF RESPONDENTS
3	1
4	1
6	8
9	1
10	2
12	5
15	4
16	2
18	1
20	1
48	1
Not codable	2
	29

Average: 11.9 hours
Median: 12 hours

Table 5.27. *Length of the oral and written examination*
(A.22)

HOURS	RESPONDENTS: ORAL EXAMINATION	RESPONDENTS: WRITTEN EXAMINATION
1	6	0
2	27	0
3	4	1˙
4	37*	1
5		1
6		8
8		6
9		3
12		5
14		1
15		3
16		2
18		5
20		1
		37†
Not codable		11
		48

* Average: 1.9 hours.
† Average: 10.7 hours. Median: 9 hours.

Table 5.28. *Number of fields required for the preliminary*
(A.22)

NUMBER OF FIELDS	RESPONDENTS	PERCENT
1	1	1.7
3	7	11.9
4	13	22.0
5	11	18.6
6	3	5.1
7	3	5.1
8	1	1.7
9	20	33.9
Not codable	29	
	88	

$N = 59$

Table 5.29.   *Fields in which recent recipients of the doctorate*
(D.26)   *were examined at their preliminary*

NUMBER OF FIELDS REQUIRED	CANDIDATES EXAMINED	PERCENT
1	8	.4
2	41	2.3
3	197	11.0
4	299	16.7
5	270	15.1
6	145	8.1
7–9 fields in English and American Literature	616	34.5
7 to "all" in English Literature	174	9.4
Modern Literature only	5	.3
American Studies	26	1.5
Medieval Studies	5	.3
No answer	94	
Total	1880	

N = 1786

Table 5.30.   *Choice of fields permitted recent recipients for their*
(D.27)   *preliminary examination*

CATEGORY	NUMBER OF RESPONDENTS	PERCENT
Choice allowed	1176	65.5
No choice allowed	620	34.5
No answer	84	
Total	1880	

N = 1796

Table 5.31.   *How chairmen assume graduate students prepare*
(A.24)   *for preliminary examination*

ANSWERS	NUMBER OF RESPONDENTS	PERCENT
Consults advisor or chairmen	22	26.5
Uses reading list or syllabus	11	13.3
Has access to old examinations	41	49.4
Is prepared by his courses	3	3.6
Department's descriptive brochure	7	8.4
Department's sample examination	9	10.8
Grapevine	13	15.7
I do not know	9	10.8
No answer	5	

N = 83

Table 5.32.   *How recent recipients of the doctorate prepared for*
(D.28)   *preliminary examinations*

| | NUMBER OF RESPONDENTS | | | |
	MALES	FEMALES	TOTAL	PERCENT
Sought advice of professors	689	147	836	44.5
Sought advice of students	895	142	1037	55.2
Used department syllabus	449	95	544	28.9
Used department examination files	666	122	788	41.9
Studied course notes	1006	246	1252	66.6
Others "Read! Read!"	107	27	134	7.1

N = 1880

Table 5.33.   *Whether or not the examiners on the preliminary*
(A.23)   *committee have taught the student being examined*

CATEGORY	NUMBER OF RESPONDENTS	PERCENT
Yes	8 ⎫	
Usually	44 ⎬	59.1
No	36	40.9
	88	

N = 88

Table 5.34.   *Number of times a student may fail his preliminary*
(A.25)   *examinations*

NUMBER OF TIMES	NUMBER OF RESPONDENTS	PERCENT
1	59	69.4
2	19	22.4
"Depends"	2	2.4
"Unspecified"	5	5.9
No answer	3	
Total	88	

$$N = 85$$

Table 5.35.   *Changes possible in this examination, according to*
(A.27)   *chairmen*

	NUMBER OF RESPONDENTS*	
CATEGORY	YES	NO
Eliminate it	1	65
Reduce it in scope	25	41
Increase it in scope	3	45

* The eighty-eight responding chairmen often marked more than one box.

Table 5.36.   *Changes possible in this examination, according to*
(B.24)   *graduate professors*

CATEGORY	NUMBER OF RESPONDENTS				
	YES	PERCENT	NO	PERCENT	
Eliminate it	46	6.0	719	94.0	$N = 765$
Reduce it in scope	338	45.1	411	54.9	$N = 749$
Increase it in scope	236	36.7	407	63.3	$N = 643$
No answer 11					

Table 5.37.   *Suggestions of chairmen of graduate departments for*
(A.28)   *improving the preliminary examination*

SUGGESTIONS	NUMBER OF RESPONDENTS
A standardized objective test	1
Reduce number of fields	19
Reduce time	4
Test for skill not knowledge	1
Omit minor	1
Reduce comprehensive and add a minor	1
Total	27

Table 5.38.   *Success of recent recipients on their first attempt*
(D.29)   *at the preliminary examinations*

CATEGORY	NUMBER OF RESPONDENTS			PERCENT
	MALES	FEMALES	TOTAL	
Passed	1313	278	1591	86.3
Failed	223	30	253	13.7
No answer	28	8	36	
Total	1564	316	1880	

N = 1844

Table 5.39.   *Opinions of recent recipients of the doctorate on the*
(D.30)   *value of the preliminary examination*

CATEGORY	NUMBER OF RESPONDENTS					
	MALES	PERCENT	FEMALES	PERCENT	TOTAL	PERCENT
They are valuable	1216	81.7	260	87.8	1476	82.7
They are not valuable	144	9.7	18	6.1	162	9.1
They are doubtful in value	128	8.6	18	6.1	146	8.2
No answer	76		20		96	
Total	1564		316		1880	

N = 1488   N = 296   N = 1784

Tabulations for Chapter 6

Table 6.1. (D.36)   *Length of dissertations submitted by recent recipients of the doctorate*

	NUMBER OF RESPONDENTS			
LENGTH	MALES	FEMALES	TOTAL	PERCENT
150 pages or shorter	121	33	154	8.3
151–300 pages	820	175	995	53.4
301–500 pages	513	86	599	32.1
Over 500 pages	97	19	116	6.2
No answer	13	3	16	
Total	1564	316	1880	

N = 1864

Table 6.2. (D.31)   *Reasons given for selecting the area of their dissertation by recent recipients of the doctorate*

	NUMBER OF RESPONDENTS			
CATEGORY	MALE	FEMALE	TOTAL	PERCENT
Attractive	1218	249	1467	78.0
Good professor	871	193	1064	56.6
Superior opportunity for research	366	85	451	24.0
Good future for specialist	301	47	348	18.5

N = 1880

Table 6.3. (D.32)   *How recent recipients of the doctorate found the subject of their dissertations*

	NUMBER OF RESPONDENTS			
CATEGORY	MALE	FEMALE	TOTAL	PERCENT
Found it myself	1026	175	1201	64.1
Professor proposed it	182	42	224	11.9
Both	354	96	450	24.0
No answer	2	3	5	
Total	1564	316	1880	

N = 1875

Table 6.4.   *Success of recent recipients of the doctorate with their*
(D.33)   *first dissertation subject*

	NUMBER OF RESPONDENTS			
CATEGORY	MALE	FEMALE	TOTAL	PERCENT
Successful	1295	262	1557	83.2
Unsuccessful	261	54	315	16.8
No answer	8	0	8	
Total	1564	316	1880	

N = 1872

Table 6.5.   *Assistance given to recent recipients of the doctorate*
(D.35)   *by their dissertation directors*

	NUMBER OF RESPONDENTS			
CATEGORY	MALE	FEMALE	TOTAL	PERCENT
As much as needed	881	197	1078	57.3
Very little	561	96	657	34.9
Not at all	122	23	145	7.9
Total	1564	316	1880	

N = 1880

Table 6.6.   *Attitude of recent recipients toward work required*
(D.37)   *to compose the dissertation*

	NUMBER OF RESPONDENTS					
CATEGORY	MALE	PERCENT	FEMALE	PERCENT	TOTAL	PERCENT
Exciting and absorbing	1048	67.0	243	76.9	1291	68.7
Painful but necessary	256	16.4	30	9.5	286	15.2
Useful but tedious	394	25.2	61	19.3	455	24.2
Serves no useful purpose	37	2.4	3	.9	40	2.1
Other answers	22	1.4	2	.6	24	1.3

N = 1564   N = 316   N = 1880

Table 6.7. *Opinion of graduate professors on value of dissertations*
(B.30)   *read by them*

NUMBER OF RESPONDENTS[*]

EVALUA-TION IN PERCENT	SUBSTANTIAL CONTRIBUTIONS	ADEQUATE BUT NOT TOO IMPORTANT	OF LITTLE VALUE
0	109	22	158
5	46	5	13
10	156	22	105
15	24	11	28
20	77	28	76
25	89	41	80
30	19	25	38
35	5	15	7
40	30	90	38
45	2	16	5
50	83	172	61
55	0	5	3
60	19	75	4
65	2	14	6
70	4	36	9
75	5	53	9
80	3	50	6
85	2	1	5
90	8	21	10
95	0	2	3
100	6	43	3

[*] No answer by 221 respondents.

Table 6.8. *Attitudes of departmental chairmen on substitutions*
(A.30)   *for the traditional doctoral dissertation*

CATEGORY	NUMBER OF RESPONDENTS	PERCENT
A work of half the size	60	75.9
Several publishable papers	30	38.0
By a survey or digest of scholarship in some area	10	12.7
By a series of lectures for undergraduates	2	2.5
By something else[*]	7	8.9
No answer	9	

N = 79

[*] Not half, but fewer pages; one publishable paper; bibliographies; a piece of writing that shows aptitude for scholarship and criticism.

Table 6.9.   *Attitudes of graduate professors on substitutions for the*
(B.31)   *traditional doctoral dissertation*

CATEGORY	NUMBER OF RESPONDENTS	PERCENT
A work of half the size	958	88.4
Several publishable papers	603	55.6
A survey of scholarship	226	20.8
A series of lectures for undergraduates	69	6.4
Something else*	107	9.9
Let it alone	29	2.7
No answer	86	

N = 1084

* Editions, handbooks, bibliographies, public lectures, course
syllabus and plans, research on the teaching of English, literary
essays, creative work (novel, poetry, and so forth).

Table 6.10.   *Opinion of the recent recipients of the doctorate on the*
(D.51)   *substitution of several publishable articles for the*
traditional dissertation

CATEGORY	MALE	PERCENT	FEMALE	PERCENT	TOTAL	PERCENT
			NUMBER OF RESPONDENTS			
Yes	932	67.6	183	63.1	1115	66.8
No	447	32.4	107	36.9	554	33.2
No answer	185		26		211	
Total	1564		316		1880	

N = 1379   N = 290   N = 1669

Table 6.11.   *Whether or not recent recipients were required*
(D.40)   *to take a final oral on their thesis*

CATEGORY	MALE	FEMALE	TOTAL	PERCENT
	NUMBER OF RESPONDENTS			
Yes	1308	281	1589	85.0
No	248	33	281	15.0
No answer	8	2	10	
Total	1564	316	1880	

N = 1870

Table 6.12.   *Attitude of recent recipients toward the final oral*
(D.41)   *examination*

CATEGORY	NUMBER OF RESPONDENTS	PERCENT
A real defense	561	35.3
A sustained examination of competence	336	21.1
Neither	692	43.5
No answer	291	
Total	1880	

N = 1589

Table 6.13.   *Attitude of recent recipients of the doctor's degree*
(D.43)   *toward their graduate program*

CATEGORY	NUMBER OF RESPONDENTS	PERCENT
No complaints	563	30.1
Complaints	1307	69.9
No answer	10	
Total	1880	

N = 1870

Table 6.14.   *Most valuable aspects of the doctoral program in order*
(D.42)   *of importance according to the judgment of the*
                      recent recipients

			RANK				
CATEGORY	FIRST	PER-CENT	SEC-OND	PER-CENT	THIRD	PER-CENT	TOTAL
Courses	608	32.4	363	19.3	262	13.9	1233 (65.6%)
Independent study	408	21.7	338	18.0	223	11.9	969 (51.5%)
Dissertation	327	17.4	440	23.4	364	19.4	1131 (60.2%)
Teaching	118	6.3	257	13.7	186	9.9	561 (29.8%)
Association with professors	177	9.4	308	16.4	295	15.7	80 (41.5%)
Association with other students	96	5.1	217	11.5	236	12.6	549 (29.2%)
Other reasons	18	1.0	15	.8	21	1.1	54 (2.9%)

N = 1880

Table 6.15.   *Subjects of complaint about the doctoral program*
(D.43)   *by recent recipients of the doctorate*

SUBJECT OF COMPLAINT	FREQUENCY	PERCENT
No guidance	64	4.9
Attitude of department (narrow, pickish, non-literary, pedantic, autocratic, scornful, and so forth)	56	4.3
Either too many courses or too many units required	108	8.3
Too many fields to cover	24	1.8
Undergraduates in graduate courses	16	1.2
Seminars (unrelated, boring, stupid topics)	56	4.3
Courses (badly taught, dull)	256	19.6
Old and/or Middle English useless	188	14.4
History of Language and/or Philology useless	144	11.0
Bibliography course useless	60	4.6
Language examinations (too many languages, no choice of languages, better to learn one, all useless)	424	32.4
German particularly useless	56	4.3
Prelims of no value	144	11.0
Dissertation useless	132	10.1
Director of dissertation incredible	20	1.5
Final oral of no value	60	4.6

N = 1307

Table 6.16.   *Attitude of recent recipients toward the worth of their*
(D.44)   *doctoral studies*

CATEGORY	MALE	PERCENT	FEMALE	PERCENT	TOTAL	PERCENT
		NUMBER OF RESPONDENTS				
Worth it	1405	89.8	302	95.6	1707	90.8
Not worth it	90	5.8	6	1.9	96	5.1
Do not know	69	4.4	8	2.5	77	4.1
Total	1564		316		1880	

N = 1880

Tabulations for Chapter 7

Table 7.1.   *Attitudes of chairmen of graduate departments on the*
(A.37)   *doctorate as an indication of competence for teaching*

CATEGORY	NUMBER OF RESPONDENTS	PERCENT
Necessary to teach underclassmen	3	3.8
Necessary to teach upperclassmen	34	43.6
Necessary to teach graduate students	77	98.7
No answer	10	

$$N = 78$$

Table 7.2.   *Attitudes of graduate professors on the doctorate as an*
(B.34)   *indication of competence for teaching*

CATEGORY	NUMBER OF RESPONDENTS	PERCENT
Necessary to teach underclassmen	76	7.1
Necessary to teach upperclassmen	430	40.2
Necessary to teach graduate students	1007	94.2
Ph.D. has no value for teaching	63	5.9
No answer	109	

$$N = 1069$$

Table 7.3.   *Attitude of recent recipients of the doctorate on the*
(D.45)   *Ph.D. as an indication of competence for teaching*

CATEGORY	NUMBER OF RESPONDENTS	PERCENT
Necessary to teach underclassmen	84	4.5
Necessary to teach upperclassmen	552	29.4
Necessary to teach graduate students	1545	82.2
No answer	335	

$$N = 1545$$

Table 7.4.   *Graduate professors' characterization of the doctoral*
(B.34)   *training offered by their departments*

CATEGORY	NUMBER OF RESPONDENTS	PERCENT
More specialized than broad	338	32.7
More broad than specialized	648	62.7
A proper balance	48	4.6
No answer	96	
Not codable	40	
	1170	

N = 1034

Table 7.5.   *Graduate professors' characterization of the preparation*
(B.22)   *of their doctoral graduates*

CATEGORY	NUMBER OF RESPONDENTS	PERCENT
Better prepared for teaching than for research	189	17.5
Better prepared for research than teaching	190	17.6
Well prepared for both	699	64.8
No answer	92	
	1170	

N = 1078

Table 7.6.   *Attitude of recent recipients of the doctorate on the*
(D.46)   *value of research in teaching*

CATEGORY	NUMBER OF RESPONDENTS	PERCENT
Research interest makes for better teaching	1178	67.5
Research interest does not make a better teacher	566	32.5
No answer	136	
Total	1880	

N = 1744

Table 7.7.   *Departments permitting students to take doctorate*
(A.34)   *without teaching experience*

CATEGORY	NUMBER OF RESPONDENTS	PERCENT
Some have no experience	28	33.7
All have experience	55	66.3
No answer	5	
Total	88	

N = 83

Table 7.8.   *Departmental provisions in pedagogy for doctoral students*
(A.33)

CATEGORY	NUMBER OF RESPONDENTS	PERCENT
Supervised teaching	72	84.7
A course in pedagogical methods	27	31.8
Other knowledge or experience necessary for teaching underclassmen	17	20.0
No answer	3	

N = 85

Table 7.9.   *Departmental provisions for familiarizing doctoral*
(A.35)   *candidates with the nature of their duties in*
colleges and junior colleges

CATEGORY	NUMBER OF RESPONDENTS	PERCENT
Make provisions	51	59.3
Make no provisions	35	40.7
Yes and no	1	
No answer	1	
Total	88	

N = 86

Table 7.10.   Departmental methods of instructing doctoral candidates
(A.36)   about their college and junior college duties

CATEGORY	NUMBER OF RESPONDENTS	PERCENT
We do it informally; they can talk to us about it; we have an annual meeting with finishing Ph.D.'s and so forth	34	38.6
Occasional formal gatherings with either a lecturer or a panel	6	6.8
A formal course, a noncredit seminar, and so forth	13	14.8
We do nothing or no answer*	35	39.8
	88	

N = 88

* Assumed to be same answer.

Table 7.11.   Chairmen's description of the means by which one of
(A.31)   their doctoral graduates secures a teaching post

CATEGORY	NUMBER OF RESPONDENTS	PERCENT
Our placement bureau	37	43.0
Departmental effort	41	47.7
Major professor's effort	71	82.6
Student's effort	78	90.7
MLA meeting	19	22.1
ADE brochure	2	2.3
Not answered	2	

N = 86

Table 7.12.   *Graduate professors' description of the means by which*
(B.32)   *one of their doctoral graduates secures a teaching post*

CATEGORY	FIRST	SECOND	RANKS THIRD	FOURTH	FIFTH	TOTALS
University's placement bureau	104	242	226	128	0	700
Commercial place-ment bureau	4	10	20	20	54	108
Department's organized effort	226	142	128	14	4	514
Major profes-sor's effort	242	430	190	32	0	894
Student's own effort	432	364	164	42	1	1003

No answer: 62

Table 7.13.   *Chairmen's report on percentage of their Ph.D.'s who*
(A.32)   *secured a teaching post unworthy of their training and*
                  *ability during the last five years**

CATEGORY	NUMBER OF RESPONDENTS	PERCENT
Less than 1%	28	43.0
1 to 10%	16	24.6
10 to 20%	9	13.8
20 to 50%	8	12.3
50 to 100%	4	5.1
No answer	20	
Not codable	3	
Total	88	

N = 65

* These percentages represent about 338 badly placed Ph.D.'s.

Table 7.14.   *Graduate professors' report on percentage of their Ph.D.'s*
(B.33)   *who secured a teaching post unworthy of their training*
                 and ability during the last five years

CATEGORY	NUMBER OF RESPONDENTS	PERCENT
None	329	46.9
5 to 20%	211	30.1
20 to 50%	109	15.5
50 to 75%	16	2.3
75 to 99%	19	2.7
100%	18	2.6
No answer or no students*	468	
Total	1170	

N = 702

* Assumed to be same answer.

Table 7.15.   *Attitude of college chairmen on the employment of*
(C.21)   *former majors who have earned Ph.D.'s*

CATEGORY	NUMBER OF RESPONDENTS	PERCENT
Are inclined to employ them	64	18.4
Are not inclined to employ them	284	81.6
No answer	15	
Total	363	

N = 348

Table 7.16.   *Means used by college chairmen to seek new staff*
(C.33)   *appointees*

RANKS

CATEGORY	FIRST	SECOND	THIRD	FOURTH	FIFTH	SIXTH	SEVENTH	TOTALS
Older graduate departments	123	62	41	22	6	1	0	255
Newer graduate departments	15	42	35	31	23	7	0	153
Teacher's agencies	14	16	16	11	10	18	8	93
AAUP or ADE advertisements	26	41	48	33	13	7	1	169
Direct applications	181	65	50	24	7	2	0	329
MLA, CEA, SMLA and so forth meetings	31	61	54	45	26	11	2	230
Other means*	28	16	26	12	7	0	0	89

* Referrals, friends in graduate departments, write to colleagues, staff suggestions, "grapevine," search committee, ask reliable alumni, direct contact, travel to recruit, follow up on our majors, church agencies, cooperative college agencies, send out the word, sound out former applicants, recruit successful secondary teachers, professional gossip, beat the bushes, advertise, hire wives of prospective staff appointee, encourage our majors to get Ph.D.'s and return.

Table 7.17.   *Qualities and skills taken into account by college*
(C.34)   *chairmen when making appointments*

| | WEIGHT | | |
CATEGORY	MUCH	SOME	LITTLE OR NONE
Teaching skill	335	28	0
Literary talent	30	214	106
Personal attractiveness	83	220	60
Religious interest	36	76	228
General knowledge of English and American Literature	300	63	0
Special knowledge of English and American Literature	192	144	24
Research interest and activity	70	217	68
Administrative ability	0	79	284
Interest in community matters	12	127	219
Broad general culture	198	121	44

N = 363

Table 7.18.   *Estimates of college chairmen on the present doctoral*
(C.44)   *program*

CATEGORY	NUMBER OF RESPONDENTS	PERCENT
Totally satisfactory	10	3.0
Needs some improvement	218	65.1
Needs much improvement	82	24.5
Needs complete overhaul	25	7.5
No answer	28	
Total	363	

N = 335

Appendix: Of the 39 chairmen who, not having Ph.D.'s, answered this
question, the answers were:

Totally satisfactory	1	2.6
Needs some improvement	21	53.8
Needs much improvement	10	25.6
Needs complete overhaul	7	17.9

N = 39

Of the 18 chairmen with Ph.D.'s who thought that the program needs a complete overhaul, the following information serves to explain their reasoning.

ELAPSED TIME (IN YEARS)
BETWEEN THE A.B. AND PH.D.
Average time: 14.1
Median time: 10.0

AGE AT TAKING THE DEGREE
Average age: 37.6
Median age: 38.0
Extremes: 25 to 53

Of the institutions at which they teach, 10 do not support advanced study or research and 5 attach small or no importance to publication when granting promotions or tenure. About 55 percent of the full, associate, and assistant professors on their staffs have Ph.D.'s. Of the ten chairmen who voted the program as totally satisfactory, their elapsed time to the Ph.D. from the A.B. was 10+ years and the median time was 9 years. They took the degree at an average and median age of 34. The upper members of their staffs are 50.4% Ph.D.'s, but only 3 of their institutions do anything to aid research; in fact, in 2 of these institutions, there is no importance given to research in considering promotion or tenure; in the other 8 cases some, or much importance is given to research.

Table 7.19.   *Suggestions of college chairmen for improving the training*
(C.45)   *of people who wish to teach but do not plan to d﹐ research*

| | NUMBER OF RESPONDENTS | | | | NO | |
CATEGORY	YES	PER-CENT	NO	PER-CENT	AN-SWER	
Let universities develop a degree emphasizing teaching and not research	222	67.3	108	32.7	33	N = 330
Let colleges train their own teachers with a strong M.A. program	28	10.0	252	90.0	83	N = 280
Let universities develop an intermediate degree between the M.A. and the Ph.D.	154	57.5	114	42.5	95	N = 268
Let universities restore the former status of the M.A.	120	54.1	102	45.9	141	N = 222

Table 7.20. *College chairmen's success in employing Ph.D.'s*
(C.32)

CATEGORY	NUMBER OF RESPONDENTS	PERCENT
They are difficult to employ	276	76.0
They are not difficult to employ	87	24.0
Total	363	

N = 363

Table 7.21. *College chairmen's estimate of the reasons for difficulty*
(C.32) *in employing Ph.D.'s*

CATEGORY	NUMBER OF RESPONDENTS	PERCENT
There are too few of them	146	52.9
They are too expensive	86	31.2
Too few and too expensive	44	15.9
Other reasons	24	
No answer	63	
Total	363	

N = 276

Table 7.22. *College chairmen's estimate of the number of Ph.D.'s they*
(C.31) *would appoint if accreditation requirements and status*
competition between colleges were eliminated

CATEGORY	NUMBER OF RESPONDENTS	PERCENT
Would appoint fewer	17	4.9
Would appoint more	36	10.3
Would appoint same number	295	84.8
Do not know	8	
No answer	7	
Total	363	

N = 348

Table 7.23. Number of appointments made by college chairmen
(C.27) in the period, 1960–1965

NUMBER OF APPOINTMENTS	NUMBER OF RESPONDENTS	TOTAL APPOINTMENTS
0	7	
1 to 9 (Average 4.6)	246	1134
10 to 65 (Average 30.9)	110	3402
Total	363	Total 4536*

* General average 12.5.

Table 7.24. Training of appointees to college positions in the period,
(C.28–29) 1960–1965

CATEGORY	NUMBER OF APPOINTEES	PERCENT
Ph.D. granted	806	17.8
ABD. status	775	17.1
Less than ABD. status	2955	65.1
Total	4536	

N = 4536

Table 7.25. Number of staff appointments chairmen of college
(C.30) departments intend to make by 1971

(a) AT THE PH.D. LEVEL

NUMBER OF APPOINTMENTS	NUMBER OF RESPONDENTS	PERCENT
None	9	2.5
No answer or do not know	45	12.4
1754 appointments*	309	85.1

N = 363

* An average of 350 Ph.D.'s per year. The range of appointments is from one to sixty; but 60 of the responding chairmen
hope to add 10 or more Ph.D.'s during this period.

(b) AT LESS THAN THE PH.D. LEVEL

NUMBER OF APPOINTMENTS	NUMBER OF RESPONDENTS	PERCENT
None	18	5.0
No answer or do not know	83	22.9
1864 appointments	262	72.2

N = 363

Table 7.26. *Attitude of the college chairmen toward the*
(C.23)   *comprehensiveness of their English program*

CATEGORY	NUMBER OF RESPONDENTS	PERCENT
It is comprehensive enough	264	73.5
It is not comprehensive enough	95	26.5
No answer	4	
Total	363	

N = 359

Table 7.27. *Areas in which college chairmen (161 respondents)*
(C.24)   *would like to expand their programs*

AREAS	NUMBER OF RESPONDENTS
Old English	15
Medieval Literature	19
Chaucer	2
Renaissance Literature	9
Spenser	1
Shakespeare	1
Seventeenth Century	5
Milton	5
Restoration	1
Eighteenth Century	9
Nineteenth Century	6
American Literature	27
Drama	15
Novel	6
Contemporary Literature	20
Comparative or World Literature	29
Advanced Writing	16
Criticism	12
Teaching of English	2
Linguistics and Modern Grammar	84

Table 7.28.   *Weight given by college chairmen to amount of*
(C.43)   *publication when considering promotion or tenure*

CATEGORY	NUMBER OF RESPONDENTS	PERCENT
We attach much importance to this	30	8.3
We attach some importance to this	242	67.0
We attach no importance or little to this	89	24.7
No answer	2	
Total	363	

N = 361

Of the 30 institutions placing much importance on publication, 7 give no aid; 1 plans to give aid; and 23 do give aid. Of the 89 institutions placing little or no importance on publication, 39 give no aid; 1 plans to give aid; and 49 do give aid.

Table 7.29.   *Attitudes of college chairmen toward attracting and*
(C.41)   *holding Ph.D.'s on their faculties*

CATEGORY	NUMBER OF RESPONDENTS	PERCENT	PERCENT OF PH.D.'S NOW ON STAFF
We will do nothing in the foreseeable future	70	19.7	34.3
We do not find it necessary to do anything yet	65	18.3	42.0
We are planning to do something	28	7.9	39.2
We are doing something	192	54.1	58.7
No answer	8		
Total	363		

N = 355

Table 7.30. *What colleges that attempt to attract and hold Ph.D.'s do**
(C.42)

CATEGORY	NUMBER OF RESPONDENTS	PERCENT
Sabbaticals (full or half pay after 3, 5, or 6 years)	121	63.0
Summer grants for travel	64	33.3
Grants for research	79	41.1
Released time	29	15.1
Loans	1	.5

N = 192

* Some colleges do more than one thing.

Table 7.31. *Number of ABD's on reporting college staffs*
(C.38)

CATEGORY	NUMBER OF RESPONDENTS	PERCENT
None	52	14.5
Some (1011 ABD's)	306	85.5
No answer	5	
Total	363	

N = 358

Average: 3.3 per department. Extremes: 1 to 23.

Table 7.32. *College chairmen's estimate of the number of their*
(C.39)   *ABD's who will become Ph.D.'s*

CATEGORY	NUMBER OF ABD.'S	PERCENT
Will finish	735	72.7
Probably will not finish	276	27.3
Total	1011	

N = 1011

Table 7.33.   *Interest of college chairmen (363 reporting) in keeping*
(C.40)   *ABD's once they have taken doctorates*

CATEGORY	NUMBER OF ABD'S	PERCENT
Will keep or hope to keep	651	88.6
Will not keep or hope to keep	84	11.4

N = 735

Table 7.34.   *Means by which college chairmen aid staff members*
(C.36)   *working for the doctorate*

CATEGORY	NUMBER OF RESPONDENTS	PERCENT
Paid leaves	192	55.0
Unpaid leaves	200	57.3
Lighter loads	48	13.8
Grants	14	4.0
Loans*	12	3.4
Nothing	22	6.3
No answer	14	

N = 349

* In some colleges these loans are redeemed if the teacher returns to the institution for a fixed term after taking his degree.

Table 7.35.   *Attitude of college chairmen on government grants that*
(C.37)   *would enable their ABD's to finish the doctorate*

CATEGORY	NUMBER OF RESPONDENTS	PERCENT
Favor grants	246	84.5
Do not favor grants	9	3.1
Do not know	36	12.4
No answer	72	
Total	363	

N = 291

Table 7.36.   Attitude of graduate professors on the percentage of
(B.20)   students of eight or more years' standing likely to
               complete doctorates

PERCENTAGE	NUMBER OF RESPONDENTS	PERCENT
0 to 10	305	34.0
10 to 25	304	34.0
25 to 50	199	22.2
Over 50	288	9.8
No answer	274	
	1170	

N = 896

Table 7.37.   Attitude of graduate professors on correlation between
(B.19)   elapsed time to the doctorate and academic success

CATEGORY	NUMBER OF RESPONDENTS	PERCENT
Minimum time results in successful career	525	51.6
Minimum does not result in success	127	12.5
No correlation between elapsed time and success	365	35.9
No answer	153	
Total	1170	

N = 1017

Table 7.38.
(A.15)
Opinion of graduate department chairmen on percentage by which they could increase their doctoral enrollment without increasing either the size of their staffs or the teaching loads*

PERCENTAGE	RESPONDENTS	AVERAGE NUMBER OF STUDENTS AND RANGE	
Not at all	37		
1 to 10	25	8.3	2 to 30
10 to 25	15	16.6	5 to 52
25 to 50	5	14.4	6 to 27
50 to 100	2	112.5	25 to 200
Over 100	1	10.0	
No answer	3		
	88		

N = 85

* The statistics indicate that a total of 730 additional students could be accommodated.

Table 7.39.
(A.41)
Opinion of chairmen of graduate departments about the effect of the proliferation of graduate departments since 1900

CATEGORY	NUMBER OF RESPONDENTS	PERCENT
It has had a good effect	19	25.3
It has had a bad effect	37	49.3
It has had no effect	8	10.7
I do not know	11	14.4
No answer	13	
	88	

N = 75

Table 7.40.   *Opinion of graduate professors about the effect of the*
(B.38)   *proliferation of graduate departments since 1900**

CATEGORY	NUMBER OF RESPONDENTS	PERCENT
ANTE-1955 GROUP		
Good effect	111	18.6
Bad effect	299	50.1
No effect	60	10.1
Cannot say	68	11.4
No answer	59	9.9
Total	597	

N = 597

	NUMBER	PERCENT
POST-1955 GROUP		
Good effect	77	15.6
Bad effect	184	37.3
No effect	56	11.3
Cannot say	89	18.1
No answer	87	17.6
Total	493	

N = 493

	NUMBER	PERCENT
NON-PH.D.'S		
Good effect	14	17.5
Bad effect	30	37.5
No effect	6	7.5
Cannot say	11	13.8
No answer	19	23.8
Total	80	

N = 80

* Total response: Good effect = 202 or 17.2%; bad effect = 513 or 43.8%; no effect = 122 or 10.4%. "No answer" was taken into account since it is the equivalent of "cannot say."

(N = 1170)

Table 7.41.   *Attitude of the recent recipients of the doctorate on the*
(D.48)   *effect of the proliferation of graduate departments*
                since 1900

CATEGORY	NUMBER OF RESPONDENTS	PERCENT
Has reduced standards	745	39.8
Has not reduced standards	258	13.7
Cannot say	818	43.5
No answer	59	3.1
Total	1880	

N = 1880

Table 7.42.   *Attitude of graduate department chairmen about the*
(A.38)   *source of a junior appointee's doctorate*

CATEGORY	NUMBER OF RESPONDENTS	PERCENT
Of importance	64	79.0
Of no importance	17	21.0
No answer	7	
Total	88	

N = 81

Table 7.43.   *Attitude of graduate professors toward the source of*
(B.37)   *a tenure appointee's doctorate*

CATEGORY	NUMBER OF RESPONDENTS	PERCENT
Prefer a Ph.D. from a long-established program	446	42.8
Prefer a Ph.D. from a new program	3	
No preference	591	56.8
No answer	130	
Total	1170	

N = 1040

Table 7.44.   *Attitude of chairmen of graduate departments toward*
(A.40)   *the source of a tenure appointee's doctorate*

CATEGORY	NUMBER OF RESPONDENTS	PERCENT
Prefer a Ph.D. from a long-established program	58	86.5
Prefer a Ph.D. from a new program	4	5.8
No preference	5	7.4
No answer	21	
Total	88	

N = 67

Table 7.45.   *Attitude of graduate professors toward the source*
(B.36)   *of a junior appointee's degree*

CATEGORY	NUMBER OF RESPONDENTS	PERCENT
Of importance	791	79.2
Of no importance	208	20.8
Not codable	24	
No answer	147	
Total	1170	

N = 999

Table 7.46.   *Opinion of graduate professors on the ability and*
(B.35)   *training of Ph.D.'s produced by the top twenty*
                    departments in the Cartter Report

CATEGORY	NUMBER OF RESPONDENTS	PERCENT
Better than average	891	84.9
No better than average	159	15.1
Not codable	19	
No answer	101	
Total	1170	

N = 1050

Table 7.47.
(D.47)

Opinion of recent recipients of the doctorate on the ability and training of Ph.D.'s produced by the top twenty departments in the Cartter Report

CATEGORY	NUMBER OF RESPONDENTS	PERCENT
Better than average	891	48.9
No better than average	218	12.0
Do not know	713	39.1
No answer	58	
Total	1880	

N = 1822

Table 7.48.
(D.47)

Opinion of recent recipients on the training and ability of Cartter and non-Cartter Ph.D.'s according to the source of their own doctorates

CATEGORY	CARTTER PH.D.'S	PERCENT	NON-CARTTER PH.D.'S	PERCENT	TOTAL
Better than average	708	61.7	183	27.1	891 (47.3%)
No better than average	65	5.7	153	22.7	218 (11.6%)
Do not know	374	32.6	339	50.2	713 (37.9%)
No answer	—	—	—	—	58
Totals	1147		675		1880

N = 1147   N = 675   N = 1822

Table 7.49.
(A.42, B.39)

Opinion of chairmen and graduate professors on the certifying of graduate departments by a central agency

CATEGORY	CHAIRMEN	PERCENT	GRADUATE PROFESSORS	PERCENT
Should be certified	25	32.5	446	40.8
Should not be certified	52	67.5	648	59.2
Not codable	—	—	23	—
Not answered	11	—	53	—
Totals	88		1170	

N = 77   N = 1094

Tabulations for Chapter 8

Table 8.1.
(B.46)
Opinion of graduate professors on granting a four-year doctorate without lowering standards

CATEGORY	NUMBER OF RESPONDENTS	PERCENT
It can be done	729	70.2
It cannot be done	310	29.8
Not codable	12	
No answer	119	
Total	1170	

N = 1039

Table 8.2.
(D.49)
Opinion of recent recipients on granting a four-year doctorate without lowering standards

CATEGORY	NUMBER OF RESPONDENTS	PERCENT
It can be done	792	48.4
It cannot be done	846	51.6
No answer	242	
Total	1880	

N = 1638

Table 8.3.
(D.50)
Opinion of recent recipients as to whether or not a four-year doctorate should have teaching internship

CATEGORY	NUMBER OF RESPONDENTS	PERCENT
It should	505	66.9
It should not	250	33.1
No answer	37	
Total	792*	

N = 755

* Answered only by those who affirmed Table 8.2.

Table 8.4. *Opinions of college chairmen about their policies toward*
(C.46) *a staff member with an intermediate degree*

CATEGORY	YES	PER-CENT	NO	PER-CENT	NO ANSWER	
Would appoint him	317	89.3	38	10.7	8	N = 355
Would retain him even if he did not earn Ph.D. in stated time	214	66.9	106	33.1	43	N = 320
Would promote him if he were a good teacher	230*		107	31.8	26	N = 337

* This figure breaks into qualified and unqualified assents. Some
172, or 74.8 percent, give an unqualified "yes"; 58, or 25.2
percent, qualify their response with "not to a professorship";
"to an assistant or associate professorship only"; "not if I could
get a Ph.D."; "only if the administration would permit it."
N = 230

Table 8.5. *Opinion of recent recipients of the doctorate as to where*
(D.52) *holders of intermediate degrees should be employed*

NUMBER OF RESPONDENTS

CATEGORY	YES	PERCENT	NO	PERCENT	NO ANSWER
At a university	350	23.3	1154	76.7	376 N = 1504
At a state college	1254	78.7	339	21.3	287 N = 1593
At a liberal arts college	1270	77.4	371	22.6	239 N = 1641

Table 8.6. *Opinion of recent recipients of the doctorate as to whether*
(D.53) *they would have taken an intermediate degree if it would*
have brought them the same post and prospects they now
have

CATEGORY	NUMBER OF RESPONDENTS	PERCENT
Would have taken it	296	15.7
Would not have taken it	1366	72.7
No answer (implies doubt?)	218	11.6
Total	1880	

N = 1880

Table 8.7.   *Opinion of graduate professors as to whether or not*
(B.40)   *an intermediate degree makes sense*

	NUMBER OF	
CATEGORY	RESPONDENTS	PERCENT
It does	682	62.8
It does not	404	37.2
Not codable	38	
No answer	46	
Total	1170	

N = 1086

Table 8.8.   *Opinion of graduate professors as to how the*
(B.41)   *intermediate degree should be defined*

	NUMBER OF	
CATEGORY	RESPONDENTS	PERCENT
On the course to the Ph.D.	119	12.3
A terminal degree	188	19.4
Both	664	68.4
Not codable	21	
No answer	178	
Total	1170	

N = 971

Table 8.9.   *Opinion of graduate professors as to whether there should*
(B.43)   *be a time limit for the conversion of an intermediate*
                  degree into a Ph.D.

	NUMBER OF	
CATEGORY	RESPONDENTS	PERCENT
There should be a limit	589	59.8
There should not be a limit	376	38.2
Not codable	30	
No answer	175	
Total	1170	

N = 985

Table 8.10.   *Time limits on the intermediate degree's conversion*
(B.44)   *into a Ph.D. as suggested by graduate professors*

YEARS	NUMBER OF RESPONDENTS	PERCENT
1	2	—
2	35	5.9
3	101	17.1
4	85	14.4
5	234	39.7
6	39	6.6
7	40	6.8
8	14	2.4
9	1	—
10	38	6.5
Total	589*	

N = 589

* Number approving limit in Table 8.9.

Table 8.11.   *Opinion of graduate professors as to whether or not a stu-*
(B.42)   *dent with an interim degree from X University should be*
               able to present only a dissertation to Y University and be
               given a Ph.D.

CATEGORY	NUMBER OF RESPONDENTS	PERCENT
It should be permitted	331	35.4
It should not be permitted	604	64.6
Not codable	7	
No answer	228	
Total	1170	

N = 935

Table 8.12.　　　*Opinion of chairmen of graduate departments as to*
(A.39)　　　　　*whether or not their departments would approve the*
　　　　　　　　appointment of holders of intermediate degrees to definite
　　　　　　　　ranks

CATEGORY	YES	PERCENT	NO	PERCENT	NO ANSWER
To an instructorship	57	76.0	18	24.0	13
					N = 75
To an Assistant Professorship	18	26.5	50	73.5	20
					N = 68

Table 8.13.　　　*Opinion of chairmen of graduate departments whether or*
(A.39)　　　　　*not an appointed holder of an intermediate degree would*
　　　　　　　　be given tenure or not

CATEGORY	YES	PERCENT	NO	PERCENT	NO ANSWER
As an instructor	12	21.4	44	78.6	32
					N = 56
As an Assistant Professor	10	25.0	30	75.0	48
					N = 40

Table 8.14.　　　*Opinions of graduate professors as to whether or not their*
(B.45)　　　　　*departments would appoint the holder of an intermediate*
　　　　　　　　degree to definite academic ranks (statistics based on high-
　　　　　　　　est rank checked by respondents)

CATEGORY	NUMBER OF RESPONDENTS	PERCENT
Would not appoint at all	129	15.0
Appoint as instructor	469	54.7
Appoint as Assistant Professor	195	22.7
Appoint to a post with tenure	64	7.2
Cannot say	93	
No answer	220	
Total	1170	

N = 857

Table 8.15.   *Attitude of college chairmen toward postdoctoral*
(C.47)   *work for the best young Ph.D.'s*

CATEGORY	NUMBER OF RESPONDENTS	PERCENT
Favor it	332	93.5
Might favor it	2	.6
Do not favor it	21	5.9
No answer	8	
Total	363	

N = 355

Table 8.16.   *Attitude of graduate professors toward postdoctoral*
(B.48)   *work for the best young Ph.D.'s*

CATEGORY	NUMBER OF RESPONDENTS	PERCENT
Favor it	347	34.2
Might favor it	83	8.2
Do not favor it	586	57.7
No answer	154	
Total	1170	

N = 1016

Table 8.17.   *Graduate professors' estimate of what percentage of*
(B.49)   *their dissertation students could be recommended for*
                   postdoctoral work

PERCENTAGE	NUMBER OF RESPONDENTS	PERCENT
0	192	28.2
5 to 25	385	56.5
30 to 50	67	9.8
60 to 80	13	2.0
95 to 100	25	3.7
Not codable	34	
No answer	454	
Total	1170	

N = 682

Table 8.18.   *Opinions of recent recipients of the doctorate as to what*
(D.54)   *should be asked of a postdoctoral fellow*

CATEGORY	NUMBER OF RESPONDENTS	PERCENT
Be held to a curriculum	260	15.7
Be an assistant to a professor as in the sciences	218	13.1
Be allowed to use his time as he pleases	1183	71.2
No answer	219	
Total	1880	

N = 1661

The Questionnaires

STUDY OF DOCTORAL PROGRAMS IN ENGLISH
sponsored by
THE MODERN LANGUAGE ASSOCIATION OF AMERICA
under a grant from
THE DANFORTH FOUNDATION

Project Director: Don Cameron Allen
SIR WILLIAM OSLER PROFESSOR OF ENGLISH
THE JOHNS HOPKINS UNIVERSITY

A. QUESTIONNAIRE FOR DEPARTMENTAL CHAIRMEN OR DIRECTORS OF GRADUATE STUDY

This is Part 1 of a four-part questionnaire. It is directed to departmental chairmen and directors of graduate study in universities that confer the Ph.D. in English. Parts 2, 3, and 4, which are coordinated with Part 1, are to be sent to professors of graduate courses in English, to chairmen of English departments in colleges that do not grant the doctorate in English, and to recent recipients of the Ph.D. degree in English, respectively.

1. Name _____
     LAST   FIRST   MIDDLE

2. Age at last birthday _____   3. Sex: (   ) M   (   ) F

223

4. Source and date of your degrees:

Earned Degrees	Year of Award	Awarding Institution
Bachelor's Degree		
M.A.		
Ph.D.		
Other:		

5. Teaching experience:

Institutions	Ranks	Dates

We need to know more about the institutions from which graduate students come and how these students are recruited and selected. We should also know how they are evaluated at the various stages in their training. If you have any comments not brought out or suggested by these questions, please state them on a separate sheet of paper.

Note: The introductory material and the first five questions are the same in all the questionnaires and hence are not repeated.

6. Indicate, if possible, by approximate percentages the sources of your resident graduate students for the current year.

Your university*	_____%
Another university*	_____%
Colleges* with enrollments of 1000 or more	_____%
Colleges* with enrollments of under 1000	_____%
A foreign institution	_____%

* For the purposes of this study, "university" means an institution that has a doctoral program in English, and "college" means an institution that does not have a doctoral program in English.

7. If your department attempts to recruit graduate students, mark the areas in which you recruit (Rank 1, 2, 3, in order of importance).
    a) (   ) Your own institution
       (   ) Regionally
       (   ) Nationally
    b) Please describe what is done. _____

8. How many majors in English did you graduate last year? _____

9. How many of them went on to graduate study in English? _____

10. How many of your current graduate students are devoting full time to study? (Exclude those teaching or otherwise employed.) _____

11. How many of your graduate students are part-time? (Include those teaching.) _____

12. About how many additional persons does your department consider to be doctoral candidates? _____

13. Do you have a quota on total graduate enrollment in English?
( ) Yes ( ) No

14. If *yes*, what is it? _____

15. Without increasing your total staff or your teaching load, by what percent do you think your doctoral enrollment could be increased?
a) ( ) Not at all
( ) 1–10%
( ) 10–25%
( ) 25–50%
( ) 50–100%
( ) Over 100%
b) This percent equals _____ number of students.

16. How are new graduate students of English selected in your university?
( ) By the university admissions office
( ) By the Graduate Dean's office
( ) By the Director of English Graduate Studies
( ) By a departmental committee
( ) By all the graduate teachers in the department
( ) By other means (specify): _____

17. When you look at the record of an applicant for doctoral study, by which of the following items is your decision about him most influenced?) Rank 1, 2, 3, 4, etc., in order of importance.)
( ) General academic record
( ) Academic record in English
( ) Academic record in ancient and/or modern languages
( ) Graduate Record Examination scores
( ) Letters from other professors
( ) Student's letters or submitted papers
( ) Student's extracurricular honors
( ) Source of previous degree(s)
( ) Other factors (specify): _____

18. Indicate your department's approximate attrition rate:

	Zero	Under 10%	10–25%	25–50%	Over 50%
a) Before the M.A. or equivalent	_____	_____	_____	_____	_____
b) After the M.A. or equivalent	_____	_____	_____	_____	_____

19. A certain number of your doctoral candidates drop out. Among those you have known personally what seem to be the reasons? (Check three most important factors.)
    ( ) Marriage
    ( ) Insufficient funds
    ( ) Domestic problems
    ( ) Loss of interest
    ( ) Illness
    ( ) Poor preparation
    ( ) No real ability
    ( ) Other reasons (specify): _____

20. What is the earliest point at which you personally can predict with some feeling of assurance that a student will not take a Ph.D.? (Check one.)
    ( ) At the end of his first year in your department
    ( ) Before the preliminary doctoral or comprehensive examinations
    ( ) At the preliminary doctoral or comprehensive examinations
    ( ) When he submits the first draft of his thesis
    ( ) At some other point (specify): _____

TRAINING
21. Please list all courses required for the Ph.D., including those required for the M.A.

_____

_____

_____

_____

_____

_____

_____

PRELIMINARY EXAMINATION*

22. Will you describe the nature of your department's examination: Its scope, duration, whether it is written or oral or both. _____

_____

_____

23. Have all the members of the examination committee taught the student under examination?

( ) Yes ( ) Usually ( ) No

24. How do your students know what to expect in the way of questions?

_____

_____

_____

25. How many times may one of your students fail this examination? _____

26. a) What proportion of your students decide or are forced to withdraw from graduate study after failing to pass these examinations? _____%

b) This percent represents _____ students.

27. In your opinion, is this part of the doctoral requirements something that should be:

	Yes	No
Eliminated?	( )	( )
Reduced in scope?	( )	( )
Increased in scope?	( )	( )

28. If you marked *yes* to "reduced in scope," or "increased in scope," what, thinking in terms of your department's examination, would you advise?

_____

_____

_____

LANGUAGES

29. a) Are you in favor of a foreign language requirement?

( ) Yes ( ) No

b) If *yes*, on what grounds do you feel such a requirement is justified?

( ) Languages are research tools.

( ) A knowledge of languages is an essential of a liberal education.

* By this is meant an examination the passing of which qualifies a student to continue to his doctorate by writing and submitting a dissertation.

c) Most departments require a candidate for the doctorate to pass a reading test in two languages. Would you think that an ability to read with comprehension and appreciation the literature of one language is a better requirement?   ( ) Yes   ( ) No

DISSERTATION

30. In your opinion, should the average doctoral thesis in English (over 300 pages) be replaced: (Mark as many as you please.)
    ( ) By a work of half the size?
    ( ) By several publishable papers?
    ( ) By a survey or digest of scholarship on some author, period, or topic?
    ( ) By a series of lectures for advanced undergraduates?
    ( ) By something else? (specify) _____

The purpose of the following questions is to elicit your opinions on the value of the training for the Ph.D. in English and American literature, on the proliferation of graduate departments of English, and on the various plans advanced to increase the supply of junior college, college, state college, and university teachers of English.

31. By which of the following means does one of your department's new Ph.D.'s get a teaching position? (Check not more than 3.)
    ( ) University's placement bureau
    ( ) Commercial placement agencies
    ( ) Departmental placement bureau
    ( ) Major professor's efforts
    ( ) Student's own effort
    ( ) Placement bureau of MLA

32. a) In the last five years, about what percent of your own Ph.D.'s have found positions that seem to you unworthy of their talents and training? _____%
    b) This percent represents _____ Ph.D.'s.

33. Does your department provide its Ph.D. students with
    ( ) Supervised teaching experience?
    ( ) A course in pedagogical methods?
    ( ) Other knowledge or experience necessary for teaching underclassmen? (Describe.) _____

34. Do any of your department's new Ph.D.'s go to a teaching position without teaching experience?   ( ) Yes   ( ) No

35. Does your department make any attempt to acquaint doctoral candidates with the nature of their duties in colleges and junior colleges? ( ) Yes   ( ) No

36. If *yes,* please elaborate: _____

_____

_____

37. Do you feel that *in general* only a person with Ph.D. training is competent to teach: (Check as many as applicable.)
    ( ) Underclassmen?
    ( ) Upperclassmen?
    ( ) Graduate students?

38. Is the source of the degree a major consideration when you are making junior appointments to your department?   ( ) Yes   ( ) No

39. a) Would your department be inclined to appoint as instructor or assistant professor a holder of a degree intermediate between the M.A. and the Ph.D.?
    Instructor ( ) Yes ( ) No   Asst. prof. ( ) Yes ( ) No
    b) If *yes,* would you be inclined to give tenure to such appointees?
    Instructor ( ) Yes ( ) No   Asst. prof. ( ) Yes ( ) No

40. When you are considering a major appointment, if all other qualities are the same, would you be inclined to give preference to a candidate (mark as many as applicable):
    ( ) Who has a Ph.D.?
    ( ) Who has a Ph.D. from a long-established graduate program?
    ( ) Who has a Ph.D. from a new graduate program?
    If none of the above factors would make a difference, check here ( )

41. The number of graduate departments of English has grown from 20 in 1900 to well over 100. What effect do you think this has had on the Ph.D. in English? _____

_____

42. Do you think that graduate departments in English should all be certified by a central agency?   ( ) Yes   ( ) No

43. The formula presented below was worked out by Professor Warner Rice as a means of estimating the cost of subsidizing a four-year Ph.D. program if students teach one course a quarter or semester in each of their last three years. So that we may gain some notion of the total national cost of subsidizing a four-year Ph.D., would you use the formula to give us your estimates, based on your optimum number of graduate students and your own fees and allowances, of how much it would cost your department to support such a program.

    Year 1 _____
    Year 2 _____
    Year 3 _____
    Year 4 _____

Supplement to Questionnaire A

PROFESSOR RICE'S FORMULA

N   number of students, which decreases in successive years because of drop-outs.
X   the cash grant paid the student
Y   the stipend paid him for teaching

Year
1. $N(X +$ allowances + tuition and fees$) =$ subsidy
2. $.9N(X +$ allowances and fees $- Y) =$ subsidy
3. $.8N(X +$ allowances and fees $- Y) =$ subsidy
4. $.8N(X +$ allowances and fees $- Y) =$ subsidy

For example:
1. $20(\$2000 + \$800 + \$600) = \$68,000$
2. $18(\$2500 + \$800 + \$600 - \$1600) = \$41,400$
3. $16(\$3000 + \$800 + \$600 - \$1600) = \$44,800$
4. $16(\$3500 + \$800 + \$600 - \$1600) = \$52,800$

The cost of supervision should be added to the total. For the first year there will be no supervision, but, assuming that less supervision will be needed in the third and fourth year, the following formula can be used.

Years
2. $N \times \$600 =$ cost
3. $N \times \$300 =$ cost
4. $N \times \$200 =$ cost

Q 43   (Using Professor Rice's formula, how much would it cost your department to support such a program?)

	YEAR 1	YEAR 2	YEAR 3	YEAR 4	TOTAL
Alabama	62,000	50,000	42,400	49,600	204,000
U. of Arizona	143,200	79,380	90,560	110,560	423,700
Arizona S.U.	51,000	37,500	40,300	45,500	174,300
Auburn	85,100	35,000	42,900	49,600	212,600
Baylor	23,400	19,500	15,600	11,700	70,200
Boston	217,500	157,950	159,375	167,775	702,600
Brandeis	53,000	38,700	34,400	34,400	160,500
Brown	960,000	792,000	688,000	736,000	3,176,000
U.C. Berkeley	320,000	210,060	186,720	186,720	903,500
U.C. Davis	65,700	14,490	12,600	12,600	105,390

	YEAR 1	YEAR 2	YEAR 3	YEAR 4	TOTAL
U.C.L.A.	149,433		. . . not applicable . . .		
U.C. San Diego	185,000	147,000	128,000	128,000	588,000
Catholic U.	40,800	37,880	35,450	37,400	151,530
Columbia	376,000	338,400	277,600	277,600	1,269,600
Cornell	138,000	95,000	84,000	94,000	411,000
Emory	57,715	19,500	26,000	13,580	116,795
Florida	49,500	28,980	29,250	41,800	149,530
Fordham	87,500	35,200	40,000	57,600	220,300
Harvard	250,000	225,000	215,000	210,000	900,000
Howard	78,400	70,000	68,000	68,000	284,400
U. Illinois	82,500	133,650	192,650	276,150	684,950
U. Iowa	139,600	91,680	88,160	100,160	419,600
Johns Hopkins	80,000	72,000	64,000	. . . not applicable . . .	
U. Kansas	66,000	53,800	41,200	34,400	195,400
Kansas S.U.	45,000	35,000	20,000	22,000	122,000
Kentucky	60,000	36,000	40,000	48,000	184,000
Louisiana S.U.	128,076	135,205	96,575	77,260	437,116
Loyola	30,000	33,300	31,200	34,400	128,900
Maryland	119,280	104,484	84,788	74,112	382,664
Massachusetts	136,000	103,400	99,200	112,000	450,600
U. Michigan	71,450	36,240	39,900	46,300	193,890
Minnesota	102,000	62,100	67,200	79,200	310,500
Mississippi	44,400	43,200	43,200	43,200	174,000
Nebraska	87,500	38,000	28,500	28,500	182,500
N.Y.U.	390,000	261,000	200,000	64,000	915,000
SUNY Albany	65,625	34,550	40,500	56,500	197,175
SUNY Binghamton	112,800	54,600	57,750	52,250	277,400
N. Illinois U.	9,600	4,200	2,400	0	16,200
Notre Dame	100,000	58,250	61,000	66,000	285,250
Ohio S.U.	204,000	124,000	124,400	158,400	610,800
Oregon U.	0	67,554	38,448	31,248	137,250
U. of Penn.	115,500		. . . not applicable . . .		
Princeton	73,500	40,000	33,500	7,500	154,500
Purdue	144,000	108,800	112,000	124,000	488,800
Rochester	68,000	36,600	32,000	35,200	171,800
St. Johns	40,800	51,000	42,400	44,000	178,200
St. Louis	240,896	160,312	125,664	120,564	647,436
U. S. California	532,000	442,000	537,000	632,000	2,143,000
U. S. Carolina	140,000	82,800	86,400	96,000	405,200
U. S. Illinois	64,000	64,600	66,800	40,000	235,400
Stanford	182,800	49,744	46,144	39,744	318,432
Syracuse	80,000	64,000	66,000	74,000	284,000
Temple	204,000	102,600	115,200	144,000	565,800

	YEAR 1	YEAR 2	YEAR 3	YEAR 4	TOTAL
Tennessee	80,000	43,200	28,800	25,600	177,600
Texas	180,000	162,000	160,000	192,000	694,000
Texas Tech	60,000	35,040	36,000	39,600	170,640
Utah	60,000	35,000	40,000	45,000	180,000
Vanderbilt	80,000	46,800	49,600	52,800	229,200
Virginia	300,000	250,000	200,000	170,000	920,000
Washington	499,485	148,800	216,750	301,750	1,166,785
Wayne State	155,000	94,000	104,000	172,000	525,000
Western Reserve	240,500	140,490	121,680	112,080	614,750
U. Wisconsin	1,875,000	1,282,500	1,296,250	1,466,250	5,920,000

B. QUESTIONNAIRE FOR TEACHERS OF GRADUATE COURSES IN ENGLISH

6. In what year did you first teach a course to which graduate students were admitted? _____

7. In what year did you first direct a doctoral dissertation? _____

8. Approximately how many doctoral dissertations have you directed? _____

9. Current distribution of classroom time:
   Graduate instruction   _____%
   Undergraduate instruction _____%

10. In an ordinary term or quarter, what is the average student enrollment:
    In your undergraduate/graduate courses? _____
    In your undergraduate courses?   _____
    In your graduate courses?   _____
    In your seminars?   _____

We need to know more about the recruitment and selection of graduate students and about how they are evaluated at various stages in their training. If you have any comments not brought out or suggested by these questions, please state them on a separate sheet.

11. What is your personal policy with *promising* undergraduates who wish to continue to the doctorate?
    ( ) Urge them to remain with your department
    ( ) Advise them to go elsewhere

12. When you look at the record of an applicant for doctoral study, by which of the following items is your decision about him most influenced? (Mark 1, 2, 3, etc., in order of importance.)
    ( ) General academic record
    ( ) Undergraduate record in English

( ) Undergraduate record in ancient and/or modern languages
( ) Source of previous degree(s)
( ) Graduate Record Examination scores
( ) Letters from other professors
( ) Student letters or submitted papers
( ) Student extracurricular honors
( ) Other factors: (specify) _____

13. A certain number of your doctoral candidates drop out. Among those you have known personally, what seem to be the reasons? (Mark three most important factors in order of importance.)
( ) Insufficient funds
( ) Domestic problems
( ) Loss of interest
( ) Lack of physical or emotional force
( ) Poor preparation
( ) No real ability
( ) Other reasons: (specify) _____

14. How would you compare the ability and preparation of the general run of graduate students now in your institution with those of your own generation?
( ) Superior
( ) Inferior
( ) About the same

15. If you marked "superior" or "inferior," please indicate those areas in which you think improvement or worsening has taken place.

IMPROVEMENT	WORSENING	PREPARATION
( )	( )	Knowledge of English and American Literature
( )	( )	Knowledge of Classical Languages
( )	( )	Knowledge of Modern Languages
( )	( )	Knowledge of Humanistic Fields (Art, History, Music, Philosophy)
( )	( )	Other areas: _____

IMPROVEMENT	WORSENING	CHARACTERISTICS AND SKILLS
( )	( )	Intelligent, careful reading
( )	( )	Precise, lucid writing
( )	( )	Intellectual curiosity
( )	( )	Powers of synthesis or analysis
( )	( )	Critical taste
( )	( )	Other characteristics or skills: _____

Since the beginning of the Ph.D. program in American universities, complaint and criticism have been loud. It has been stated that the process was a sort of initiation rite, that it took more time and energy than it was worth, that it guarantees nothing measurable about its products, and that, considering the subsequent careers of most Ph.D.'s, it is very unrealistic. Perhaps the answers to the following questions will enable us to look more clearly at the problems, but we shall appreciate any additional ideas or opinions you are moved to record.

TIME
16. What was the elapsed time between your B.A. and Ph.D.? _____ years

17. Approximately how was this time spent?
    a) Full-time graduate study: _____ years
    b) Part-time graduate study: _____ years
    c) Full-time teaching: _____ years
    d) Part-time teaching: _____ years
    e) Military service: _____ years
    f) Other employment: _____ years

18. Do you consider the time you spent actually working for your doctorate:
    ( ) Reasonable?   ( ) Too long?

19. In your experience, do those who take the minimum amount of time generally have more successful careers as college and university teachers than those who take longer?
    ( ) Yes   ( ) No   ( ) No difference

20. Among the students known to you, how many of those who have been working towards a doctorate for eight years or more are likely ever to finish?
    ( ) 0–10%
    ( ) 10–25%
    ( ) 25–50%
    ( ) Over 50%

21. What is the earliest point at which you can predict with some feeling of assurance that a student will not take a Ph.D.? (Check one.)
    ( ) At the end of his first year in your department
    ( ) Before the preliminary examination
    ( ) At the preliminary examination
    ( ) When he submits the first draft of his thesis
    ( ) At some other point: _____

_____

TRAINING
22. When a student has taken a Ph.D. in your department, do you regard him as:

( ) Better prepared for teaching than research?
( ) Better prepared for research than teaching?
( ) About as well prepared for one as for the other?

23. How would you characterize the training that your department gives its Ph.D. candidates?
( ) More specialized than broad
( ) More broad than specialized

PRELIMINARY EXAMINATION*

* By this is meant an examination the passing of which qualifies a student to continue to his doctorate by writing and submitting a dissertation.

24. In your opinion, is the preliminary examination as one of the doctoral requirements something that could be:
Eliminated? ( ) Yes ( ) No
Reduced in scope? ( ) Yes ( ) No
Increased in scope? ( ) Yes ( ) No

25. If you marked *yes* to "reduced in scope" or "increased in scope" what, thinking in terms of your department's examination, would you advise?

LANGUAGES
26. a) Are you in favor of a foreign language requirement?
( ) Yes ( ) No
b) If *yes*, on what grounds do you feel such a requirement is justified?
( ) Languages are research tools
( ) A knowledge of languages is an essential of education
c) Most departments require a candidate for the doctorate to pass a reading test in two languages. Would you think that an ability to read, write, and speak one language is a better requirement?
( ) Yes ( ) No

27. Do you feel that work in any of the following is a justifiable requirement for students who will specialize in modern literature?
( ) Old English
( ) Middle English Language and Literature
( ) Modern English Grammar

28. If so, would you express your reasons? _____

29. During the last academic year, about how many times have you:
a) Assigned reading in one of the required foreign languages? _____
times

b) Heard a seminar report or read a term paper in which the student needed to use one of the required foreign languages? _____ times

c) Read something in one of the languages you had to know for your degree? _____ times

30. Approximately what percent of the theses your department has accepted and you have read are in your personal judgment:

A substantial contribution to scholarship or criticism? _____%

Adequate but not too important contributions? _____%

Of little value as a whole or in substantial part? _____%

31. In your opinion, could the average doctoral thesis in English (over 300 pages) be replaced: (mark as many as you please)

( ) By a work of half the size?

( ) By several publishable papers?

( ) By a survey or analysis of scholarship on some author, period, or topic?

( ) By a series of lectures for advanced undergraduates?

( ) By something else? (specify) _____

The purpose of these questions is to elicit your opinions on the value of the training for the Ph.D. in English and American literature, on the proliferation of graduate departments of English, and on the various plans advanced to increase the supply of junior college, college, state college, and university teachers of English.

32. By which of the following means does one of your department's new Ph.D.'s get a teaching position? (Mark as many as you like, in order of importance.)

( ) University's placement bureau

( ) Commercial placement agencies

( ) Departmental placement bureau

( ) Major professor's efforts

( ) Student's own efforts

33. In the last five years, about what percent of your own Ph.D.'s have found positions that seem to you unworthy of their talents and training? _____%

34. Do you feel that *in general* only a person with Ph.D. training is competent to teach: (Check as many as applicable)

( ) Underclassmen?

( ) Upperclassmen?

( ) Graduate students?

35. In the Cartter report, "An Assessment of Quality in Graduate Education," twenty departments of English (listed alphabetically below)

were rated as "leading" both in effectiveness of graduate program and in quality of graduate faculty: California (Berkeley), Chicago, Columbia, Cornell, Duke, Harvard, Illinois, Indiana, Johns Hopkins, Michigan, Minnesota, North Carolina, Northwestern, Pennsylvania, Princeton, Stanford, Washington (Seattle), Wisconsin, UCLA, Yale.

Do you think that Ph.D.'s produced by most of these departments are better on the average in ability and training than those trained by other departments?　( ) Yes　　( ) No

36. Is the source of a teacher's doctorate a major consideration when you are making a junior appointment?　( ) Yes　　( ) No

37. When you are considering a tenure appointment, if all other qualities are the same, would you be inclined to give preference to a candidate:
( ) Who had a Ph.D. from a long-established graduate program?
( ) Who had a Ph.D. from a new graduate program?
If neither of the above factors would make a difference, check here. ( )

38. The number of graduate departments of English has grown from 20 in 1900 to well over 100. What effect do you think this has had on the Ph.D.?

39. Do you think that departments granting the Ph.D. in English should be certified by a central agency?　( ) Yes　　( ) No

40. Do you think that a degree intermediate between the M.A. and the Ph.D., which represents the completion of all requirements except the dissertation, is a sensible way of solving the teacher shortage?
( ) Yes　　( ) No

41. If such a degree is established, should it be considered:
( ) A terminal degree?
( ) On the way to the Ph.D.?
( ) Both?

42. If it is an interim degree, should it be transferable so that the holder could earn it at X university, but submit his dissertation and take his Ph.D. at Y university?　( ) Yes　　( ) No

43. Many graduate departments of English now have time limits for various phases of the Ph.D. training course. Should there also be a time limit on proceeding from an intermediate degree to a Ph.D.?
( ) Yes　　( ) No

44. If you marked *yes*, about what time limit would you be inclined to propose? _____ years

45. Would your department be inclined to appoint a holder of such a degree:

( ) To an instructorship?
( ) To an assistant professorship?
( ) To a post with tenure?

46. At various places in this questionnaire, you have answered questions about the reduction of certain traditional requirements for the Ph.D. Considering your answers to 24, 25, 26, 27, 28, 31, do you think it possible to give a four-year doctorate to a greater number of students without lowering standards?   ( ) Yes   ( ) No

47. If *yes*, please give your arguments. _____

48. Postdoctoral work in English is now being offered at a few universities. Do you think your department would be interested in doing it?
( ) Yes   ( ) No

49. Assuming that work of this sort is established in the leading graduate departments and properly financed, about what percent of the young Ph.D.'s whose theses you have directed or helped direct would you nominate for this additional training? _____%

C. QUESTIONNAIRE FOR CHAIRMEN OF ENGLISH DEPARTMENTS IN LIBERAL ARTS COLLEGES* AND OTHER INSTITUTIONS WITHOUT DOCTORAL PROGRAMS IN ENGLISH

* For the purposes of this questionnaire, "college" means an institution that does not grant the doctor's degree in English.

NOTE: In answering *questions 6 through 10,* please give all figures as of the fall term (semester, quarter) of the year concerned.

6. Approximately how many students are currently enrolled in your institution?
a) Full-time students _____ b) Part-time students _____

7. How many of these students are enrolled:
a) In required English courses? _____ b) In elective English courses? _____

8. Please indicate any change in the number of students enrolled in *elective* English courses since 1964.
( ) *Increase*   ( ) *Decrease*
Percent of increase since   Percent of decrease since
fall 1964: _____   fall 1964: _____
Average increase per year   Average decrease per year in
in numbers: _____   numbers: _____
( ) *No change*

9. What is the number of juniors and seniors majoring in English as of fall 1966? _____

10. Please indicate any change in the number of English majors since fall 1964.

( ) *Increase*   ( ) *Decrease*
Percent of increase since   Percent of decrease since
1964: _____   1964: _____
Average increase per year   Average decrease per year in
in numbers: _____   numbers: _____
( ) *No change*

11. a) Does your department offer an M.A. in English or American Literature?   ( ) Yes   ( ) No
    b) If you marked *yes*, when did you begin? _____

12. If you offer such a degree, how many candidates:
    a) Obtained the degree in the last five years? _____ b) Are now working for the degree? _____

13. If you answered *no* to question 11, do you have any immediate plans:
    a) For offering an M.A.? . . . ( ) Yes   ( ) No   b) For offering a Ph.D.? . . . ( ) Yes   ( ) No

14. If any of your majors of the last two years have gone on to work for Ph.D.'s, please name the universities in which they have enrolled.

_____

_____

15. Since 1961 about how many of your departmental majors have gone on to work towards a Ph.D.? Total number: _____ Percent: _____

16. Is the interest of your majors in securing a doctorate in English:
    ( ) Increasing?   ( ) Decreasing?   ( ) Steady?

17. Is it a policy of your department to encourage qualified majors to study:
    a) For the M.A.?   ( ) Yes   ( ) No
    b) For the Ph.D.?   ( ) Yes   ( ) No

18. Have you developed any programs or methods for preparing qualified majors for the problems they will encounter in graduate work?
    ( ) Yes   ( ) No

19. If *yes*, please describe them: _____

_____

_____

20. Do you and your colleagues make a special effort to send your better majors to the universities from which you have your own degrees?
    ( ) Yes   ( ) No

21. When you are making an appointment, do you give preference to one of your former students who has gone on to graduate school?
    ( ) Yes   ( ) No

22. What is the average teaching load in your department? _____
hours a week _____ students a term

23. Do your programs in English and American Literature seem to you sufficiently comprehensive in coverage?　( ) Yes　　( ) No

24. If you could expand your offerings, what areas would you add?

25. Please supply the following information about the regular members of your department.

Rank	Number in Rank	Number with Ph.D.
Professor		
Associate Professor		
Assistant Professor		
Instructor		

26. If you share personnel with another department or departments, please name the departments.

27. How many full-time members of your regular staff have been appointed as replacements or additions during the last five years? _____ appointments

28. How many of these appointees had completed their Ph.D.'s when they began teaching with you? _____

29. How many of these appointees:
a) Have completed all doctoral requirements except the dissertation?
_____
b) Have taken their doctorates since you appointed them? _____

30. Approximately how many new appointments do you expect to be making in the next five years:
a) At the doctoral level? _____ b) At less than the doctoral level? _____

31. Were it not for accreditation and competition for staff, would you be inclined to appoint:
( ) Fewer Ph.D.'s?　　( ) About the same number as now?

32. If you are finding it difficult to obtain teachers who have completed the Ph.D., would you suggest a reason?
( ) They are in too short supply
( ) They are too expensive for our budget
( ) Other reasons (specify) _____

33. How do you secure new department members? (Mark 1, 2, 3, etc., in order of importance.)
( ) Apply to older graduate schools
( ) Apply to newer graduate schools
( ) Apply to teachers' agencies
( ) Use AAUP or ADE facilities
( ) Consider direct applications
( ) MLA annual meeting
( ) Other means (specify): _____

34. Check the degree of importance you attach to each item below in considering candidates for positions in your department.

	Much Importance	Some Importance	Little or No Importance	
a)	( )	( )	( )	Teaching skill and experience
b)	( )	( )	( )	Literary talents
c)	( )	( )	( )	Personal attractiveness
d)	( )	( )	( )	Religious interest
e)	( )	( )	( )	General knowledge of English and American Literature
f)	( )	( )	( )	Special knowledge of fields of English and American Literature
g)	( )	( )	( )	Research interest and activity
h)	( )	( )	( )	Administrative ability
i)	( )	( )	( )	Interest in community matters
j)	( )	( )	( )	Broad general culture

35. What is the highest rank to which you can promote a teacher who has yet to complete his Ph.D.?

36. Does your institution encourage regular staff members working on their Ph.D.:
( ) With paid leaves of absence?
( ) With unpaid leaves of absence?
( ) By other means? (specify) _____
( ) Not at all?

37. If your institution has no means for helping these staff members, would it welcome some government or foundation project that would aid them?　( ) Yes　　( ) No　　( ) Don't know

38. How many of your regular staff members have completed all the Ph.D. requirements except the dissertation? _____

39. In your opinion, how many of these will finish? _____

40. Of those who finish:
    a) How many will you keep on your staff? _____
    b) How many can you not keep? _____

41. Because of academic competition for trained staff, many colleges are offering professional opportunities and scholarly facilities (paid leaves, research grants, etc.) to attract and keep young Ph.D.'s. What is the situation at your institution?
    ( ) We are doing so   ( ) We do not find it necessary yet
    ( ) We are planning to do so   ( ) We will not do so in the fore-
                                         seeable future

42. If you marked "we are doing so" or "we are planning to do so," what are you doing or what do you plan to do?

    _____

    _____

43. Some institutions without doctoral programs make the publication of books and articles a criterion for tenure and promotion. What is the attitude of your institution?
    ( ) We attach much importance to publication
    ( ) We attach some importance to publication
    ( ) We attach little or no importance to publication

44. What do you think about the usual doctoral program as preparation for the college English teacher?
    ( ) Altogether satisfactory   ( ) Needs some improvement
    ( ) Needs much improvement   ( ) Needs complete overhaul
    (Please extend your opinion in the space at the end of this question-naire or on a separate sheet.)

45. The following are suggestions for improving the graduate training of people who plan to make a career of English teaching without research. Please indicate your agreement or disagreement with each item.
    Agree   Disagree   No opinion
    ( )   ( )   ( )   Let colleges train their own teachers
                                      with strong M.A. programs
    ( )   ( )   ( )   Let the universities develop a Ph.D.
                                      emphasizing teaching and not re-
                                      search.
    ( )   ( )   ( )   Let the universities develop an inter-
                                      mediate degree between the M.A.
                                      and the Ph.D.
    ( )   ( )   ( )   Let the universities restore the former
                                      status of the M.A.
    (If you have suggestions other than those mentioned above, please write them down on a separate sheet.)

46. In order to solve the teacher shortage, it has been proposed that an intermediate degree be established for students who have completed

all the work for the Ph.D. except the dissertation. This new degree could be considered an interim degree or a terminal degree.

a) Would you appoint the holder of such a degree to your staff?
( ) Yes ( ) No

b) Would you retain him if within a stated time he did not take a Ph.D.? ( ) Yes ( ) No

c) Would you promote him if he did not take a Ph.D. but was in all other respects satisfactory? ( ) Yes ( ) No

47. Some universities are now establishing a postdoctoral program which will permit a young Ph.D. in English who has held the degree not more than five years to spend a year or more of study and research at a university. Would you be willing to grant one of your young men or women leave to enter such a program? ( ) Yes ( ) No

48. If *yes*, what, in your opinion, would be the value of such a program to your college?

_____

_____

49. If you answered *no* to question 47, please state your objections to such a program for college teachers.

_____

_____

D. QUESTIONNAIRE FOR RECENT RECIPIENTS OF THE PH.D. IN ENGLISH

6. If married, give year of marriage. _____

7. How many of your children were born before you received your Ph.D.? Number of children: _____ ( ) Not applicable

8. At what time did you decide to get a Ph.D. in English?
( ) Before entering college
( ) By the junior year
( ) By graduation
( ) While working toward the M.A.
( ) After the M.A.

9. The most important factor in the selection of the graduate school from which you received your Ph.D. was: (check one)
( ) Academic
( ) Financial
( ) Geographical

10. If you checked "academic," what factors influenced you most?
( ) The reputation of the university
( ) The reputation of the department

( ) The reputation of the professor in your field
( ) A program that appealed to your special interest
( ) Other factors: _____

11. Do you consider the elapsed time between your B.A. and Ph.D.:
( ) Reasonable?   ( ) Too long?

12. If *too long,* how many years in your opinion are *reasonable?* _____
years

13. If *too long,* what caused the delay? (Mark as many causes as applicable.)
( ) Poor graduate guidance
( ) Military service
( ) Foreign language requirements
( ) Finances
( ) Change of academic interest
( ) Dissertation
( ) Other causes: _____

_____

14. About how much time elapsed between your entrance into graduate work and the passing of your preliminary examination?* _____
years

15. About how much of this time was full-time study? _____ years

16. About how much time elapsed between the beginning and completion of your doctoral dissertation? _____ years

17. Indicate about how much time between your B.A. and Ph.D. was spent in

Teaching { Teaching fellow _____ years
{ Full-time teacher _____ years
Other employment: (specify and indicate elapsed time)

_____   _____ years
_____   _____ years
_____   _____ years

18. If you had at least one year of uninterrupted work for the doctorate, where did you obtain financial support? (Indicate all sources.)
( ) Parents or relatives
( ) Wife or husband
( ) Grant or fellowship
( ) Loan
( ) Personal savings

_____

* By this is meant an examination the passing of which qualifies a student to continue to his doctorate by writing and submitting a dissertation.

The following questions deal with the character of your doctoral training.

19. If certain courses were specifically required for your doctorate, will you please list them?

_____

_____

20. In what respect were your courses of greatest value?
( ) In passing the preliminary examination
( ) In writing the dissertation
( ) In teaching
( ) In other ways (specify): _____

_____

21. In what languages did you pass tests? _____

22. Which, if any, of these languages did you learn after starting graduate work?

_____

23. Did you use any foreign languages in your graduate courses?
( ) Yes   ( ) No

24. Did the research for your dissertation require a knowledge of a foreign language?   ( ) Yes   ( ) No

25. In which of the following areas have you used one of these languages (or another you learned for other reasons) since receiving your doctorate?
( ) In teaching preparations
( ) In research
( ) In leisure reading
( ) None

26. What fields or areas of English and American literature were you required to know for your preliminary examination? _____

_____

27. Were you allowed to choose the fields in which you were examined?
( ) Yes   ( ) No

28. How did you prepare for the examination? (Check as many items as applicable.)
( ) Sought the advice of professors
( ) Sought the advice of students
( ) Used department syllabus
( ) Used department files of former examinations
( ) Studied graduate course notes

29. Were you given a full pass on your first try?   ( ) Yes   ( ) No

30. What value does the preliminary examination have, in your opinion, for the student examined?

_____

_____

31. Why did you select the special field of your dissertation? (Mark as many as applicable.)
( ) Intellectual attractiveness
( ) Good professor in that area
( ) Superior opportunities for research
( ) Promising future for specialists
( ) Other reasons: _____

32. How did you get your special topic?   ( ) Found it myself
( ) Professor proposed it   ( ) Both

33. Was your first topic successful?   ( ) Yes   ( ) No

34. If unsuccessful, what happened? _____

_____

35. How much did your director help you in the preparation of your dissertation?
( ) As much as needed
( ) Very little
( ) Not at all

36. How long was your dissertation? (Check one.)
( ) 150 pages or less
( ) 151–300 pages
( ) 301–500 pages
( ) More than 500 pages

37. Did the research required for your dissertation make you feel that work of this nature:
( ) Is exciting and absorbing?
( ) Is a painful but necessary requirement?
( ) Is a useful but tedious requirement?
( ) Serves no useful purpose?

38. Has your dissertation been published as a monograph or article(s)?
( ) Yes   ( ) No

39. Since taking your degree, how many articles, monographs, or books have you had accepted for publication that in no way depend on your dissertation? _____articles _____monographs _____books

40. Were you required to take a final oral?   ( ) Yes   ( )No

41. a) In your opinion, was your final oral, if you took one,

( ) A real defense of your thesis?
( ) A substantial examination of your general competence?
( ) Neither of the above?
b) If you marked "neither of the above," will you give your opinion in the space below?

_____

_____

_____

42. What do you now regard as the most valuable aspects of your doctoral training? (Mark up to three in order of importance, with "1" representing the most important factor.)
( ) Courses
( ) Dissertation
( ) Teaching experience
( ) Association with professors
( ) Association with other students
( ) Independent study
( ) Other valuable aspects: _____

43. Please indicate any aspects of your graduate training that you now think were valueless or unrealistic. _____

_____

44. Considering your present position and prospects, would you say that the time and money you invested in your doctorate was "worth it"?
( ) Yes   ( ) No

_____

Although the Ph.D. in English and American Literature has been criticized from the beginning as no guarantee of culture, scholarship, or pedagogical competence in its recipients, the demand for Ph.D.'s now exceeds the production of Ph.D.'s by three times. To meet this demand some of the older graduate departments are considering the elimination of some traditional requirements that now seem unrealistic. Other departments are thinking about new degrees between the M.A. and Ph.D. that will be acceptable to other institutions. English departments that once limited themselves to undergraduate work or to nothing beyond a program for the M.A. are adding a program for the Ph.D. The latter phenomenon is not unusual. Within the last seventy-five years the original dozen graduate departments granting the doctorate has grown to more than a hundred. The following questions are intended to elicit your opinions on the current situation, but we shall be glad to have you set down other ideas or make a fuller statement on a separate sheet.

45. Do you feel that *in general* only a Ph.D. is competent to teach: (check as many as applicable)

( ) Underclassmen?
( ) Upperclassmen?
( ) Graduate students?

46. Do you think that a Ph.D. actively engaged in scholarly or critical writing is likely to be a better teacher than one who is not?
( ) Yes ( ) No

47. In the Cartter report, "An Assessment of Quality in Graduate Education," twenty departments of English (listed alphabetically below) were rated as "leading" both in effectiveness of graduate program and in quality of graduate faculty: California (Berkeley), Chicago, Columbia, Cornell, Duke, Harvard, Illinois, Indiana, Johns Hopkins, Michigan, Minnesota, North Carolina, Northwestern, Pennsylvania, Princeton, Stanford, Washington (Seattle), Wisconsin, UCLA, Yale.
Do you think that Ph.D.'s produced by these departments are better on the average in ability and training than those trained by other departments? ( ) Yes ( )No ( ) Don't know

48. Do you think that the proliferation of graduate departments of English has resulted in reducing the standards for the Ph.D.?
( ) Yes ( ) No ( ) Can't say

49. Do you think that a Ph.D. like the M.D., and given for four years of graduate work, is desirable? ( ) Yes ( ) No

50. If you checked *yes*, should such a degree necessarily include supervised teaching? ( ) Yes ( ) No

51. Do you think that a satisfactory Ph.D. could be given if the dissertation requirement were limited to a collection of publishable articles?
( ) Yes ( ) No

52. Do you think that a degree between the M.A. and Ph.D. (e.g., M.Phil., D.A.) that represents the "all but dissertation" situation is feasible as a qualifying degree for teaching in:
Universities with doctoral programs
in English? . . . . ( ) Yes ( ) No
State colleges? . . . . ( ) Yes ( ) No
Liberal arts colleges? . . . . ( ) Yes ( ) No
Two-year colleges? . . . . ( ) Yes ( ) No

53. If you could have secured your present post and prospects with such a degree, would you have gone on to a Ph.D.? ( ) Yes ( ) No

54. When a new Ph.D. is appointed a postdoctoral fellow, should he:
( ) Be held to some sort of curriculum?
( ) Be assistant to a professor as in the sciences?
( ) Be allowed to use his time as he pleases?